58648
Martin

PE
1429
M3
1968

JI

D1265021

The Logic and
Rhetoric of Exposition

PE
1429
M3
1969

The Logic and Rhetoric of Exposition

HAROLD C. MARTIN · Union College

RICHARD M. OHMANN · Wesleyan University

JAMES H. WHEATLEY · Trinity College

THIRD EDITION

58648

HOLT, RINEHART AND WINSTON, INC.

New York · Chicago · San Francisco · Atlanta · Dallas
Montreal · Toronto · London · Sydney

Copyright © 1963, 1969 by Holt, Rinehart and Winston, Inc.
Copyright © 1957, 1958 by Harold C. Martin
All Rights Reserved
Library of Congress Catalog Card Number: 79–75916
SBN: 03–078595–2

Printed in the United States of America
9   8   7   6   5   4   3   2   1

FONTBONNE LIBRARY

PE
1429
M3

PREFACE

Every writer, from rankest amateur to professional, knows occasions on which his writing goes well. Words come unbidden; sentences follow each other as obediently as a brood of ducklings; and paragraphs shape themselves with ease. On such occasions, writing is all pleasure; but the occasions are few. Most of the time even professional writers sweat over their work, pace the floor, tear up what they have written, and lament the day they ever committed themselves to such a career. That does not stop them from continuing any more than a bruising contest keeps the professional football player out of the next game, because they know from experience that whatever the difficulties there will be at least the satisfaction that comes from having completed the job.

The experienced writer, however, has one thing going for him that the amateur lacks—the knowledge that an obstacle may yield if he shifts strategy and tries a new tact. He knows this not only from practice but from his awareness that all writing has a good amount of game-element. He is a sort of verbal chessplayer with a half-dozen possibilities open to him for the next move, and he has the added advantage of being able to start the whole game over again if he finds he is working himself into a checkmate position.

A book to help the inexperienced writer needs above all to give him a means to understand the game he is playing: the moves available to him, the strategies and tactics that work best, the reactions and counter-plays he can expect from a good opponent. Unless he gets into the writing as he gets into a game, the writer seldom releases enough adrenalin to give a spirited performance. In this book we have tried in two ways to stimulate that kind of performance. We treat composition as an action; and, especially in the first chapters, we draw our examples from contemporary experience, not because they are topical but because they have to do with events and attitudes that should ring a bell in the mind of the user and reinforce his sense that, in writing, he is himself engaged in an event-making activity.

This is not a book of formulas and rules; it does not pretend to be a complete and ready handbook for correction of every fault ticked off by the instructor who reads your compositions. It is fundamentally a book for thinking about writing. Since, especially in the first four chapters, this is a book about strategies of writing, what we have done as authors will not do the reader much good unless he works the exercises scattered through the text as he encounters them. We hope we have succeeded in explaining what we mean by "explanation," but we know from our own experience in writing that working the problems is as important as going through the text.

The first edition of this book, written eleven years ago, was revised and expanded five years later. Like the two previous versions, this one retains a two-part structure, initial chapters dealing with the conceptual acts involved in writing, subsequent chapters given over to bread-and-butter concerns. But unlike the two earlier versions, this one swings away from the classical treatments of rhetoric to make use of one that reflects more accurately and fully the speculations about language and the use of language that have characterized the past three decades. We have found the new modes of inquiry useful in our own work and believe that students will find them useful, too.

H.C.M.
R.M.O.
J.H.W.

Schenectady, New York
Middletown, Connecticut
Hartford, Connecticut

February 1969

CONTENTS

The Logic and
Rhetoric of Exposition

Part 1

chapter one / *Explanation*

To write is always to explain something to someone. Single sentences, and even sentences that don't seem to be explanations—"Shut the door," or "I like a good brawl"—contain what might be called an explanatory component. The first sentence contains the explanation that there is a door, that it is open, and that it needs shutting. Making explanations in the course of speaking and writing, and understanding them in listening and reading, is so natural that they often seem invisible. In writing formally, as you are asked to do in school and college, you have a better opportunity to notice the actual process of explanation, because you keep running into its difficulties. You are apt to start from inklings, half-understood data and the connections between them, and are then faced with the need to work toward an explanation. The process may seem so active that it looks unfamiliar.

But it is at least reassuring, and may be enlightening, to remember how very natural and indeed unavoidable explanations really are. Any speaker makes them all the time; and as with any other natural activity (such as walking) he knows a good deal about explaining without having to think about it—unless, of course, he wants to improve.

   • *Exercise 1.1:* What is the explanatory component in "I like a good brawl"? Someone once said of Mary Queen of Scots that she was "a good sort, but a bad lot." What is the explanatory component there? In saying that, what else was the speaker doing, besides explaining?

We have been speaking of explanations as an activity. Actually, there are three different senses in which one can speak of an explanation as an activity. First, an explanation is an act in the sense that it is always performed to someone, even when that someone is oneself: reminding someone of something, reporting to him, or warning him, and so forth.

Second, a written explanation is an activity in the sense that it progresses —it starts somewhere and goes by a certain route to an outcome. In this sense, a good written explanation can often be thought of as a drama. With some writers, elements in the explanation seem to function like elements in a play: antagonists and protagonists, hurdles to be leapt, heroes and allies, and villains to be outwitted. But however pale or vivid the drama, any explanation that makes sense at all progresses.

> • *Exercise 1.2:* Try to analyze a short piece of writing that comes to some conclusion—perhaps a newspaper editorial—as though it were a drama. For instance, is there a "hero-idea"? A "villain-idea"? Where does the hero get his support? The villain? Is there a single climax, or a series of them?

Finally, and most fundamentally, an explanation is an activity in the sense that one's mind is obviously at work, is *doing* something, whenever one thinks about anything, and "makes up his mind" about it. At various levels of consciousness, one is always pulling experience together into one shape or another. A person may focus momentarily on the forest instead of the tree (perhaps to test his impression of wind) so quickly and naturally that he is not aware of having briefly substituted the implicit concept *forest,* or *group,* for *tree.* Yet he *has* done something. The word "fact," as many philosophers have pointed out, derives from the Latin word *facta,* which means "made."

So fundamental a point at first glance may seem impractically far from the ordinary problems of thinking and writing. One way to test its importance is to consider the effects of an alternative view: what happens to the writer who follows contemporary usage and thinks of facts as just facts—hard little nuggets of reality waiting to be discovered and announced?

The answer seems to be that certain fundamental problems in writing are more apt to occur if one thinks of facts in such a way. A witty teacher once invented the term "cow" to describe the kind of writing that seems cowed by facts, that consists of unexplained data, quotations, "background information"—the kind of writing that simply presents the raw materials for an explanation. Suppose that 75,000 cars a day use the Los Angeles freeway. A pure example of "cow" would leave it at that. But are all those cars best understood as an example of progress, a cause of air pollution, a symptom of the "lonely crowd" or of a "lemming-complex" in American life? The cowed writer stops asking questions too soon.

His opposite, the writer whose work is often described by the slang term "bull," deals in empty generalizations, structures of explanation that are often internally confused and unrelated to situations. More facts will probably not help him, because he is not yet fully engaged in the activity of making sense. Oddly enough, he is apt to hold the same notion of facts that his cowed counterpart does, although he writes as though he has risen above them. The student who writes, "Strictly for its heuristic value, an objective consideration of data is more seminal than it is often considered," is the victim, willing or not, of a kind of verbal "spin-off," most noticeable in the phrase "is often considered."

The twin problems of "cow" and "bull" that follow from too simple a view of facts are problems in the *invention* of explanations; a more subtle problem that seems related to that view is one of the *disposition* of the explanation on paper. We are reserving matters of disposition for Chapter 4, but it is worth noticing now that our second sense of activity (see above), in which a good essay can be compared to a drama, is more difficult to attain if one thinks of facts as nuggets. Even the writer who has thought long and hard about a topic may have a "Drama Problem" in his writing, so that his essay seems to take for its model the last paragraph of a laboratory report. In leaving out all the difficulty and exploration of coming-to-know, all the inadequate ideas that had to be discarded or refuted or refined, he will sound as though he is simply "reporting the facts," even though he knows that things aren't quite that simple.

Finally, this view of facts may influence attitudes that reach far beyond questions of writing alone. "Telling it like it is" will be valuable whenever a better explanation replaces a weaker one; but as a slogan, "Tell It Like It Is" may encourage the kind of impatience with explanation itself that is a troublesome contemporary phenomenon. If there were simply a world of facts out there, waiting to be discovered, disagreement with one's own views could seem irritating—deliberate obfuscation. Among people whose perceptual equipment was in good working order, there would be no excuse for what has been called "counter-understandings of events." Presented with a different understanding from one's own, one might retaliate by dismissing the opposition (people over the age of thirty, adolescents, rednecks, the establishment) and its way of explaining things to us. One might even be led to *explain* the world by dismissing explanation itself, perhaps as a waste of time, and by favoring *action* instead. Tempting, but illusory: it isn't just playing with words to notice that an explanation which condemns explanation is fundamentally self-contradictory.

• *Exercise 1.3:* Find an example, in a popular medium, of the contemporary concern with explanation. It could be a song, or a movie, or an article. What does it see as the problem in explanation? Does it give or imply a solution? Do you agree? (Example: "The Sounds of Silence.")

1/ Concepts

In order for "counter-understandings of events" to exist—let us call them counter-explanations—an explanation must be composed of elements which *could,* in some way, be different from what they are. The usual name for the individual elements which make up an explanation is **concept**—often defined as "mental construction." As we have seen, the notion of construction need not mean that in one's dealings with the world he "makes it all up." **Concept** is simply a name for the divisions one makes in experience, from the simplest and least reflective perception up to and beyond the most abstruse consideration of the nature of Democracy.

Some concepts are purely mental constructions, in that they do not correspond to anyone's actual experience: *infinity* and *Hades* are examples of concepts that men have fabricated for various purposes. But most concepts are constructions in another sense. They "cover" some part of actual experience, but nothing in experience forces just those concepts on people. Take a simple one: *boat.* It may seem natural or even inevitable; boats just *are* boats. Yet there is no reason at all, in logic or human psychology, why our concept *boat* could not include icebergs, rafts, floating barrels, or even corks and bottles. (A great breakthrough occurs in *Winnie the Pooh* when Pooh sees an umbrella as potentially a boat—that is, revises his concept of *boat.*) If someone objects, here, "But a bottle isn't anything like a dinghy," a fair answer is, "How closely does a dinghy resemble an aircraft carrier?" Ocean liners, kayaks, schooners, tugboats, and catamarans are all similar in some ways, but very dissimilar in others. Taken together, they hardly form a "natural class"; the taking-together is precisely an act of construction—something that the mind contributes to experience, or does to shape it.

Take a contrary situation: there are many more natural groupings for which no concept exists. Rowboats, kayaks, canoes, dinghies, and punts share some obvious features: they are hollowed-out shells; they can be powered by oars, a paddle, or a pole (a long wooden object); they are roughly the same size; and so on. Yet we have no concept that covers just this territory, or did not until now. Perhaps as you read the last two sentences you began to form a concept, to develop a mental construction.

> • *Exercise 1.4:* A good way to see how a concept works is to test it against data. If you formed a concept that covers rowboats, kayaks, canoes, dinghies, and punts (let's give the concept a name—"slet"), you should be able to tell whether it includes other kinds of boat. Is a gondola a slet? What about a barge? A trireme? A racing shell? A skiff? After you have tested the concept in this way, write a definition of "slet." Then invent one or two other concepts, and test them in the same way.

Without concepts, experience would be radically different from what it is. Even fairly rudimentary perceptions would be impossible: we would not notice a tree, but only a configuration of green, black, and gray shapes. In fact, *green, black,* and *shape* are also concepts, and we would lack even their help in organizing what we perceive. There would be no sense of repetition in experience; we could never think, "oh yes, another X." Concepts operate at the most immediate stages of experience, and operate more pronouncedly, of course, at more complicated stages of understanding. It is in this sense that they are the "elements" of explanation.

Often concepts overlap in their coverage of experience, as, for example, *house* and *home,* or *fate* and *destiny,* or *freedom* and *license.* Each of the paired concepts shares with its counterpart some of the same "power" to organize experience, and each has some distinctive characteristics of its own. There are houses that are not homes, and also homes that are not houses (think of some examples). When two concepts at first seem the same, you can often discover important differences between them by imagining circumstances in which you would use one or the other. J. L. Austin tells the following story to discriminate between *by accident* and *by mistake:*

> You have a donkey, so have I, and they graze in the same field. The day comes when I conceive a dislike for mine. I go to shoot it, fire: the brute falls in its tracks. I inspect the victim, and find to my horror that it is *your* donkey. I appear on your doorstep with the remains and say—what? 'I say, old sport, I'm awfully sorry, &c., I've shot your donkey *by accident*'? Or '*by mistake*'? Then again, I go to shoot my donkey as before, draw a bead on it, fire—but as I do so, the beasts move, and to my horror yours falls. Again the scene on the doorstep— what do I say? 'By mistake'? Or 'by accident'?
>
> J. L. AUSTIN, *Philosophical Papers*

- *Exercise* 1.5:   Try the same kind of test for *fate* and *destiny*. Then explore a
  group of allied concepts like *forest, woods, grove,* and *jungle* by changing
  the details of an imagined tree-scape, and seeing at what point you would
  switch from calling them, say, a grove to calling them a wood.

Of course, "power" is a metaphor—concepts have no power until they
are *used* by someone. In use, concepts can be powerful indeed. As we
write, for instance, important social and political lines are drawn according to how people refer to urban riots: are these riots an instance of
rebellion? lawlessness? insurrection? anarchy? civil disorder? black
power? crime in the streets? (Imagine the political beliefs of someone
who would choose each of these concepts.)

Later in this chapter, we shall consider some of the uses of definition
of concepts, and the means by which they may be located. But first it
may be well to gain a clearer sense of concepts in action. And oddly
enough, one of the best ways to get a sense of concepts in action is to
watch them when they are less fiercely and emotionally engaged—in fact,
when they are at play, in games, jokes, and puzzles. Without the sets of
concepts we call rules, games couldn't exist. No two games of football
are exactly alike, but without the rules which make the game possible, a
touchdown would be simply the act of a man in an odd-looking costume
carrying a funny-shaped ball over a white line. No framework of rules, no
game—and little meaning to his action.

Jokes are a special case of games, because they play with concepts
themselves, and one of the reasons for laughter must be the pleasure to
be found in such play. Of course, taste in jokes varies among people;
what strikes one as funny in one situation may bore him in another, and
explanation or analysis of a joke is notoriously ineffective if the speaker's
purpose is simply to make someone else laugh. But a little reflection will
usually confirm the fact that what was pleasing in a joke was at least in
part the manipulation not only of single concepts but often of whole sets
of concepts.

Consider puns, for instance. Although most people have been taught
to groan when they hear one, frequently they find themselves laughing
at one. If puns are "the lowest form of humor" it may be because the
structure of a pun is often very simple: the pun-word represents the
point of intersection between two concepts. There's the old one about
the charming thief, for instance, who had "very taking ways." It cap-
italizes on an accident of the English language: The same word happens—in defiance of logic—to stand for the concept *stealing*, as well as
the concept *charming*. Perhaps a bad pun is one that brings two concepts
together in an uninteresting way, so that there is no surprise in seeing

them brought together, and no pleasure in seeing the connection grow and deepen as one thinks about it. A first cousin to the pun is the joke that plays with whole phrases ("Listen, Your Highness, don't send any more knights through that gigantic hand; let your *pages* do the walking through The Yellow Fingers"). Such reversals may overcome some of the weakness of simple puns by being a little more elaborate, as well as by coming at the end of an anecdote. A more complicated structure occurs in the famous line of Oscar Wilde, "Work is the curse of the drinking class,"—more complicated because it not only turns a familiar phrase around, but deliberately opposes Wilde's decadent cynicism to the pious war on alcoholism in "the lower classes." Whole sets of concepts, which seem to have a natural antipathy to each other, are brought into violent collision.

But there's more to it than that. To exclaim that "drink is the curse of the working class" is to group some people, matter-of-factly, as members of the "working class," on a social scale which presumably includes people who are not working men. Many sorts of people might have used the slogan, when it was popular, but they would all have been assuming that social scale in doing so. They would also have been fervently condemning, in quasi-theological terms, the "curse" that demon rum levied upon this group, condemning it because it prevented working men from working or because it used up the wages they did earn. Besides sympathizing with these unfortunates, they might have felt a certain security in repeating the slogan: perhaps the security of not belonging to the working class; perhaps the security of moral indignation at the supposed curse, which sounds simple enough to require no very careful thought; and perhaps the security of being invulnerable. But "ah, no," Wilde seems to answer in his careful drawl, "we drinking men are cursed only by work; isn't your indignation a trifle unimaginative? Shocking though you may find it, for once try looking at such matters the way *we* see them, instead of from your own safe distance." Class structure and moral certainties, then, with perhaps an easy acceptance of others' doom, are a set of concepts for which Wilde impudently substitutes his own concept of class structure, and his own sort of "curse." (Do you suppose he was also quietly turning the Bible against some of its more thoughtless adherents, who forget that work was part of Adam's curse?)

Here's a final example of the way jokes play, often seriously, with concepts. This example belongs to the nightclub comedian's style: "Just my luck. Bought a suit with two pair of pants today, and burned a hole in the jacket." Dick Gregory says he used that as an opening to his act because it was ingratiating: it belongs to the style of comedian's jokes that makes fun of the teller. It is also clean, and there are probably other categories one could find for it. Wilde's joke was sharply-focused because it reversed a slogan; Gregory's is relatively soft-focused, and depends on the listener's letting the joke turn over in his mind and gather meanings. Like this: a two-pants suit is a sort of Ordinary Man's approach to practical riches; it seems to have an air of largesse about it, and some invulnerability to Chance and Wear—spoil one pair and you still have one. "You're safe, dig?" as Gregory might say. We've called it part of an Ordinary Man's point of view, from a more affluent role: That is we've taken the point of view of those who needn't bother erecting such defenses against wear and tear. That's part of the ingratiation, then: the speaker is "just an ordinary guy," not at all immune to misfortune, but doing what he can. He *was* relatively safe, it seemed, until he burned the jacket, and was left with two useless pairs of pants. It wasn't a two-pants suit, it was a one-jacket suit. Doubly safe in this case meant doubly vulnerable. One set of concepts: safety, largesse, the prudent triumph of the Ordinary Man. The opposite set: failure, stupidity, (the fly-in-the-ointment and the-small-print-in-the-contract), the recurrent defeat of the vulnerable. "Just my luck," says Gregory.

Moving from the pun to Gregory's joke, one might suppose that the degree of complexity of conceptual play was the most important scale on which one places jokes, but since jokes come in so many shapes and sizes, there must be other scales. Often a joke seems to belong to some category—of subject matter, for instance, or of style—and the listener probably has, at least for the moment, an approximate place for it on some scale or other. Some people seem habitually to find mother-in-law jokes funnier than jokes about children, or Yiddish humor funnier than Irish. For some, the clarity of outline in Wilde's joke is pleasing, while for others it seems too "clever"—by association as well as content too "smart-alecky"—to be really funny. And some people would put all jokes of the ready-made variety that can begin "Have you heard the one about," relatively low on their various scales of the comic; they want to catch their humor on the wing, arising out of situations rather than have it served to them on a platter. But even on the wing, the moment of comedy is a moment of play with concepts and sets of concepts.

> • *Exercise 1.6:* Analyze one or two jokes or cartoons or comic moments for
> their conceptual play.

Jokes play with conceptual sets, and scales underlie a good deal of ordinary classifying. We should pause over one more idea connected with Gregory's joke. There, the two sets constructed around safety and invulnerability are incommensurate, and that was part of the point. "Incommensurate" means "not measurable together." Two concepts are incommensurate when they belong to different sets of concepts, as apples and houses ordinarily do. (Can you think of a single set that might include both apples and houses?) Gregory could happily, smugly perhaps, at least optimistically, look at that suit as a two-pants suit; or, more sadly and wisely, he could see it as a suit with only one jacket: and the two ways of explaining the same suit are incommensurate.

A good many puzzles, with more solemn playfulness than jokes, turn on the principle of the incommensurate, so that the pleasure of the solution derives in part from sorting out the commensurate from the incommensurate. Here's a typical and perhaps familiar example. Three salesmen hire a hotel room, which the roomclerk says costs $30, so each pays him $10. After they've gone up to the room, the roomclerk realizes that the charge should have been $25 for three people, and sends a bellboy up with the extra $5. But the bellboy perhaps decides that splitting $5 three ways is too complicated; anyway, he keeps $2 and returns $1 to each of the men. Really, then, each man has paid $9 (total: $27), and the bellboy has two (total: $29). But originally there were $30! What's become of the other dollar?

The answer is that the listener was being carefully led down a blind alley, and was asked ("Really, then") to add together two figures which are incommensurate. One ($27) is the men's *payment,* and the other ($2) is the bellboy's *income*—adding them is like adding apples and anniversaries. What you *can* add is $25 (the hotel's income) and $2 (the bellboy's income) to get $27 (total income). And of course total income = total payment. Presto!

A special variety of playful confusion, which also has lessons for workaday problems, results when one of the two incommensurate concepts belongs to what is ordinarily in the background of one's thinking. Conventions in art, for example, are usually left in the background of the artwork itself, and so it would be a rare sonnet that mentioned iambic pentameter or the presence of fourteen lines. But in a recent television parody of courtroom drama, after tense shots of the stern judge, the determined prosecutor, and the frightened defendant, while the violins in the background music were dithering excitedly, there was at one point a murmur from the courtroom spectators—whereupon the judge pounded his gavel and announced, "If there is any more disturbance in the courtroom, I shall have to ask the orchestra to leave." Suddenly a background concept had been yanked into the foreground, calling up incommensurate visions of violinists hard at work in the court-room, following the progress of the trial and commenting upon it in perfect harmony.

A more complicated example of this sort of "problem" was the television commercial for a shampoo which began by showing an old-style phonograph playing a 78 rpm recording of the company's familiar sales-tune, sung by a voice reminiscent of Rudy Vallee and the 1930s. Suddenly a hand brusquely shoved the tone arm aside and smashed the record, whereupon a voice announced a change in the shampoo's secret formula, and invisible singers began a "rock" version of the old sales-tune. The commercial is more complicated than the courtroom parody primarily because the style of singing is made to stand for the effectiveness of the shampoo, but also because the commercial begins by bringing the background convention of singing commercials into foreground prominence, and ends by giving that convention its proper and "natural" role—invisibility.

Because art depends so heavily on convention—a sonnet's length, Shakespeare's soliloquies—serious arguments about art sometimes arise which are similar in form to the courtroom parody, or to the shampoo commercial. The famous eighteenth-century critic Samuel Johnson disliked Milton's poem "Lycidas," for instance, because it used conventions of the pastoral elegy such as sheep and shepherds. Since the nominal subject of the poem was the death of a friend, the use of such conventions on such an occasion seemed to Johnson a sign of insufficient grief on Milton's part. (Most modern critics not only disagree with Johnson but find positive values—foreground values rather than just background ones—in Milton's uses of convention in that poem.)

In philosophy, too, famous arguments have arisen when concepts that ordinarily belong to the background of thinking are brought into the foreground. Here are two problems which have given rise to such arguments. See if you can explain the confusion that arises from the incommensurate nature of background and foreground concepts.

1.   The Greek philosopher Zeno very nearly proved that the flight of an arrow was impossible: to travel the distance, the arrow must first travel half the distance, and before that a quarter of it, and before that an eighth, and so on down to the smallest imaginable division of space. But since there are an infinite number of points on an arc, the arrow will obviously never arrive at its destination. (Clue: the problem here is not only one of background and foreground concepts, but also of the kind of background concept involved.) Check your explanation against the one in a good encyclopedia, in the article on Zeno.

2.   A man says, "All New Yorkers are liars! Me? I live on West

Seventy-Third Street, New York City—and you can quote me." He may be quoted, but can his assertion be taken seriously? If so, how? Under the rules of such problems, one cannot "go behind" the information given, by checking upon the man or administering lie-detector tests to New Yorkers. In any case, the first problem is structural, not factual: what is one to do when a man seems to be accusing himself of being a liar?

The problem seems to present a circle, in which what the one New Yorker says about *all* New Yorkers must be false in order to be true, and vice versa. To break the circle, a distinction would have to be made between two kinds of statement, one of which is accepted as a matter of the background convention, and the other as the subject of a foreground assertion. Both kinds of statement can be questioned, but only after they have been distinguished. In effect, the New Yorker would then be saying, "All statements by New Yorkers are false [foreground assertion] except of course this one, which is a statement about such statements [background]."

• *Exercise 1.7:* For three of the following examples, analyze the use of background and foreground concepts.

a. "But you can't start before the whistle blows; that's not playing the game."
b. "But you can't call a former President a traitor; that's not playing the game."
c. "All generalizations are false."
d. "I have seen birth and death, / But had thought they were different; this Birth was / Hard and bitter agony for us, like Death, our death." (T. S. Eliot, "Journey of The Magi.")
e. "Our Supreme Court approves of pornography."
f. "Course requirements are the very antithesis to what education in a free society should be."

For the writer, sensitivity to the questions—which concepts are commensurate with each other? and in what ways?—will help to remind him that he is always dealing with concepts. It will often provide solutions to hard problems in thinking, and will sometimes suggest new directions to explore. In the following sentence, for instance, concepts ordinarily thought to be incommensurate are grouped together. "He had all the necessities of existence: two cars, a wife, and a mortgage." Evidently, a writer is not bound by the conventions which ordinarily separate incommensurate concepts. Wives and mortgages and cars *may* all be grouped together under the category "necessities of existence," but if they are, the purpose of the new grouping—irony, in this case—should be made clear to writer and reader alike.

Purpose is another subject: it is time to cast a wider net. For instance, **definition** may be defined as the location of a concept; what purposes, we will now ask, can definition help the writer to achieve?

2/ The Uses of Definition

Concepts are primarily a matter of thought, definition primarily a matter of words. So tidy a distinction, however, may disguise the rich variety of interplay between thought and words. As we turn from jokes and puzzles to the practical uses of definition, we will necessarily be discussing some of the more common and important kinds of interplay between thought and the words the speaker must use to explain and explore that thought.

William James, the American psychologist and philosopher, once described an argument between two groups of people on a camping trip. Here is the problem they debated: a man is standing a few yards from a tree, and part way up the trunk, on the other side from the man, is a squirrel. The man moves around the tree trying to see the squirrel, but the squirrel keeps moving around the trunk, staying just opposite the man. Clearly the man goes around the tree, but does he go around the squirrel? One group said yes, one said no, both were equally convinced, and the argument, like the man and the squirrel, progressed in circles. James pointed out that the disagreement was not factual, but verbal. If "to go around something" means to progress in a circle around it, regardless of what *it* does in the middle, then the man does go around the squirrel. But if "to go around something" means to move from the front of it, to one side, to the back, to the other side, and finally to the front again, then the man does not go around the squirrel. Not all James's friends were content, but it seems clear that James had attacked the problem in the best possible way. If he did not "solve" it, in the sense of proving one side right, he at least *dis*solved the problem by showing that it was an unrewarding one unless put in other terms. And of course he did so through definition.

The example is a trivial one, but the moral is not. Many puzzles of greater consequence create perplexity partly or entirely because of such confusions. Take for instance the old teaser as to whether a tree makes a sound if it falls in a deserted spot out of the hearing range of man or animal. Or the still more ancient philosophical question about the reality or unreality of objects. Instances abound in more practical matters, too. Are viruses alive? That depends partly on the definition of "alive." Is Angola entitled to independence? Any discussion of the issue must include a definition of political rights. Is such and such a law unconstitutional? The answer may hinge partly on the meaning of "unconstitutional," and it will almost certainly depend upon the definition of words in the Constitution and in previous court opinions. Whenever the facts are certain but the controversy still lumbers on unfruitfully, it is wise to take a fresh look at the key terms of the controversy and their meanings —at words and concepts. Students and others who like firm answers may weary of the rejoinder, "It's all a matter of definition." And indeed, the call for definition can be tedious, question-begging, and sophistical: not every dilemma will be resolved by a clarification of terms. But clarity of terms is essential to every important argument, and definition offers a powerful means of brushing away intellectual cobwebs.

Many questions, like those in the preceding paragraph, cannot even be intelligently posed without definition. It is hopeless to ask how much poverty there is in the United States unless there is some acceptable definition of poverty. Especially in problems of classification, definition is a prerequisite. Thus, before deciding which organizations were subversive, the Attorney General first had to define "subversive," implicitly or explicitly (he defined the word too loosely, to many people's taste). A well known House committee decides at intervals whether certain activities are "un-American." The censors, and sometimes the courts, are asked to determine what books and movies are "obscene" or "blasphemous." As these decisions have serious practical consequences, so do the definitions they incorporate. Meteorologists cannot say how many *hurricanes* there were last year without definition; nor can critics decide when the *novel* arose as a literary form; nor teachers decide which students have done *satisfactory* work; nor the man on the street decide whether what he is about to do is *wrong*. Problems of all sorts, including many that students write about, are likely to become manageable only after a certain amount of defining.

Dilemmas, questions, and problems of classification often call for definition as a means to an end; some difficulties faced by the writer call for definition as an end in itself. Perhaps he is uneasy about the popular use of a certain word—as the architect Richard Neutra was about the verb "own." Neutra thought it absurd to speak of a man as owning a house that was built, not for his individual needs, but to the specifications of a mass-produced stereotype, a house with no privacy in a row of identical houses, a house with a thirty-five-year mortgage. Ownership should imply more psychological control and more personal involvement than that, he argued. His problem was specifically one of definition, or rather of redefinition.

Similarly, a writer may wish to propose a new definition of a term in common use, even though the conventional definition is not so much wrong as incomplete or puzzling. This happens often in science: in a sense, men knew for a long time what electricity was, but scientists could not rest content with the layman's definition. In humbler pursuits, too, conceptual reform often comes with redefinition. There was a revolution in social work and penal practices when theorists began to think of a criminal not as an inherently bad man, but as the product of his environment. And definitions of education continue to proliferate, though everyone knows what education is, after a fashion. To define such terms is to attack conceptual and practical matters at their center.

Now and then, the writer encounters a phenomenon, a complex of events, a way of behaving or thinking, which has persisted for some time and been vaguely noticed, but which has never been isolated, fenced in, and given a label. If he wishes to concentrate his attention on such a phenomenon, to analyze it, and to understand it, he will save a great deal of inconvenience and wordiness by naming it. No doubt, there have always been people who wash their hands every ten minutes, or couldn't stop chewing their nails, or just had to touch every other lamppost, but the psychologist who gathered such quirks and oddities together under the heading "compulsive" behavior performed a service for his colleagues and users of the language generally by providing a shorthand term and a definition. Innovation of this sort can often be much more than a procedural shortcut. By coining and applying such terms as "repression," the "Oedipus complex," the "id," the "death wish," Freud opened the door to a whole new way of understanding the human mind, though the patterns of behavior referred to by his terms were probably as ancient as the family. To name and define is to reinterpret, as well as to reduce complexity.

* *Exercise 1.8:* Invent a word to serve as a noun or adjective expressing some substance or quality for which at present there is not a proper word in English. (It has been noted, for example, that there is no dignified but unpretentious word in English meaning "the regular male companion of a young, unmarried female"—what is rather embarrassingly called a "boy friend.") Without defining the word you invent, use it in a paragraph until its meaning becomes clear. Then write a definition.

Sometimes, too, naming and defining are ways of overcoming newness and strangeness. History sometimes repeats itself; but it also dazzles the observer with novel arrangements of people and institutions, which only become "thinkable" as names and definitions are minted and pass into currency. "Cold war," "iron curtain," "balance of terror"—terms like these, though they sometimes lead to oversimplification, have helped postwar Americans to orient themselves within the turmoil of move and countermove brought on by the rise to power of Soviet Russia and the development of atomic weapons. Similarly, an obscure social upheaval assumed new clarity and shape for outsiders when Jack Kerouac labeled and defined the "beat generation." (In fact, one doubts that the movement itself would have flourished so vigorously without the rallying point of a title.) The chance to make the new familiar through language does not present itself only to public men and novelists; even a student grappling with an assigned theme is likely to find that some obstacles melt away if he confronts them with name and definition.

The need for defining may also arise, not from the encounter with experience, but from the necessity of making words behave properly. Perhaps the writer wishes to introduce a technical term, say "entropy," one with which his readers may be unfamiliar. Clearly, if the word is to perform its function for him, he must define it before he proceeds. Or perhaps he wants to restrict the meaning of a common word to suit his purposes. It is within his rights, in an essay on traffic deaths, to use the word "accident" to mean "collision caused by a driver's carelessness or miscalculation" (thereby excluding murder, suicide, mechanical failure, and so forth); but, if he takes this liberty with the word, he has an obligation to spell out for the reader just how much he has narrowed down the usual meaning, an obligation to define "stipulatively," as we shall call it. Again, it often happens that a writer imports a term from another field and uses it metaphorically or analogically in his own. Thus Matthew Arnold christened the English middle class "Philistines"; and literary critics have come to speak of the "tension" in a poem between two attitudes, image clusters, patterns of structure, and so on. Since a metaphor or analogy never creates an exact equivalence, the writer who first takes such a leap must make it clear how much and how little of the original meaning he has carried along with him. These are procedures which will from time to time concern every writer except the most slavishly conventional. In bending language to one's special purposes, it is often expedient to define.

Definition has a common use, too, in studies of other writers' thoughts. It would be difficult to describe the theme of Book I of *The Faerie Queene* without knowing what Spenser meant by "grace." Such concepts can be so central to the outlook of a man or an age that they deserve full-scale definition. Whole books have been devoted to the idea of progress, to Shakespeare's concept of nature, to the notion of romanticism, and so forth. In literary criticism, intellectual history and philosophy, a great deal depends on understanding precisely how men have used their favorite terms, for the structures of human belief are accessible to the student only through examination of the words men use to express those beliefs.

Finally (to make an end of this survey) defining serves the writer well even when he does it privately, never committing his definition to paper. For his very competence with language will be in part a consequence of adequate control over words and meanings. That is not the same as saying he should have a "big vocabulary." The matter is not nearly so much one of extent as of discrimination and control. If, for instance, he doesn't know the difference between "obedience" and "servility," his style will be flabby, wavering, and unpersuasive. Nor can his thought be lucid if it wallows in vague and ambiguous language. The writer who protests, "You understood me, even if I didn't use the right word" is fooling himself and shirking the arduous job of writing plainly. Similarly, the writer who claims, "I know what I mean, but I can't put it into words" is mistaking a half-formed intuition for a fully explicit thought. Of course all writers, to one degree or another, possess a "feeling" for the words of their native languages; but even the most accomplished poet or novelist must puzzle over the appropriateness of this or that word. The neophyte will never grow as a writer without a constant effort to master the words he half-knows, and to study those with which he is barely acquainted. He must get accustomed to the constant effort to define, if only for himself.

3/   Conventional Defining

What we have said about the various needs that press a writer to define and about the complexities of meaning should make it abundantly clear that defining may require more than a word, more than a sentence or paragraph, perhaps more than an entire volume. Even in the face of such elaborateness, much can be done to make defining efficient and comprehensible. If it could not, men would move blindly in the welter of experience, and, moreover, would find themselves frequently unable to transmit to others or receive from them any account of experience at all.

But of course defining is, to begin with, a procedure with a firm place in daily life and ordinary discourse. A conventional (and highly useful) pattern of definition has grown up, one that may conveniently serve as our starting point. Roughly, the pattern is that of an equation, an equivalence between an unknown and something known, between an x and a y where y is something that is already familiar. This is the pattern most often found in dictionaries—an assertion of the sameness in meaning conveyed by two or more words:

> *institution,* n. 1) an organization or establishment for the promotion of a particular object, usually one for some public educational, charitable, or similar purpose; 2) the building devoted to such work; 3) a concern engaged in some activity, as a retail store, broker, or insurance company; 4) *Sociol.* an organized pattern of group behavior, well-established and accepted as a fundamental part of a culture, such as slavery; 5) any established law, custom, etc.; 6) *Colloq.* any familiar practice or object; 7) act of instituting or setting up; establishment: the institution of laws; 8) *Eccles.* a. the origination of the Eucharist, and enactment of its observance, by Christ. b. the investment of a clergyman with a spiritual charge.

> *American College Dictionary*

Even conventional definition, as the example shows, can be a highly refined procedure; and, as our experience with the use of good dictionaries makes clear, it is not always so illuminating as might be hoped. For one thing, a good dictionary presents many *y*'s for the *x* whose meaning its user wishes to know, and he is sometimes perplexed as to which he is to choose. More than that, the *y*'s themselves may often be as unfamiliar to him as the *x* from which he begins. If, for example, he finds that an equivalent for "profuse" is "prodigal," he may plunge further into darkness; conversely, if he finds "imperturbable" equated with "not perturbable," he gets nowhere at all. Reliable dictionaries, of course, have many ways of obviating the awkwardness illustrated by the equivalents, or synonyms, for "profuse" and "imperturbable." Yet their best devices will often not be helpful enough unless the user understands the nature of the process of defining.

A definition has two initial components: the term-to-be-defined (*definiendum*) and the defining term (*definiens*). In the example given above, "institution" is the *definiendum,* and each part of the lengthy series of words and phrases following it is *a definiens,* a defining term. It is immediately apparent that the *definiendum* is usually limited to a single grammatical unit, generally to a single word. To ask, "What is an ecclesiastical institution?" is probably to imply that one already knows what "institution" means and wants only to know what it means when it is modified by the word "ecclesiastical"; or it is to ask for two definitions, one for each word in the *definiendum.* Certainly it would be bizarre to ask for a definition of "all the ecclesiastical institutions in seventeenth-century Italy which were neither corrupt nor moribund," or any such oversized *definiendum.* The simplicity required in the *definiendum,* however, is neither expected nor desired in the *definiens.* In it one may properly anticipate more than one word, more than one grammatical unit, more than one logical division.

Consider this simple definition: "A gig is a two-wheeled, horse-drawn passenger vehicle." The *definiens* is compounded of four informative expressions: "two-wheeled," "horse-drawn," "passenger," and "vehicle." Of the four, one is a noun, and refers to a class of objects meant to include the referent of the *definiendum.* If it alone is used ("A gig is a vehicle"), there is indeed a definition, and for some purposes that definition may be adequate. That it may not be, this colloquy makes apparent:

> INQUIRER: What is a gig?
> RESPONDENT: A gig is a vehicle.
> I: Oh, I understand. A gig and a wagon are the same thing.
> R: Not at all. A gig is designed to carry passengers.
> I: Well, a wagon may carry passengers.
> R: Yes, but a gig is designed especially to carry passengers, and a wagon is designed to carry freight rather than, or in addition to, passengers.
> I: Well, then, a gig is a special kind of wagon.
> R: No, it's really not a wagon at all. Its particular function is different. A wagon carries passengers only incidentally. That is not what it is designed to do.
> I: I think I understand you now. A gig is a carriage.
> R: That's more like it, but there is another difference I forgot to mention. Most carriages have four wheels, and a gig has only two.
> I: Is a gig, then, like a bicycle?
> R: Not at all. For one thing, the two wheels on a gig are joined by an axle and operate in parallel; the two wheels of a bicycle are placed one behind the other and are connected not by an axle but by a rigid frame which permits one to follow the other or, as a matter of fact, one to precede the other. Besides that, I said "passengers," not "passenger."
> I: My brother and I often ride together on a bicycle.
> R: True, but a gig is *designed* to carry more than one passenger, and a bicycle is not.
> I: *Must* there be more than one passenger in a gig?
> R: No, there need not be, but a gig is designed to accommodate more than one, though generally not more than two or three without crowding. It has only one seat, and a carriage has one or more.
> I: Now I know what you mean. When I was in Japan I rode on gigs, but the name used for them there is "rickshaws."

R: A rickshaw is a different thing because it is pulled along by a human being.

I: Could an ox or a dog draw a gig?

R: Neither one, I think. An ox requires a yoke, and a gig has shafts; and the shafts are too far apart and too far raised from the ground to be attached by harness to a dog. At any rate, a gig is designed to be drawn by a horse.

I: I conclude, then, that a gig is a vehicle for one or more passengers, operating on two wheels joined by an axle, and drawn by a horse. Why didn't you say so in the first place?

In short, the task of definition is far from complete when only the class term has been supplied.

The example is not so preposterous as it may seem in the form of a dialogue. The backing and filling illustrate quite accurately the mental process of framing a definition, and it is to avoid such roundaboutness in exposition that a pattern of formal definition is useful. Compressed, the *definiens* turns out to have two parts: in addition to the class term (vehicle), it needs one or more distinguishing terms to set it off from other objects (wagon, carriage, bicycle, rickshaw) in the same class. The defining term, then, is a composite. It names (*a*) what the referent of the defined term has in common with other objects (class term) and (*b*) what differentiates it from other objects in the same class (distinguishing terms).

If the Respondent had first answered the Inquirer's question by saying, "A gig is a thing," the process would, of course, have been even longer. From this one may infer that the class to be used in the defining term should be as limited as it can be without excluding "gig," the *definiendum*. The limitation can be stated in this way: the class word of the *definiens* should be of the order of generality *next above* the *definiendum*. To find that class word may in itself be no easy matter, but unless it, or one near it, is found, the definer makes for himself exactly the kind of difficulty the Respondent would have had with the Inquirer had he started with "thing" instead of with "vehicle."

Selection of the distinguishing terms presents similar difficulties. The Respondent might have described the vehicle as "made of wood and metal," for instance, but had he done so he would have added little that is helpful, since wood and metal are less specific properties of the object he has in mind than are its two-wheeledness or its limited carrying capacity or its mode of locomotion. On the other hand, if the Respondent had added the distinguishing term, "with red leather upholstery," he would have erred in the direction of being *too* specific, for not all gigs are so nattily equipped. The general rule for choice of distinguishing terms is that they should be the ones that most strikingly set off the object referred to by the *definiendum* from other objects in the same class.

One more part of the definition requires attention. What of the equation sign between the *definiendum* and the *definiens,* of the word "is" in the original definition of "gig" and in the definition finally arrived at? Considering the false leads and the tediousness of that definition, one might say that it more nearly represents an intention than a certainty. The definer intends, when he is done defining, that the expressions on each side of the word "means" or the copula ("is") will balance perfectly, like the two pans of a scale in which one measures out a quantity of potash by putting a metal weight of known quantity in one pan and sifting potash into the other until the indicator of the scale rests at dead center. Since measuring an amount of potash is much simpler than measuring words, it is natural to regard with suspicion this indication of equivalence between the two sides of a definition. Indeed, it is not uncommon to hear people say that there are no such things as synonyms or synonymous expressions in language and that a precise definition is, therefore, impossible. For the practicing writer such an assertion is academic, to say the least. He is much less concerned to know whether or not a precise definition is possible than to know what degree of precision is necessary for the answer demanded by the question "What is *x*?" Potash can be measured in truckloads, on a feed-store weighing scale, or in delicate balances in the laboratory, but there will be varying degrees of accuracy.

If uneasiness about the copula persists, one may be tempted to look on it less as a statement of equivalence than as a command, as though the definer were saying not *"x is y,"* or *"x means y,"* but "Use *x* to mean *y*." There does exist a recognizable strategy, usually called **stipulative definition,** which proceeds in just that way: "Use *x* to mean *y*." It is a dangerous but often useful strategy. Lewis Carroll pointed to the dangers, in *Alice in Wonderland,* when he had Humpty Dumpty explain to Alice that *he* used the word "glory" to mean "a nice knock-down argument." The possibilities of confusion are clearly great, best symbolized by Humpty's famous and chaotic end in the nursery rhyme. But stipulative definition is sometimes not only useful but necessary. A central concept in existentialism, for instance, is that of the absurd—though the absurdity referred to is far more consequential than the everyday incongruities and tomfooleries which the word "absurd" ordinarily calls to mind. In chemistry, "salt" means not only sodium chloride but a number of similar compounds as well; and think of "work" in physics. In any of these cases a writer might need to stipulate a definition, depending on the makeup of his audience, in order to pursue the subject at all. Just because it is so special a case, however, the nature of stipulative definition will not account for the other and more frequent kinds of definition which assert, rather than command one to accept, an equivalence between terms—and, by inference, an equivalence between the concepts to which they refer.

We have taken nouns ("gig," "institution") for our sample *definienda*, and indeed, the writer will more frequently have cause to define a noun than one of the other parts of speech. But notice that the conventional method of definition serves as well for verbs, adjectives, and adverbs, with slight modifications:

> To *gerrymander* is to set the boundaries of political districts in a way strongly favorable to one party, by arranging them in grotesque and complicated shapes.
>
> *Arrogant* means proud and confident to excess.
>
> *Decidedly* means pronounced, definitely.

In dealing with adjectives and adverbs, the definer is likely to offer one or more near-synonyms, rather than a class term and several distinguishing terms. And with pronouns, auxiliary verbs, articles, prepositions, and so on, the conventional method breaks down more seriously—consult dictionary entries for some of these words to see what subterfuges are necessary. Still, none but a lexicographer has much occasion to define "the," "could," "in," and the like, and for most practical purposes the standard form is adequate:

$$\textit{definiendum}\text{—}\begin{array}{c}\text{``is''}\\\text{``means''}\end{array}\text{—}\underbrace{\text{class term} + \text{distinguishing terms.}}_{\textit{definiens}}$$

- *Exercise 1.9:* Often a definition can be reinforced by distinguishing the object referred to from others with which it might be confused. Define the first word in each of the groups below, making proper distinctions between it and the others in the group:

  a. planet, star, asteroid, meteor
  b. sonnet, ode, quatrain, rondeau
  c. capitalism, socialism, communism
  d. rectangle, parallelogram, trapezoid
  e. deviation, difference, variation

4/   Patterns of Definition

In practice, so basic a formula as the one we have just considered would be confining if the writer littered his page with formal applications of it. In any field of discourse, precision and clarity are the goals in definition, not obedience to a formula. The writer needs—and the reader will be grateful for—other ways of forwarding the public or private task of defining. Consider this example, from a handbook of terms used in literary criticism:

> *Atmosphere* is the mood pervading a literary work, setting up in the reader expectations as to the course of events, whether happy or (more commonly) disastrous. Shakespeare establishes the tense and fearful atmosphere of *Hamlet* by the terse and nervous dialogue of the opening; Coleridge engenders a strange compound of religious and superstitious terror by his manner of describing the initial scene of "Christabel"; and Hardy, in *The Return of the Native,* makes Egdon Heath an immense and brooding presence which reduces to pettiness and futility the human struggle for happiness for which it is the setting.
>
> M. H. ABRAMS, *A Glossary of Literary Terms,* based on the original version by Dan S. Norton and Peters Rushton (New York: Holt, Rinehart and Winston, Inc., 1957).

Abrams begins with a compact definition in conventional form; the first sentence alone pins down the term rather neatly. But the examples are by no means superfluous. The first two suggest two different ways of building atmosphere (dialogue and description). The third indicates how important a function atmosphere can have in a literary work. And all three explain the concept further by illustrating the language that critics use to speak of atmosphere ("tense and fearful," "compound of religious and superstitious terror," "immense and brooding presence").

Such an example makes it possible to move away from the somewhat confining formula of conventional definition and look at the process of defining in the fulness that is valuable in writing. Good exposition employs methods that are various beyond the power of any simple formula to describe. A brief discussion of some of them, in orderly fashion, will be useful.

The simplest in form is also the one most common to an abridged dictionary: **definition by synonym.** Putting aside the claim that no two words have the same meaning, one can recognize in synonyms an essential device for conveying meaning. To say that "heroism" means "bravery" does not indeed exhaust the possibilities of meaning for the word "heroism," but it directs the mind effectively toward one range of possible meanings. Anyone who knows what "bravery" means, but not "heroism," would at least be led part way to understanding by such a definition. And, after all, no definition could take him all the way: only a full acquaintance with the behavior of the word could do that. Synonyms are useful in defining, and the search for semantic perfection should not make the perfectionist lose sight of that fact.

> • *Exercise 1.10:* How near do the following pairs come to being exact synonyms? What are the differences between the two members of each pair?
>
> a. gourmet—gourmand
> b. confident—optimistic
> c. vacillate—waver
> d. unintentional—inadvertent
> e. correct—proper
> f. suggest—imply

Where synonyms do not satisfy because the *definiens* is as little agreed upon or as hard to pin down as the *definiendum,* **definition by analysis** will help. This is the kind of definition used in the discussion of "gig" above, one in which the *definiens* includes mention of the class of objects to which the *definiendum* belongs and of the characteristics that distinguish it from other members of that class. Like definition by synonym, it, too, is commonly found in abridged dictionaries, though much less elaborately than a writer may like in his own work. In definition by analysis, the definer comes closer than in any other means to the search for full meaning that is the primary end of the use of language as an instrument of inquiry. The resources of the analytic definition are exhausted only when there remain no more questions to ask, no more distinctions to make. It may do its job adequately in one sentence or may fail to come to the end of it in a volume. Whether a sentence or a volume is needed depends on the purpose the definition is meant to serve and on the perceptiveness of the definer.

The **synthetic definition** is like the analytic definition in naming a class word and distinguishing characteristics; it differs in the fact that the distinguishing characteristic *depends on* the class. To define the "pre-Cambrian" as the "earliest geological period" is to define synthetically; so, also, is to define "electron" as "one of the smallest particles of matter." Synthetic definitions are concise, but often they fail to supply as much information as one would wish. Think how much more a beginner would need to know about pre-Cambrian age or about electrons in order to understand the definition. The synthetic definition is incomplete, but it is at least emphatic—it calls attention to just one characteristic of the thing in question, and if that characteristic is important enough, such a definition can be highly economical.

Earlier in this chapter we mentioned the frustration caused by definitions like " 'imperturbable' means 'not perturbable.' " Still, **definition by negation** sometimes has its uses. Remember, for instance, how much of it proved necessary in the dialogue on "gig." Similarly, it might be helpful in some situations to be told that the crocodile is not (technically) an amphibian. But notice that such definitions do their work only when the audience already knows rather a lot about the things or concepts involved—knows, for instance, what the biological characteristics of amphibians are. Negation is, at best, a helpful aid to definition, never more than a way station.

The four methods of definition reviewed so far—by synonym, by analysis, by synthesis, and by negation—all fit the pattern of equivalence ($x = y$). One other kind of definition lies at the edge of this group; it may be called **definition by likeness** (by comparison, simile, or analogy). One of Robert Frost's most impressive sonnets begin with the line

"She is as in a field a silken tent,"

and goes on to explore the simile. Of course the value of the definition hinges on the power of the image to suggest, of itself and through connotations developed in the poem, important qualities of "she"; fragility, resilience, strength, sensitivity, serene aloofness, surprising stability. This may be a roundabout way to define, or it may strike to the heart of the matter, depending on the skill and discrimination of the writer (who should be secure in his mastery of connotations before he attempts this sort of definition). But in less imaginative forms, definition by likeness is within the reach of every writer, and highly pertinent, for all its indirection. The ways in which marriage is like an armed truce, or a pretty girl like a melody, or a peccary like a pig, are important and illuminating, even though no comparison will match up *definiendum* and *definiens* point for point (if it did, it would be an equivalence, and the word "like" would be out of place). Moreover, it is important for the definer who chooses this method to spell out the ways in which, say, a peccary is *not* like a pig. Definition by likeness is never complete, but it can be dramatic, suggestive, and vivid.

Of the methods of definition that remain to be discussed, some may lend themselves to expression as equivalences, but that form does little justice to their nature. Essentially they focus attention in a certain way, or suggest operations to perform, or illustrate the *definiendum* in action. Consider first the least important of these methods, **ostensive definition,** or definition by showing. It is much more common in speech than in writing, since it must be accompanied by a gesture, or the equivalent: "What is a cam shaft?" "That, right there." The writer may, however, get the result by using pictures or symbols: "This is an ampersand: &." Or he may direct attention to the thing in question through verbal instructions: "If you look for a minute at a bright light and then close your eyes, what you will see is an after-image." The speaker or writer, in defining this way, does not offer an equivalent for the *definiendum,* but points to an instance, from which his audience can generate its own definition.

This method is closely related to **definition by example,** the difference being that one who defines by example mentions or describes an instance, rather than actually showing one. "What is a *Bildungsroman?*" "Well, books like *Great Expectations, The Red and the Black,* and *A Portrait of the Artist as a Young Man.*" "Oh, you mean a novel about growing up." "Yes, that's it." The definer does not specify the properties of his *definiendum,* but leaves that task to the audience. Of course, his several examples may have more than one characteristic in common, some of which are irrelevant to the term defined, and for this reason definition by example is most reliable when accompanied by a standard analytic definition. However, it can stand alone if the audience knows the object, but not the name of it: "Lepidoptera are lunas, monarchs, fritillaries, swallowtails, and so on." Definition by example relies upon the fact that every class has what logicians call an *extension* —a set of individual members—as well as an *intension*—a set of shared characteristics which unites the members. When a writer produces examples, he is listing part of the extension of the class, but his purpose is to guide the reader to an understanding of the intension. The best way to do this, obviously, is to spell out the intension, and use the examples as supplementary material. But if, for some reason, the writer wishes to let his examples carry the whole burden of definition, he has two responsibilities. First, he should offer enough examples to allow correct generalization (he might even list the whole extension, if the class is a small one); and second, he should make sure that his examples are typical and illuminating (for defining purposes, selling the Brooklyn Bridge is a much better example of "fraudulence" than selling a shoddy piece of furniture because the new "owner" of the bridge has nothing at

all to show for his money). These cautions should not obscure the un-
equaled usefulness of examples in defining. Not only do they give body
and clarity to a writer's definitions; they are indispensable aids to per-
suading, since a concrete instance often captures the reader's interest and
imagination when a generalization fails to do so.

> • *Exercise 1.11:* How does the following definition work? It is possible to
> deduce from it an analytic definition? What is gained and lost by the
> attempt?

> July 3, 1943
>
> We received a letter from the Writers' War Board the other day asking
> for a statement on "The Meaning of Democracy." It presumably is our duty
> to comply with such a request, and it is certainly our pleasure.
>
> Surely the Board knows what democracy is. It is the line that forms
> on the right. It is the don't in Don't Shove. It is the hole in the stuffed shirt
> through which the sawdust slowly trickles; it is the dent in the high hat.
> Democracy is the recurrent suspicion that more than half of the people are
> right more than half of the time. It is the feeling of privacy in the voting
> booths, the feeling of communion in the libraries, the feeling of vitality
> everywhere. Democracy is the score at the beginning of the ninth. It is an
> idea which hasn't been disproved yet, a song the words of which have not
> gone bad. It's the mustard on the hot dog and the cream in the rationed
> coffee. Democracy is a request from a War Board, in the middle of a morn-
> ing in the middle of a war, wanting to know what democracy is.
>
> E. B. WHITE, *The Wild Flag*

The other kinds of definition without equivalence do their work by
revealing the object or the word in action. **Definition by function** is an
extremely common type, especially useful when the object, person, and
so on, is known primarily for what it does: "A detergent cleans"; "A
podiatrist studies and treats disorders of the foot." Closely related, but
often more complex, are what scientists call **operational definitions,**
definitions which express the meaning of a term by listing the operations
one must perform in order to see if the term applies. Take these simple
instructions: "Measure the three sides of a triangle; if they are equal
in length, the triangle is equilateral." Many of the terms in science can
be operationally defined—"mass," "precipitate," "relativity"—and scientists tend to prefer such definitions because they make it possible for
any investigator to confirm the results of another, and because they
incorporate, not only knowledge, but the means of arriving at knowledge.

Definition by context is much like operational and functional definition, but the definer, instead of describing the behavior or use of things, illustrates the behavior or use of the term itself. The quotations (on pp. 43–44) drawn from the *Oxford English Dictionary* to illustrate meanings of "nice" are examples of definition by context; they show the word in action, giving thereby a richer insight into its meanings than analytic definition alone. Partly, the meaning of a word is a function of its interaction with other words: What adjectives apply to "proposition"? Can "astonish" have an inanimate noun for direct object? If one does not know the answers to these questions, he will not be able to use the words appropriately, nor will he fully understand them. "Famulary" means "of or pertaining to servants"; so says the dictionary. But what does one do with the word? Does one speak of "famulary duties"? "famulary men and women"? "famulary quarters"? "famulary virtues"? Can something be "exceedingly famulary"? Only definition by context could resolve these problems. It goes without saying that children first learn words largely from contextual appearances, and though this method is cumbersome in itself, it is often an indispensable aid to defining, even in prose that is far from childlike.

There are more ways of defining than these ten, but these are perhaps the most important. And indeed, it may seem that ten are too many. How is the writer ever to get on with his business if he must ponder such a battery of methods every time he wishes to define a term? Actually, the matter is not as complex as that. As we have indicated, the various patterns of definition have their peculiar virtues and flaws; each is particularly appropriate in some contexts, and quite out of place in others. The very needs which lead the writer to define will in part determine which method or methods he selects, as will his rhetorical purpose, his relationship to his reader. The important thing is for him to have the patterns at his command and to understand how each of them works. Once he has achieved that much mastery, framing a definition will become more a matter of solving individual writing problems than a matter of memory and labored choice.

- *Exercise 1.12:* How would you go about defining these words, given the stated purpose or problems?

  a. genius (You want to analyze the role of genius in public life.)
  b. realistic (You are faced with a disagreement as to whether *Moby-Dick* is realistic.)
  c. syndrome (You want to decide whether a certain journalist is justified

in using the word to describe President Richard M. Nixon's style of
speaking.)
  d. lip-service (You want to analyze a new attitude of college students
     toward social issues, an attitude for which there is as yet no convenient
     name, and lip-service comes close without being quite right.)

5/ Structures of Explanation

Definition is concerned with locating the concept; once located, it
will take its place in a larger structure of explanation. In addition to
thinking about concepts in isolation, then, we should begin to consider
such questions as how they fit together, what kinds of combinations there
are, and what happens to a concept when it enters into combination with
others.

Some kinds of structures have very little effect on the concepts which
constitute them. *Lists,* for instance, are usually just collections of elements, perhaps alphabetized for handy sorting out. If they are alphabetized, the principle of order—the alphabet—is meant to be arbitrary,
to tell us nothing about the elements in the list except their place in the
handy order we have imposed. Lists are also extensible: nothing in their
makeup prevents new elements from being added on or fitted in.

It is because they make so few claims to order that lists are often
useful, but that strength is sometimes a weakness, when the concepts
being listed seem to require greater coherence of treatment. Well into
the last century, some philosophers felt challenged by the fact that an
encyclopedia simply lists, alphabetically, the elements of human knowledge. Some felt it was almost an insult to so noble a subject as human
knowledge to organize it alphabetically: surely it ought to be possible
to put first things first—mathematics, or theology—and then to show
how the rest of knowledge followed from such a fountainhead.

Had they been able to achieve their dreamed-of structure, they would
have produced an elaborate *hierarchy,* with a place for everything man
has learned, and a reason for its being at that place and not another.
Earlier, when discussing jokes, we spoke of scales underlying much of
our ordinary classifying; a hierarchy is an elaborate and reasoned-out
scale. The elements in a hierarchy, unlike those on a list, are to some
extent defined by the position they hold: physics, in an ordering of
human knowledge, would be understood differently if it preceded biology. A common example of hierarchies is the table of organization
of a business or a military service, where the principles of organization

are power, authority, and responsibility, and where (for instance) a vice-president in charge of sales is defined in part by his formal relation to his superiors and inferiors. Above all, a hierarchy aims to be complete—without an office boy unaccounted for.

Between lists and hierarchies belong two other familiar kinds of structure: (1) the simple *chronicle,* which is a list of events organized on the principle of succession in time, and (2) the *taxonomy,* which makes an order based on complexity (*phyllum, genus, species* in biology) but, unlike a hierarchy, suggests nothing about superiority or inferiority in rank.

Even so brief and selected a list of structures may suggest useful questions to the practicing writer. Is he writing a simple chronicle, or is he introducing the organizing principle of causation, or of purpose? If one of the latter, how will he defend its introduction? Again, how much completeness, and of what kind, will he be aiming for? Is he writing a section of what would be a larger taxonomy, or part of a list? Is the extraordinary length of some of Faulkner's sentences, for instance, or the falsetto singing of The Beatles, an item on a list of characteristics, or the surface expression of some deeper characteristic? Finally, how dependent upon each other are these elements, and what is the nature of that dependence? Such questions can lead far indeed—sometimes too far to be useful for some purposes—but it is the failure to ask *any* such questions which results in the kind of writing called "cow," mentioned earlier in the chapter.

> • *Exercise 1.13:* (1) The summary volume of the University of Chicago's Great Books series is called the *Syntopicon.* How does it organize the Great Ideas? Take the first four: can you think of some other ways they might be organized? Are any of your ways better? Why? (2) The Dewey Decimal System replaced, in most libraries, earlier systems of classification. Besides standardizing catalog numbers, what were some of its virtues as a system, compared with the ones it replaced? Why is it now being replaced by the Library of Congress system? (3) Construct a set of terms for the "field" of a particular physical activity, such as sewing or tree-climbing. Choose an activity that doesn't yet have a terminology, or whose present terminology is inadequate. In tree-climbing, for instance, should you divide the process into "hunch" and "reach," or would "knees up," "knees grip," "hands up," "hands grip" be a better series?

The Pentad. The structures of explanation which we have considered so far are conceived extrinsically, as though they are the result of "standing back" from any real explanation, in order to see it in its broad outlines. They are independent of any subject-matter, and could organize discussions of nations or of hit songs. A more limited and intrinsic approach to structures of explanation has been suggested by the American philosopher and critic Kenneth Burke. Borrowing from Aristotle, Burke suggests that human beings possess a framework for concepts having to do with *human actions,* a framework which he calls "the pentad." This fivesome—compare the word "triad"—is rather like the rules of the game of explanation, the rules by which anyone instinctively plays whenever he sets about explaining human action. The five elements which a complete explanation of human action would include are these: Act, Scene, Agent, Agency, Purpose. There is the Act, or what was done; the Scene in which it occurred; the Agent or actor who did the act; the Agency he used in performing the act, such as the gun and getaway car for the holdup; and the Purpose of the Act, such as getting even with society. Act, Scene, Agent, Agency, Purpose—The terms seem simple because the model from which they are drawn fits so many ordinary circumstances—the model of a man physically doing something. For instance, a builder (Agent) uses a hammer (Agency) while building a house (Act), for someone to live in (Purpose) down the street (Scene). With the same ease we follow and construct much more complicated explanations. Suppose the radio reported that the government (Agent) had passed a law requiring registration of fire-arms (Act), in order to reduce the number of gun-crimes (Purpose) in the nation (Scene), the law to be enforced by local police (Agency). The reporter would be using the same framework for concepts, but the concepts would now be much more abstract, which is to say that both the concept and the relations between them invite and repay investigation. Consider some of the questions that might be raised here with the aid of the pentad:

1. Is democracy in danger in the situation described by the reporter? It might be if the government were acting as Agent, rather than as Agency of the people. Or is the government, in this case, really acting representatively, that is, as Agency, so that thinking of it as Agent is just a convenient device?
2. Similarly, is treating the government as a single Agent just another shorthand device, or does the term "government" tend to cover over deep divisions among the White House, Attorney General's Office, FBI, and Congress, or within any of those groups? If there are divisions, are they evident in the Act itself? Will they have any bearing on the ability of the Act to achieve the Purpose?

American soldiers, but the quality and meaning of their sympathy, if not its intensity, evidently varied with the rest of their terms.

* *Exercise 1.14:* In most versions of the so-called domino-theory of the Vietnamese war, the Scene is Southeast Asia. America (Agent) is supporting (Act) the Saigon government (Agency) in order to prevent the spread of Communism (Purpose) across Southeast Asia. Construct a version of this argument which still defends the American role in the war, but which replaces one or more terms in the framework. (Narrow the scene to Vietnam, for example, or change the Agency to American soldiers.) What changes does the adjustment require in the other terms? Now construct an argument *attacking* the war or the U.S. role in it, and analyze it in terms of the pentad.

Coherence and Sequence.   Looking at explanations of human actions as entities, it is clear that an explanation is not just a collection of five separate concepts loosely bundled together. Instead, an explanation has a shape and coherence of its own, which is produced by emphasizing two or three of the five elements, and stressing the connections between them. There is the familiar scene-act connection, in explanations which claim that somebody did something because he had no choice in that situation: the situation or Scene required that particular Act to be performed. "Bravely (or wretchedly, or gratefully) he kissed her—he had no choice." Or the same event might be explained by stressing the Agent-Act connection: "Isn't that just like him"? "That's him all over."

Both of these explanations employ the kind of connection we ordinarily call *cause,* but evidently there are different kinds of cause, depending on the sorts of concepts being connected. When we explain an action as the result of the Scene—a fire, for instance—we might be imagining cause as the connection between a stimulus and a response. If we say he did something because that's the sort of person he is, "cause" might be translated as "appropriate expression."

Both our kinds of cause might be called *static,* to distinguish them from more sequential, or *dynamic,* explanations. There are explanations which emphasize the Act-Agent connection, for instance, where the Act a man performs is said to change the kind of man he is. Consider the fellow who breaks a life-long rule against borrowing in order to meet a particular emergency. Having repaid the loan, does he return to his firm principle or, having found he can get in and out of debt, decide to acquire a credit card? If the latter, his act of borrowing has changed him not simply into one-who-borrowed but into a persistent borrower.

Or one might stress the Act-Scene sequence, in which the Act changes the Scene. Kenneth Burke tells the story of a woman serving on a volunteer committee which met in the evening around a large table, in an area separated from the rest of the office by a railing. As her disagreement with the rest of the committee increased, she first grew silent, then got up from the table, walked outside the railing to where the coats were piled, put her coat on, faced the group, and announced her resignation. This story can be told, as we have just tried to tell it, item by item, one act simply following another. Told that way, however, the story does not quite make sense. With the help of the Act-Scene connection, one can better understand the sequence, and write about it more coherently. The disillusioned volunteer, one might say, performs a series of physical Acts which make the physical Scene conform to her inner, emotional state of disagreement; outside the railing and dressed for the street, she evidently feels herself in a position—in a new Scene—which makes possible for her the new Act of resignation. To use the pentad in this way is to look for principles of coherence in what would otherwise be a mere succession of events.

> • *Exercise 1.15:* (1) Without using the names for the pentadic terms (Act, Scene, and so forth), rewrite in two or three paragraphs our first version of the committeewoman's story, trying to imply the principles of coherence which you find most plausible. (2) Think of some other possible connections between terms of the pentad, and give examples. Is each of your connections primarily static or dynamic? Which of these possibilities are you most used to hearing and using?

Sequences and progressions are the most difficult—and often the most interesting—kinds of connections to think about. Our final example of sequence is of a more familiar type: the movement from one relatively static explanation to another one. Imagine a judge who explains a candystore robbery by emphasizing the connection between the Scene, the Agent, and the Act: the slum-Scene produced the kind of boy (Agent) who "naturally" did the Act. So far, the prognosis is acquittal. But the judge is perhaps not happy with this formulation of the situation, since it would make the Law, which he serves, useless and irrelevant. So he moves to a new explanation of the situation, by imagining a new Agent, Society: "Nevertheless, Society cannot allow its enemies to go unpunished, or chaos will follow." The question is, how does the judge move from one explanation to the other?

• *Exercise 1.16:* Write an essay in which, with the help of the pentad, you either bridge the judge's gap, or construct a different explanation for him. What explanatory connections, for instance, might the judge establish between the Society which he sees threatened, and the slum which is presumably a part of it?

Models and World-Views. Nearly everyone is agreed that World War II was to some extent the result of World War I—more specifically, the result of the terms of the armistice of 1918 and of the peace treaty of 1919. But what exactly is the connection? More fundamentally, what sort of connection makes a convincing explanation? Many of the explanations have drawn on common-sense psychology. They first locate the cause in Germany (the Agent) and then ascribe to Germany certain emotions which depend on everyday notions of what motivates individual people. In this case, Germany is supposed to have felt ashamed over losing World War I, angry at the harsh terms of peace which the Allied Powers imposed, and jealous of the victors. Using the model of a person, then, who is motivated by ordinary kinds of emotion, and using the Agent-Act connection, the following explanation seems to make perfect sense: Germany started World War II in order to get even with the victors of World War I, just as a vindictive person might have done.

The historian A. J. P. Taylor, discussing the effects of the armistice and the peace treaty, offers quite a different kind of explanation. True, he says, many Germans did resent the terms of these agreements.

> But the armistice had another side. It tied the Germans in the immediate present; it tied the Allies for the future. They were anxious to ensure that the German nation acknowledged defeat; and therefore the armistice was concluded with representatives of the German government, not with a military delegation. The Germans duly acknowledged defeat; in return—and almost without realizing it, the Allies recognized the German government. . . . More than this, the Allies not only recognized the German Reich; its continued existence now became essential to them if the armistice were to be maintained. The Allies were transformed, without conscious intent, into Allies of the Reich against anything which threatened to destroy it—against popular discontent, against separatism [division of Germany into smaller states], against Bolshevism.
>
> This was carried further by the peace treaty, again without deliberation. . . . The treaty was designed to provide security against new German aggression, yet it could work only with the co-operation of

the German government. Germany was to be disarmed; but the German government would arrange this—the Allies only provided a Control commission to see that the disarmament had been carried out. Germany was to pay reparations; again, the German government would collect the money and pay it over—the Allies merely received it. Even the military occupation of the Rhineland [a part of Germany] depended on German co-operation. The civil administration remained in German hands; and German refusal to co-operate would produce a state of confusion for which the peace treaty made no provision. In the immediate situation of 1919 the peace treaty seemed crushing and vindictive; a *Diktat* or a slave-treaty as the Germans called it. In a longer perspective, the most important thing in the treaty is that it was concluded with a united Germany. Germany had only to secure a modification of the treaty, or to shake it off altogether; and she would emerge as strong, or almost as strong, as she had been in 1914.

The Origins of The Second World War, Fawcett, pp. 27–28

In Mr. Taylor's explanation, we seem to be moving in a world quite different from the common-sense psychological one. Strange sorts of events occur, and odd effects follow from apparently straightforward acts. The collective Agent, the Allies, had clear purposes—providing for peace and their own security—and so they performed the Acts of imposing the armistice and of forcing Germany to sign a peace treaty. So far, so good for the Allies. But their Acts, Mr. Taylor shows, had a logic independent of the purpose for which they were performed. Because a peace treaty is not the same as a battle, because it is a joint act, an apparently triumphant treaty may be curiously self-defeating. The Act has consequences of its own, primarily that of strengthening the defeated opponent. If in addition the opponent is the technical Agent expected to carry out the provisions of the Act, he gains further strength.

In a way, ascribing these results to the Act depends just as much on matters of common sense and belief as ascribing jealousy to a nation would. What Mr. Taylor provides is a means of understanding the unlucky inadvertence of large-scale, international events. In the world he describes, governments act primarily out of self-interest, but it is a self-interest blind to the formal properties of events. Between a government's Act and the achievements of its purpose, Mr. Taylor interposes a realm of intricate and surprising logical structures which surround the Act— or sometimes, the failure to act—itself. Because the consequences are unexpected, Acts in Mr. Taylor's world seem to have a kind of power in themselves; and governments seem to be like men stumbling blindfolded in a room full of dangerous machinery which they have created and have set in motion.

> • *Exercise 1.17:* Try to describe one of the following events in such a way that the Act performed has surprising effects—surprising to the Agent who performs the Act. You might cast your account in the form of a narration.
>
> a. Telling a clothing salesman that he has bad breath.
> b. Promoting a petition to end parietal hours.
> c. Announcing your discovery that the poet Shelley was a girl.
> d. Asking one's harassed mother what time dinner will be ready.

Here is another example of a historical explanation, with a different world-view—a newspaper essay by the syndicated columnist Holmes Alexander, which ran under the headline "The Energy of Affluence." (We will number the paragraphs for easier reference.)

1. Washington—President Johnson lacks an ability to make himself understood in foreign policy, but this is not to say that he doesn't have what it takes.
2. LBJ holds two beliefs which are the foundation rocks of his thinking in international matters, and he has a special capacity in addition to these.
3. First, the President regards our war against communism as an open-ended struggle. It is not a game limited to nine innings, 60 minutes, 10 rounds, five sets, four chukkars or any other frame-work. The contest, as he sees it, goes on forever.
4. Second, the President, being no Fancy Dan of a philosopher, sees the Communist hatred of capitalistic America with ranchhouse clarity. The struggle will not conveniently come to an end so long as we are the haves and they are have-nots. "We've got too much that they want," the President puts it.
5. Moreover, as a self-made millionaire in a wealthy nation, Mr. Johnson has an unusual understanding of the American nature. We are not, as shallow thinking supposes, merely accumulators of material riches and world power.
6. The dynamics of history have generated an energy that makes Americans different from other peoples on earth.
7. This energy of affluence characterizes the U.S.A. far more truly than our alleged acquisitiveness and our current frenzy for social welfare. And it is this energetic push, better understood by the Texan

President than by his immediate predecessors, which has made contact with the Communist world.

8. Lyndon Johnson, among other things, is the examplar of a compulsive activity in America. It is a force which wouldn't consider giving up anything of value. It drives forward, not for the purpose of accumulating more, but because it does not have the built-in capacity to stop.

9. We have here a peculiarly American trait which is not often considered as a factor in foreign policy. Yet it is such a factor. It is a counter-factor to the Communist jealousy.

10. It is an automatic guarantee that we are not going to give up the struggle so long as we have a leader who instinctively understands the quality.

11. The Johnson foreign policy has this hidden resiliency which needs to be taken into account. It supplies a staying-power that is more than a match for the Communist determination to fight on till the end of time.

12. For though it's true, as the President often says, that the U.S.A. seeks nothing by conquest, it's also true that we are not a nation to sit back on our wealth and be corrupted by it.

13. If we are in an endless struggle, we are blessed with a faculty of inexhaustible energy and, in this respect, we are quite unlike the empires of the past, which have succumbed to the barbarians.[1]

(Hartford *Times,* June 30, 1967)

One of the reasons for the complexity of this piece is the fact that it is composed of two related arguments, the first about President Johnson, and the second about History and the American character. In the first, Johnson is a good president because he clearly *understands* two matters having to do with foreign policy, and because he personally *represents,* without having to think about it, something central to the American character and experience. In terms of the pentad, one could say that understanding is one kind of Act, and representing is another. Both kinds are meant to be praiseworthy here—both are meant to show that he has "what it takes"—but there is an important difference: to praise a man for understanding something is to credit him with being a free Agent, and a successful one. On the other hand, to praise him for unconsciously representing something valuable is to convert him into an Agency. This conversion begins here at paragraph 5, as the essay shifts to the second argument about History and the American character, although the transition is made less abrupt by such phrases as "unusual

[1] Reprinted by permission of the McNaught Syndicate, Inc.

understanding" (5) and "instinctively understands" (10). Perhaps Mr. Alexander means that President Johnson consciously chooses to act out what he already is—which would be a third kind of action.

Our analysis so far has been strictly preliminary, beginning the task of laying out the argument as it develops. You will find other connections between the two arguments: what Mr. Johnson is said to understand in paragraphs 2 and 3, for instance, is meant to help justify the existence of the peculiar energy described in the later paragraphs. But with this much introduction, you should be ready to carry on, into fairly elaborate exploration.

- *Exercise 1.18:* a. In the second argument of Alexander's piece, call "energy" the Agent, with President Johnson the Agency (however conscious a one). What is the Scene? What Acts are ascribed to the Agent; and what Acts might it be expected to perform? Are there any Acts which it might not be expected to perform? Since the argument is so general, try "plugging in" some specific acts which you can imagine a government deciding to perform.

    b. Or is the notion of a government deciding to do something incommensurate with this particular argument? When one thinks of decisions, he usually links them to Purpose: people decide to do things for some purpose, or motive. Here, we are told that greed is not the purpose; can you find a Purpose? If Purpose is largely omitted in the explanation, does anything serve in its place?

    c. Consider the phrase, in paragraph 7, "made contact." Many people speak of making contact with someone for the purpose of communication, or cooperation; military tacticians speak of a patrol making contact with the enemy. How is Mr. Alexander using the term? Support your analysis with other examples from the piece.

    d. Does your last argument suggest anything about the kind of world which Mr. Alexander imagines? How would you describe that world's elements, and the possible relations between them? Are the elements best described as people, or nations, or forces, or some other kind of entity? Make a list of the relations between these elements which are referred to by Mr. Alexander, perhaps starting with "jealousy" (paragraph 9). Do these relations seem in any way commensurate with each other—do they seem to be drawn from a particular kind of explanation of human action? How does this world differ from that of A. J. P. Taylor?

    e. In short, can you describe "ranchhouse clarity"? In so philosophical a piece, the mention of "Fancy Dan" philosophers suggests that Mr. Alexander considers his kind of philosophizing crucially different from other kinds. Try to describe the difference, as he sees it.

    f. Now write a complete essay on Mr. Alexander's piece, explaining the sources of your agreement and disagreement.

6/ Lexical Defining

In your analysis of Mr. Alexander's essay, you have reached the most general problem in the study of structures of explanation: an attempt to describe the tacit set of rules by which the "world" of his essay is put together. From such heights of generality, one can look across to other peaks belonging to the same mountain range: speech acts (Chapter Two), proof (Chapter Three), and persuasion (Chapter Four). But while here, we may pause to explore several matters adjacent to the general problem of locating concepts. The most obvious of these is the dictionary, whether pocket-sized or shelf-length.

Most people have widest acquaintance with the definitions that appear in dictionaries, that is, with *lexical* definitions, and these bear special consideration. The task of a lexicographer, contrary to popular belief, is mainly one of reporting, not prescribing. He is concerned with recording the actual meanings and uses of words, noting, to be sure, which uses are colloquial, slangy, characteristic of the uneducated, and so forth, but not dictating the way language *should* be used. He presents the meanings of a word that have had or still have currency, those that various men at various times and for various purposes have used. An abridged dictionary records as many meanings as suit its purposes and size; an unabridged dictionary purports to record all the meanings that have sound claim to attention, all that have had enough currency at any time to be considered a legitimate part of the language.

One of the editorial consultants of the *American College Dictionary* (abridged) reports that he and his colleagues tabulated 832 meanings of the word "run," but that they included only 104 of those meanings in the desk dictionary which they helped to compile. The reason for their making so drastic a reduction is obvious enough, but the grounds on which they chose one meaning rather than another for inclusion may be less evident. They might, of course, have excluded all meanings no longer current, but to do so would have been to reduce the usefulness of the dictionary for anyone dealing with the writing of past centuries. They might have limited their choice to meanings common in the general use of language, barring all technical usages. Or they might have made more or less arbitrary choices, setting down the meanings they approved or those which the etymology of the word seemed to justify. The inadequacy of any of those criteria is readily apparent. What lexicographers actually do in such a case is attempt to determine which meanings are most common in general discourse, and then to make special provision for technical, rare, purely colloquial, and dialectical meanings. If they have done their work well, the meanings they record are all proper, the equivalences true equivalences, and the definitions "good" ones.

Unabridged dictionaries are of two kinds: (1) those that record the full range of meanings detected by lexicographers, arranging them in groups to indicate similarity; (2) those that attempt to locate the earliest appearance of each meaning and to record its persistence at subsequent periods. Both kinds may, and generally do, document the meanings they list by brief quotations. The foremost American unabridged dictionary is *Webster's New International,* a large one-volume work which not only contains a much greater number of meanings for each word than an abridged dictionary but also defines a much greater number of words. Even more extensive and elaborate is the *Oxford English Dictionary,* the great historical dictionary of the English language. Its thirteen folio-size volumes make it possible to scan in one place the entire history of a word, and it is for that reason an invaluable resource for students and scholars alike. Some idea of its approach to the problem of defining can be gathered from a greatly abbreviated account of its treatment of the highly ambiguous word "nice," a word so variously used today that one would be hard put to answer quickly a demand for its definition. Since the OED is a dictionary built on historical principles, it is appropriate to rephrase the defining question to read not "What does 'nice' mean?" but "What did, and does, 'nice' mean?" A few (perhaps one-sixth) of the answers to that question are set down here:

Foolish, stupid, senseless. *Obs.* (Common in 14th and 15th c.) a. Of persons.

> 1387) Trevisa *Higden* (Rolls) VI. 23 He made the lady so mad and so nice that she worshipped him as the greatest prophet of God Almighty.

Wanton, loose-mannered; lascivious. *Obs.* c. Of dress: Extravagant, flaunting. *Obs.*

> 1563) *Homilies* II. *Idolatry* III. (1640) 72 An Image with a nice and wanton apparell and countenance.

Slothful, lazy, indolent. *Obs. rare.* b. Effeminate, unmanly. *Obs., rare.*

> 1598) Florio, *Paranimpha* . . . an effeminate, nice, milkesop, puling fellow.

Fastidious, dainty, difficult to please, esp. in respect of food or cleanliness; also in good sense, refined, having refined tastes.

> 1782) Cowper *Mut. Forbearance* 20 Some people are more nice than wise.

d. Precise or strict in matters of reputation or conduct; punctilious, scrupulous, sensitive.

1887) BARING-GOULD *Red Spider* xvii, I should get it back again ... and not be too nice about the means.

Not obvious or readily apprehended; difficult to decide or settle; demanding close consideration or thought; intricate. b. Minute, subtle; also of differences, slight, small.

1870) HOWSON *Metaph St. Paul* ii. 41 When we desire to appreciate the nicer shades of meaning.

Agreeable; that one derives pleasure or satisfaction from; delightful.

1837) MAJ. RICHARDSON Brit. Legion ix. (ed. 2) 220 The Commandant, whom I subsequently found to be a very nice fellow.

The soundness of such definitions is beyond dispute simply because the cited text is evidence that the word once had the meaning attributed to it by the lexicographer (historical lexicographers do occasionally make mistakes in definition, but their citations give the dictionary-user a chance to spot any lapses). The importance of appreciating the historical "truth" of a definition is more apparent for reading, of course, than it is for writing. A man writes, for the most part, with his own age in mind, and he defines words with the assumption that his readers will know that he means their definition to be taken as referring to his and his readers' present existence. If for any reason he prefers to use a word in a manner no longer common, he prefixes to his use of it a reminder: "When I call Miss Grundy a spinster, I use the word *in its now almost forgotten sense,* not of an unmarried woman past her prime, but of one who makes her living at the spinning wheel." But the reading of books from other periods is not made easy in this way. In dealing with them, the reader must always be aware that meanings do change and that his understanding of a passage depends on his knowing the words in it as their author knew them. To read "humorous" in these lines from Kyd's *Spanish Tragedy* as though it means "amusing" is to miss the point altogether:

> "My Lord, be not dismay'd for what is pass'd;
> You know that women oft are humorous."

Kyd's use of "humorous" is conventional for his time, and a check on the meaning of that word in the sixteenth century will provide the information needed to make the passage intelligible. Meaning in this instance, however difficult it may be to come at, is literal. When it is more than literal, when, for instance, a pun is involved, the reader may have to resort to historical knowledge of other kinds, to etymology, for example, as in these lines from Milton's *Paradise Lost*:

> "As we erewhile, astounded and amaz'd
> No wonder, fall'n such a pernicious highth."
> (1.281-2)

Both "pernicious" and "astounded" are serious puns; both mean what they still mean today in common usage, but both have additional meanings drawn from their Latin ancestry. "Astounded" comes from *ex-tonare* and thus refers to being struck by, or hurled out by, thunder, a reference to the battle in which Satan was cast out of heaven by God. "Pernicious" comes from *per-nex* and means "through death" or "death-giving," a description of the "highth" much more impressive than one is likely to understand if the word is taken only to mean "bad" or "undesirable."

7/ Form in Definition

After a writer has successfully thought out the purpose and means of his definition, he may still encounter snags in the actual wording of it, even if he uses the neat form of equivalence that is common to most definitions. One requirement of the form is that the terms on both sides of "is" or "means" be of the same grammatical class: a noun on one side of the equation demands a noun on the other, an adjective demands an adjective, and so on. The following definitions, though adequate as far as meaning is concerned, illustrate breaches of form:

> Rent is paying money to an owner for the use of his property.
> Cramming is when you study very hard immediately before an examination.
> "Flagrant" means something openly outrageous or illegal.

A simple correction in each preserves the proprieties of expression:

> Rent is money paid to an owner for the use of his property.
> Cramming is studying very hard immediately before an examination.
> "Flagrant" means openly outrageous or illegal.

Despite its neatness, the invariability of the formula $x = y$ may make it disagreeable to the writer. To avoid the mechanical balancing of *definiendum* against *definiens,* he may resort to several other patterns. He may, for instance, compress a definition in this fashion: "A square joins four equal straight lines at right angles so as to form a complete enclosure." This is the same as the analytic definition, "a square is a geometrical figure in which four equal straight lines meet at right angles so as to form an enclosure," but substituting an active verb for the copula and class term of the analytic definition considerably reduces formality. Another way of reducing formality and providing variety is to use the grammatical structure known as "apposition." This also has the advantage of reducing emphasis on the definition so that the forward movement of the discourse is not interrupted:

> Paul used the Greek term *agape,* a word meaning "brotherly love," to distinguish a kind of Christian love which he believed to be entirely different from love as the unrelieved search for fulfillment discussed in Plato's *Symposium* and deeply rooted in subsequent Greek thought.

In *"agape,* a word meaning 'brotherly love,' " there is a definition (by translation) which is presented as an appositive. The reader gets the explanation of *agape* which the definition supplies without having his attention drawn away from the principal focus of the sentence (a contrast between two concepts of love). If the writer had wished to provide the Greek equivalent for "love as the unrelieved search . . ." as he did for "brotherly love," he could have used the same device as for *agape,* or he could have set the word *eros* in parentheses after "fulfillment." If his intent had been to follow this paragraph with a discussion of the Platonic concept, he might have wished to emphasize the term for it, preparatory to beginning a discussion. To do so, he would have separated the definition from the preceding sentence in this way:

> . . . entirely different from the Platonic concept of love. That concept, given the name *eros,* was the embodiment of the human faculty of desire, of yearning, of lust to possess. It included every manifestation of powerful longing from the most sensual to the completely sublimated.

In this example of a definition to which importance has been lent by its presentation in an independent sentence, one can see also the most common device writers have for making definitions fully effective—that of adding definition to definition until a complex series of equations is established for the *definiendum.*

8/   Checks in Definition

The various ways in which a definition can be presented give the writer no excuse for failing to clarify as he goes along, unless, of course, his purpose at a given point in the discourse is to mystify or to create suspense by withholding information. He may use one means of definition only, or many; he may set down his definition with all the starkness of a mathematical equation or with the unobtrusiveness of an aside. Which means and which manner he uses will depend on his intent and on his assessment of his readers' needs.

Once the writer understands the nature of the defining process and knows how to handle definitions deftly in the regular flow of discourse, he may still need to check himself occasionally to make sure that his definitions will hold up under careful scrutiny. The process of writing is such that a writer is often carried along by his own words, the words seeming at times to come almost of themselves. So great is their impetus at such times that the writer may neither wish, nor be able, to check the rush of words. He will be convinced that the words say what he means to say and will not dare to test them at the time of the writing for fear of shutting off the flow itself. When he comes back to his work and looks at it soberly and critically, however, he may find inadequacies and contradictions where he would earlier have sworn that completeness and harmony reigned. At such times—and they are common—system is the best buckler against despair. If he can ask a series of questions about his terminology, if he can systematically test his definitions, he may swiftly discover the weaknesses and discrepancies and remedy them; if he cannot, he must write and rewrite until the sentences satisfy his inner ear. Both methods work, and most writers make use of one or the other as occasion demands.

A system of checks on what one has written is essentially negative. Like a mechanic checking an automobile engine to discover the cause of sluggish operation, the writer eliminates one by one the possible causes of disorder until he has found and corrected the faulty mechanism. This hunt for the causes of trouble is seldom as orderly an affair as a book will make it out to be, but that is true of the entire process of writing. In any case, a list of common faults in defining is helpful, even if the writer never applies the checks systematically.

OVERINCLUSION

Complete confidence about the meaning of some words, and equal confidence that others are sure to understand them as the user does, often makes the writer rather summary and careless in definition. For example, to define "patriotism" as "the feeling a man has for his country" is less than enough simply because men have many feelings about their country which are far from patriotic. This is the fault of overinclusion, of failing to qualify the class word in the *definiens* as much as it needs to be qualified. In the example given here the addition of qualifying phrases to "feeling" will help to correct the deficiency: "Patriotism is the feeling of partiality, respect, love, and pride which a man has for his country."

OVERRESTRICTION

At the other extreme, a definition may suffer from overrestriction, from being so closely confined by the class word or the qualifiers in the *definiens* that not all of the things to which the *definiendum* may properly refer are covered by it. "Kings are rulers by hereditary right" is an overrestrictive definition of the word "king" since it makes no provision for rulers who have taken thrones by force or who have been elevated to them without any hereditary claim at all. Both overinclusiveness and overrestriction can be detected by sampling, that is, by asking if all the examples one can call to mind have the attributes named or implied in the *definiens*.

DUPLICATION

It is sometimes convenient and useful, though often dangerous, to define a term simply by using a second term which has a different linguistic history but the same meaning. The definition, " 'Liberty' means 'freedom,' " uses a word of Latin origin on one side of the verb and a word of Germanic origin on the other. Where definition is needed because the *definiendum* (the word itself) is simply unfamiliar to the reader, this kind of definition may be valuable: " 'Prophylaxis' means 'cleaning' " is an example. Where definition is needed because the *definiendum* stands for something which the reader actually does not know, a definition of this kind is of little help. In general it is best avoided except in the act of translation ("Rot" in German means "red" in English) because it may appear to give information without actually doing so.

CIRCULARITY

A definition which uses the *definiendum,* or a variant of it, in the *definiens* is said to be circular. Most instances of circularity occur not in a single sentence ("Freedom is the state of being free") but in a series of sentences long enough so that the repetition of the *definiendum* is not immediately noticeable:

> *Freedom* is not easily defined except by reference to what it is not. The closest one can come, in positive terms, may be to call it "independence of action." Independent action is that which is free from coercion or control by any external agent whatsoever.

AMBIGUITY

In any writing, the danger of ambiguity is always great because words shift and multiply meanings so rapidly and because there is sometimes actually an accidental identity between the appearance or sound of words having very different meanings and origins. Think, for instance, of the differences in meaning between "herd" and "heard," or "foul" and "fowl," or between the two meanings of the word "mean," one from Medieval French, the other from Old English, in this sentence: "The average man is the mean man of the population." Definition is often thought of as the means of eradicating ambiguity, and it is true that stipulative definition, at least, does have that as its main purpose. Lexical, or historical, definition, however, does not so much eradicate as describe the essential ambiguity of words because it indicates all or a large number of the meanings which a word may have. Yet, despite the fact that definitions can seldom divorce themselves from ambiguity, there is a sense in which they must attempt to avoid it. The examples given above deal with *semantic* ambiguity, that deriving directly from the meanings of words themselves. Another kind of ambiguity, that known as syntactical, is more likely to plague the definer because it results from the careless handling of punctuation or of the order of words. To define a "willful abstainer" as "one who does not do something because he does not wish to" is to produce such ambiguity: in this instance, a simple cure is affected by placing a comma after "something." The definition "In gin rummy, a discard is a card placed by a player of no value to him in the center of the table face up in return for a card previously drawn from a face-down stack also in the center of the table" has all the words needed to make an accurate definition but they are arranged so badly that their meaning is ambiguous.

OBSCURITY

The person who defines stipulatively usually does so in order to clarify or restrict meaning. It is only a short step from stipulative defining of the right kind to another kind that is less defensible, the stipulation of bizarre and newly invented meanings for words in common use. The writer who insists on the privilege of making up his own definitions for words which, in ordinary discourse, have different meanings from the ones he attributes to them runs several risks. If the word for which he makes a private definition has strong connotations, nothing he can do will relieve it of them, no matter how he defines it. Moreover, because the writer, like his readers, is accustomed to using words with their conventional meanings, he is very likely to be caught off guard in any extended passage of writing and to find, too late, that he has used an important word both in a private sense and in the sense common to everyone. Should he be skilled enough to escape both dangers, he faces a third, that of developing a vocabulary so special and private that a reader needs a special lexicon to make use of his works. It is safe to say that a writer must have rare talents to find and keep readers willing to make such an effort for him. In most cases, such private defining is less the product of special insight than of laziness or pretentiousness; when either is the cause, the reader is fully warranted in leaving the writer to weave his web in splendid isolation.

These formal checks on one's defining are mechanical aids only. Good definitions can come only from some understanding of what is involved in the defining process. Enough has been said here to suggest the ramifications of that process and to indicate the respect it deserves from a serious writer.

- *Exercise 1.19:* Describe the faults in each of these definitions; then write a better one.

   a. When a group can maintain conformity, it is called equilibrium.
   b. Network: anything reticulated and decussated at equal intervals, with interstices between intersections (from Dr. Samuel Johnson's *Dictionary of the English Language*).
   c. Literature is the embodiment in words of a great religious or mythical system.
   d. A recluse is an eccentric.
   e. The real traitor is the man who criticizes his country in intemperate words.
   f. Verse is prose cut into lines of equal length.
   g. Osmosis is where one thing filters into another.
   h. The policy of containment can best be described as one in which the idea is to contain the spread of something uncontained.
   i. In underworld parlance, a rod is a gat.
   j. What Weber means by "charisma" is leadership.
   k. Sculpture is the representation of human or animal figures in marble.

chapter two / *Speech Acts*

1/ Words and Deeds

We have said that explanation is an activity, and we have spoken about writing in a dramatic metaphor, asking you to think of ideas as heroes and villains that move through a kind of plot. We do not use the metaphor lightly, for we hold that any piece of writing does in fact represent an action.

This is not a popular view. The vernacular has a rich store of idioms that draw a sharp line between speech and action, and make it clear that in any rating of words and deeds, words come out a feeble second best. "Just talk" and "empty words" are phrases that come to mind. A "big talker" is by implication a small doer, and therefore an object of derision. One may put him in his place by reminding him that "talk is cheap," or by rudely asking him to "put up or shut up." In more genteel circles such a fellow may be accused of "paying lip service" to his principles, instead of abiding by the wise saying that "actions speak louder than words." To be sure, the recourse to words instead of deeds may rarely count as a virtue: many would agree with Winston Churchill that it is better to "jaw, jaw" than to "war, war"; but even this preference rests on a conviction that talk is ineffectual and therefore harmless. "Sticks and stones will break my bones, but words will never hurt me."

It is true that words never broke a bone or stopped the breath. But aside from that, the idea expressed by the clichés in the preceding paragraph is nonsense of a high order. Words *are* deeds. Or to speak more exactly, the *use* of words is always a deed, and often a deed of some importance. Consider for a start, what the newspapers consider newsworthy. Even when physical and violent action troubles large parts of the world, as at this writing, the news is mostly about talk. Sunday, July 28, 1968: Only two stories on the front page of *The New York Times* report physical action, and those two only in part. The main action is verbal. For instance: (1) Senator McCarthy has said the American people feel, as they showed in the primaries, that "it is time for the killing to stop"

51

in Vietnam, and that the Democratic Party "must honor that mandate" or, by implication, lose the election. (2) Negro groups from Florida and Louisiana have filed statements with Republican officials that the convention delegations from these states have denied representation to Negroes. (3) Alexander Dubcek, the Communist party chief in Czechoslovakia, has said that his government will not take "even a step back from the road we have set out on"—that of liberalization. (4) The National Advisory Commission on Civil Disorders has said, in a long report, that urban riots are a form of social protest, widely supported by Negroes, and not the work of criminals or "riffraff." And so it goes. The only part of the paper that reports much "action," in the usual sense, is the sports section.

Why does the *Times* consider these utterances front page material? There's a temptation to suppose that the talk and writing is important only because it is a substitute for, or prelude to, or comment on the use of physical force which is just offstage: the Vietnamese war, a possible conflict between Czechoslovakia and the Soviet Union, riots and insurrection in American cities. True in part. But notice that in speaking and writing the words they did, these men and organizations already performed quite distinct actions. Reconsider:

1. Senator McCarthy used words to *infer,* but also to *warn,* as the *Times* headline duly noted. He was warning Democratic politicians that unless they responded to the public sentiment for peace, their party would fare badly at the polls. Whatever has happened subsequently, the act of warning was performed, and had its effect in the tug and pull of electoral politics.
   (Query: why was McCarthy's act not a *threat?*)
2. The groups from Florida and Louisiana performed the act of *accusing,* as well as that of *protesting.* Protest has a bad name just now—for being negativistic and ineffectual—but this particular protest, made formally, must be dealt with. It is already making an impact on Republican officials, and indirectly on the voters.
3. Dubcek's act-in-words was an *affirmation* of purpose and a *promise* (the *Times* called it a *pledge*). As such, it staked out a position for the upcoming talks between Czechoslovakia and the USSR, and thus altered, however slightly, the course of relations between those two countries. To see the force of such an act even more clearly, simply consider the consequences of not making good on the promise. No promise, no breach of promise.
4. The Advisory Commission's report performed the apparently bland act of *stating.* Yet that too counts. Against a background system of concepts that dismissed riots as the work of a small minority of delinquent types, the report's words were also a *contradiction*— much like giving the lie direct.

The italicized words name speech acts, of a particular kind that we shall call *illocutionary:* acts performed in saying something, just as in saying "Hello" one performs the act of greeting. They are actions in a quite precise and formal way, about which more later. For the moment, it will do to notice that in each case the action was performed simply by uttering or writing certain words in the right circumstances. No other physical movement was necessary, although naturally things like gesture, facial expression, and means of publication make a difference in how such acts are interpreted. The use of words was not just an accompaniment to the "real" action; the real action *was* the use of words. And what the words did is now done, not to be reversed except possibly by further acts in words.

> • *Exercise 2.1:* Work through the main stories in a newspaper or a news mag-
> azine, and note the illocutionary acts that are reported. In each case, how did
> the act alter the situation in which it was made? Might the speaker or writer
> have accomplished the same thing nonverbally? If you like, try to describe
> a major recent event as it might have happened (or failed to happen) with-
> out speech acts.

McCarthy, Dubcek, and the others performed their acts publicly and deliberately. We can be sure that they knew exactly what they were doing, and intended their actions to be reported widely. Given their positions, they could count on that result. Now, the overwhelming majority of speech acts gain little notice and have no bearing on political or diplomatic affairs, but they nonetheless count for something in the lives of the people who participate in them.

Take the act of marriage. It requires a whole network of speech acts, performed by at least three participants, in rigorously prescribed order, and often in a prescribed place. Moreover, there are papers to be drawn up and signed, to register the marriage and give it legal status. To be sure, the real meaning of a marriage for the couple, and its chances of success, do not hinge on these formalities. But although happy marriages may be built on love, the act of marrying is primarily a speech act—or rather a complex series of speech acts—and there is simply no other way to accomplish marriage in our society.

Many actions that require words proceed according to slacker conventions, but are binding nonetheless. Take the act of making a date. Any of the following exchanges—different though they are—would count as performing that act:

1. "I called to ask if you would like to go to the movies with me tomorrow night."

"I'd like to very much. Thanks."

"Great, I'll pick you up at 7:30."

2. "May I have the pleasure of your company at the cinema tomorrow evening?"

"Yes indeed, I shall be delighted to accompany you."

"Excellent. My car will stop for you at 7:30, if that hour suits your
convenience."

"It does, thank you; I shall await the event impatiently."

3. "Flick tomorrow?"

"O.K."

"7:30?"

"O.K."

No matter whether the words form complete sentences or not, or
whether the tone is familiar or decorous. If the parties go through a few
simple speech acts — *inviting, accepting, agreeing* on a time — then
the date has been arranged. Anyone who doubts the efficacy of such
words should consider the probable consequences of the boy's not showing up, or of the girl's telling him when he does show up that she has
changed her mind.

The best way to see that the words do in fact accomplish these
specific acts is to compare them with misfires like these:

1. "I've been wondering whom to ask to the movie tomorrow."

"I accept."

2. "Will you go to the movie with me tomorrow night?"

"Well, I wish I could."

3. "Would you like to see the movie tomorrow?"

"Yes, I would."

"That's interesting."

(Query: where is the failure in each exchange? What goes wrong?)

Making a date and marrying are actions that bind two people con-
tractually, and for that reason they are especially clear examples of the
word as deed. But in fact *all* exchanges of words are actions, even if
they have no contractual force. Some lines from a play will illustrate this
point. Lane, the butler, enters the room, and says:

Lady Bracknell and Miss Fairfax. (ALGERNON *goes forward to
meet them. Enter* LADY BRACKNELL *and* GWENDOLEN.)

LADY BRACKNELL.　Good afternoon, dear Algernon, I hope you are behaving very well.

ALGERNON.　I'm feeling very well, Aunt Augusta.

LADY BRACKNELL. That's not quite the same thing. In fact the two
things rarely go together. (*Sees* JACK *and bows to him with icy
coldness.*)

ALGERNON (*to* GWENDOLEN). Dear me, you are smart!

GWENDOLEN. I am always smart! Aren't I, Mr. Worthing?

JACK. You're quite perfect, Miss Fairfax.

GWENDOLEN. Oh! I hope I am not that. It would leave no room for
developments, and I intend to develop in *many directions.* (GWEN-
DOLEN *and* JACK *sit down together in the same corner.*)

LADY BRACKNELL. I'm sorry if we are a little late, Algernon, but I
was obliged to call on dear Lady Harbury. I hadn't been there
since her poor husband's death. I never saw a woman so altered;
she looks quite twenty years younger. And now I'll have a cup of
tea, and one of those nice cucumber sandwiches you promised me.

    OSCAR WILDE, *The Importance of Being Earnest*

It's easy to put labels on the sentences and clauses—Lane's *announcement,* Lady Bracknell's *greeting* and *statement* (which expresses
a hope), Algernon's *reply,* Lady Bracknell's two *statements,* which also
constitute an *objection* to Algernon's reply, and so on through Lady
Bracknell's final speech, which includes an *apology,* and *excuse,* and a
request. There is little here that borders on the contractual, but the
whole conversation is a network of illocutionary acts, each contributing
(trivially, to be sure) to the evolution of the social occasion.

> • *Exercise 2.2:* In the excerpt just quoted, how does the comedy exploit
> illocutionary acts? Which speakers attempt illocutionary acts that are sur-
> prising, in context? What instances are there of common illocutionary acts
> used for odd purposes? What does this tell about character? Try a brief skit
> of your own, in which illoculationary acts reveal character and carry forward
> plot. Or, starting from an arbitrarily chosen series of acts (such as greeting,
> commanding, defying, lamenting), write two instances of the series, one of
> which will be farcical, and one potentially tragic.

Talking is doing. So, of course, is writing. For many people talking
and writing are the main modes of action, and it is hard to think of
anyone but a hermit who does not use words to perform a good proportion of the acts that move his life along. One may lament this fact as a
token of the flabby, over-civilized lives we lead, or, more realistically,
one may accept speech acts as the common inheritance of human beings,
as an extraordinarily versatile means of social interaction, and as an art
to be mastered.

2/ The Rules for Doing Things with Words

We have just been insisting that people cannot use words without performing deeds. Now a few steps in the opposite direction: not all acts can be performed this way; nobody is capable of performing all the possible speech acts; those you *can* perform change with the time and circumstances; various foul-ups can occur in the performance; and even when you perform an act fully and properly, what happens later may keep it from being successful. Words have power, but the use of that power requires an understanding of rules and conventions. No cause for alarm: you already know these rules and conventions, though you probably could not state them (just as you know the grammar of English, though neither you nor anyone else has ever been able to state all its rules). It is worth spending some time on the rules and conventions of speech acts, both because they are interesting in themselves and because even though they rarely cause trouble in talking, they sometimes do in writing, which after all is a less familiar activity.

The best way into the subject is through examples.

1. "I hereby increase your lung capacity."
2. "I hereby divorce you."
3. "I hereby appoint you my friend."

But no. There *are* ways to increase someone's lung capacity, but speaking to him is not one of the ways. Example (2) is more subtle, for no physical or logical obstacle forbids this method of divorce—in fact, in some parts of the world it is perfectly valid. It just happens that our culture does not recognize it. Hence, no matter how many times a disgruntled spouse utters the words, he will not have managed to dissolve his marriage. Likewise, (3) is bound to be a flop, because we do not have a verbal formula for creating friends; it takes two to do that.

From these failures one may infer a first rule of speech acts:

A. A CONVENTIONAL PROCEDURE MUST EXIST FOR PERFORMING THE ACT IN QUESTION.

Even when a procedure does exist which involves the use of words, just speaking or writing the right words by no means guarantees performance of the act. For instance, what goes wrong in each of the following brief dramas?

4. *Counsel for the Defense:* "We find the defendant not guilty."

5. *Student in back row:* "Class dismissed."
6. *Urchin:* "I bet you the Denver Hilton against 5¢ that the Mets don't win the pennant."

Each of the speakers tries to perform a recognized speech act, and each uses an appropriate form of words, but none of them is the right person to use those words to that end. In ways that are usually clear enough, the conventions empower certain people to perform certain speech acts, and if the speaker does not fill the bill, his act is void. Not only the speaker, but the person he is addressing, too, must meet certain requirements:

7. *Minister, to golden anniversary couple:* "I now pronounce you man and wife."

Does he thereby marry them?

This rule, then, is:

B. THE PARTICIPANTS MUST BE THE RIGHT ONES FOR THE ACT IN QUESTION.

Notice, by the way, that this restriction applies not only to formal and contractual acts, but also to acts like *telling* (stating):

8. *Arthur, to Burt:* "A memory of early childhood is passing across your mind."

That's for Burt to tell Arthur, if so. Coming from Arthur, the words are presumptuous. He can't tell Burt what he is in no position to know, especially when it is something only *Burt* is in a position to know.

Try to infer rule C from these examples, all of which violate it:

9. "When is the Queen of Canada going to pay her next visit to the United States?"
10. "Hansel, I'd like to introduce you to my friend Gretel."
11. *Runner-up, at a political convention:* "I refuse to accept the nomination."
12. *Man in New York:* "Welcome to Brazil."

Many speech acts make presuppositions or depend for their validity upon certain circumstances. A question about the Queen of Canada presupposes that there *is* a Queen of Canada, and an introduction presupposes that the two people have not met before. No one can introduce a girl to her brother if they've been living in the same family. Similarly, it is impossible to refuse what has not been offered, or to welcome someone to a place far from where the welcomer is. In short:

C. THE CIRCUMSTANCES MUST BE APPROPRIATE.

D. THE PROCEDURES MUST BE EXECUTED CORRECTLY AND COM- PLETELY.

A person who says

13. "I'd rather be right than"

has not stated anything. Two men have not made a bet until the second has said "It's a bet" or "Done" or something of the sort, or has shaken hands with the first. And do these words constitute an invitation?

14. "I'm having a party next Saturday, Bill, and I imagine you'd enjoy it."

Possibly, but Bill had better make sure—if, indeed, he has any inclination to continue this somewhat enigmatic relationship. The example is a slight one but courts of law are crowded with cases that originate in ambiguous or incomplete speech acts.

Many speech acts call for the speaker to have certain beliefs or feelings at the time when he makes his move. Oscar says

15. "I promise to return your Geiger counter as soon as I get back from Alaska."

But he has no intention of doing so, and in fact expects to spend the rest of his days in Alaska. What can we say of his performance? He did make a promise, by speaking the right formula in the right circumstances, and he can be called to account later. Moreover, he did not simply state something false, since he did not state anything at all: he made a promise, and that is a different matter. If the owner of the Geiger counter were suspicious he would not say "That's false," but rather "You don't mean that," or something of the sort. It seems best to say that Oscar has performed a *deficient* speech act; specifically, he has promised *in bad faith*. Many speech acts can be deficient in similar ways, and they are covered by this rule:

E. THE SPEAKER MUST HAVE THE APPROPRIATE FEELINGS AND BE-
LIEFS.

(Prove this point to your own satisfaction: What are the feelings or
beliefs appropriate for a man congratulating his victorious opponent?
warning a child about playing with matches? telling a neighbor that his
house is on fire? criticizing the school president?)

Finally, some speech acts require a follow-up in order to come off
successfully, even if they are properly executed at the time and even if
the speaker has the right feelings and beliefs. Suppose that Oscar did,
after all, promise in good faith, but that he forgot to pack the Geiger
counter when he returned from Alaska. Clearly he has not fulfilled his
promise, and although he can plead good intentions, that may not entirely satisfy the owner. Or consider the endorsement of a political candidate: if the endorser changes his mind later, and tries to sabotage the
campaign, his original speech act turns out not to have been "happy."
So we have rule:

G. THE SPEAKER MUST CONDUCT HIMSELF APPROPRIATELY AFTER-
WARD.

• *Exercise 2.3:* How do the rules apply to these speech acts?

a.	Baptizing a child	f.	Pledging allegiance
b.	Declaring war	g.	Refusing an offer
c.	Saying goodbye	h.	Declaring love
d.	Praising	i.	Giving advice
e.	Excusing oneself for bumping into someone	j.	Telling a joke
		k.	Praying

For two or three of the above, construct a brief dialogue exemplifying one
or more kinds of failure.

Writing is just a way of putting speech into a more permanent form.
To be sure, most writing is more formal than most speech: if he wants
to, the writer can avoid the false starts, wrong turns, ellipses, self-inter-
ruptions, and plain mistakes that punctuate casual talk. Nonetheless,
writing depends entirely on speech for what it accomplishes, in the
sense that neither writer nor reader could make the least bit of headway
without his built-in knowledge of linguistic structures and conventions.
Likewise, the writer performs illocutionary acts that he is used to per-

forming orally, and he relies upon the same familiar set of rules—there simply isn't any other set of rules for him to use.

In a personal letter, for example, the similarity to speech is obvious. Here the writer usually has an audience of one person, as is most often the case in speech. Moreover, he usually knows that person rather well, so that he can write with some of the informality of speech, with a clear sense of the relationship that holds between him and his audience, and with a body of shared experience to make the speech situation concrete.

It is not so easy to draw on ordinary speech acts in less personal writing—essays, letters to the editor, articles, compositions. For one thing, writing of this sort uses much less than the full repertory of speech acts (greetings, declarations of love, refusals of offers, thanks, and many others will not usually come into play). But more important, the *audience* for such writing is always in one degree or another indefinite, and therefore hard to cope with. Rule B says that the participants must be the right ones, but much of the time a writer does not really know who the other participant is, or whether he is an appropriate person to be on the other end of a given speech act. A moment's reflection will show that, this being so, the writer cannot always be sure whether he himself is suited to performing that act: for the fitness of one participant depends on his relation to the other, not on some eternal and absolute qualification. Example: Gene sets out to tell Jane about diseases of the horse. But it turns out that Jane is a professor of veterinary medicine, therefore not an appropriate person to be told such things. By the same token, Gene, who has an elementary textbook knowledge of the subject, is not suited to this speech act—though he *would* be able to tell *Joan* about diseases of the horse, since she doesn't know hoof and mouth from foot-in-mouth. (Or consider, a priest is qualified to marry people, but would he be the appropriate person to marry a Bedouin to his fourth wife?) This kind of misunderstanding is much more likely to occur in writing than in speech. (Why?) And of course Rule C (the circumstances must be appropriate) also creates more puzzles for the writer than for a speaker who is in the center of quite visible circumstances. Rules E and F are more perplexing to the writer than to the speaker for similar reasons.

> • *Exercise 2.4:*   For a few hours, note the written illocutionary acts that come
> your way (signs, notices, ads, and so on) which are inappropriate or unsuc-
> cessful. What is the most common cause of failure?

There is no point in making light of such difficulties; the practiced writer, no less than the student, must contend with them. This book and its authors can stand as examples. Turn back to the first paragraph of section 2 on page 56. One sentence there begins "No cause for alarm," and constitutes an act of *reassurance*. Now the right audience for such a sentence is one that indeed feels some alarm, or nervousness, or worry. One can't reassure a person who is already assured—cheerful and confident. But of course we had no way of knowing whether you or any other reader would be disturbed in the slightest by our list of hazards that beset speech acts. Perhaps you passed it off with a shrug. Or failed to understand the dangers we referred to. Or were merely bored. Even if you did need reassurance, it is fair to ask whether we were the appropriate people to reassure you. We know this subject reasonably well, and therefore felt in a position both to warn and to reassure, but bear in mind that the fitness of you and us for participation in the speech act depends on our relation to each other, not on the authors' competence alone: if the writing in this book has not persuaded you to invest some authority in us, then our attempt at reassurance was simply miscalculated—for we do not otherwise know each other, and unless you trust whatever you read in print, you could have no other reason for trust than your opinion of what you were reading. As a matter of fact, some of these difficulties occurred to us at the time, and we intended our "no cause for alarm" as a slightly whimsical overstatement, with a bit of self-mockery in it. But probably that mild joke was even harder to bring off, because it depended on two things: your sensing the same awkwardness that we felt in the speech situation, and, furthermore, your thinking that we were capable of spoofing ourselves—or at least that we were *more* likely to spoof ourselves than to be quite so pompous and self-important as "no cause for alarm" implied. In short, what we were attempting to do with that little phrase is the sort of thing that works easily between friends who know each other's styles of irony and humor, and the sort of thing that even a stranger can usually manage with the aid of gesture and facial expression. But it is not so easy in writing, when the writer and the reader are at a distance and unknown to each other.

One more example: in the next sentence we wrote that "it is worth spending some time on the rules and conventions of speech acts, both because they are interesting in themselves and because even though they rarely cause trouble in talking, they sometimes do in writing, which after all is a less familiar activity." The most obvious business of the sentence is *stating* several things, and that in itself presents few problems. But notice that we were also *pleading* and *advising*, especially in "it is worth spending some time . . ." and in "they are interesting in themselves." We were pleading (in a soft voice, to be sure) for you to give the next few pages your attention, and advising you that it would be worth your while to do so. These are tricky matters. All the same obstacles of the rule B variety rise up here (do we have the authority to advise you, and so on). Furthermore, rule C may stand in the way of these speech acts. When X advises or pleads with Y, one of the "appropriate circumstances" is that Y is free to do what X wants, or not to do it. (You can't advise a legless man to stand up and walk.) But this is a textbook. Presumably you are reading it as part of the required work for a college course. If so, then we were advising you, and pleading with you, to do something you have little choice about. That may be all right, as a courteous pretense, in the same way that people sometimes say "would you like to bring me the file?" when they really mean "bring me the file." But it raises a question about the relationship between a textbook writer and his audience that we cannot confidently answer: is it appropriate, or for that matter *honest,* to write as if to a reader who has chosen to read this book, for fun or for betterment, when we know that most of the readers are under some compulsion, not only to read the book, but even to study the subject? And what about rules E and F? When we wrote that it is "worth" spending some time on these rules, and that they are "interesting" in themselves, we were making a very general claim. "Worth" it for everyone? "Interesting" to everyone? We must admit that we doubt it, great as our own interest in the subject is. So strictly speaking, the speech act violated rule E, in the interest of coaxing you into the pages to follow. As for rule F, it calls for the writer "to conduct himself appropriately afterward." In this case, that can only mean *making* the chapter interesting and worth your while. Have we done so? Probably so, for some, and not, for others. When judged by rule F, then the speech act probably had mixed success.

In being so critical of our own words, we are not denigrating ourselves as writers. Rather, the difficulties we have spoken of challenge anyone who writes to an unknown and mixed audience, and no one can entirely surmount them. It is good, therefore, to be conscious of them, and to cope with them as frankly as possible. That is partly a matter of "skill" in writing, but partly, also, a matter of basic human relations, and even of morality.

> • *Exercise 2.5:* The task of a student writing a composition is no less subtle than that of an author writing a textbook. Think about the following questions:
>
>   a. When you write an essay, your instructor is its first audience: do you actually write as if you were communicating personally to him or her?
>
>   b. If so, how does rule B apply to illocutionary acts such as statements?

c. If not, what other audience do you have in mind?

d. What do you know or assume about that audience?

e. Is that audience sometimes imaginary? If so, how does rule B apply?

f. What are the actual *circumstances* of your speech acts in a composition?

g. Do you write as if you were a student in a required course, or a free agent? If the former, doesn't that prevent you from writing freely and confidently? If the latter, are you being entirely honest?

h. Apply rule E to a composition you have already written: did you always have the appropriate feelings and beliefs? Did you ever put down on paper what you thought somebody wanted to hear, rather than what you wanted to say?

Try writing your next short composition in three versions: one addressed only to your instructor, taking into account what you know about him or her and the relationship that holds between you; a second to an audience of your classmates; and a third as if for publication in a magazine of wide circulation. Be as honest as possible. After you have finished, compare the three versions to see how rules B, C, E, and F affected your writing.

3/ Assertions and Truth

For obvious reasons, in exposition there is not much call for the illocutionary acts of baptism, swearing allegiance, renouncing one's legal rights, placing under arrest, and the like. Even less legalistic and dramatic acts like praising, apologizing, and refusing play a relatively minor role. Their place is in the flow of social interchange, where relationships are constantly being altered and adjusted, and where each response calls for a counter-response.

In this very distinction, however, is an implicit piece of advice: when you *want* your writing to suggest the flow of social interchange, when you want it to involve the reader as a social being with emotional responses as well as intellectual, it's a good idea to vary the pattern of illocutionary acts. And in general, writing that draws the reader into a dramatic relationship with the writer will be more lively than writing that does not. Here is D. H. Lawrence writing about Benjamin Franklin:

> It's a queer thing, is a man's soul. It is the whole of him. Which means it is the unknown him, as well as the known. It seems to me just funny, professors and Benjamins fixing the functions of the soul. Why the soul of man is a vast forest, and all Benjamin intended was a neat back garden. And we've all got to fit in to his kitchen garden scheme of things. Hail Columbia!

The soul of man is a dark forest. The Hercynian Wood that scared the Romans so, and out of which came the white-skinned hordes of the next civilization.

Who knows what will come out of the soul of man? The soul of man is a dark vast forest, with wild life in it. Think of Benjamin fencing it off!

Oh, but Benjamin fenced a little tract that he called the soul of man, and proceeded to get it into cultivation. Providence, forsooth! And they think that bit of barbed wire is going to keep us in pound forever? More fools them.

Studies in Classic American Literature

Trace the illocutionary acts in this passage, and the ways they involve the reader; then compare it with this version of the last two paragraphs:

No one knows what will come out of the soul of man, which is a dark forest with wild life in it. To fence it off was impertinent for Benjamin. Yet he did fence a little tract that he called the soul of man, and proceeded to get it into cultivation, speaking, absurdly, of Providence. People who think that human beings can be permanently confined to such a tract of land are quite foolish.

The pace is still quick (and somewhat erratic), but much of the vitality has disappeared. Lawrence's original keeps alive the movement of speech acts, to an astonishing extent, and it would take a great gain in rational force to compensate for the loss of dramatic and personal force that our revision brought about.

All the same, most of the sentences in most expository writing perform the act of *stating,* and for that reason we shall give special attention here to assertions, and to the obligations they impose upon the writer.

Assertions are peculiar in that they focus attention doubly on "circumstances." It is easy to see why. Recall rule C: "The circumstances must be appropriate." If the act is refusing, we noted, then a necessary circumstance is that the refuser has been offered what he is refusing. Similarly, one who states must be in a position to state: circumstances will not allow us to *state* that a 40-mile-an-hour wind is blowing at the North Pole just now. But the assertion also hangs on circumstances in another way. Even if we were stationed at the North Pole with the proper instruments, and said "There is a 40-mile-an-hour wind blowing," circumstances might disqualify the assertion in another way—for example, the circumstances that in fact the wind was blowing only twenty miles an hour. No matter whether we lied or were simply the innocent victims of snow-blindness; our assertion fails.

This peculiar second link between assertions and circumstances is, of course, that of *truth,* and a fair definition of "assertion" is "a sentence that is either true or false." It sounds simple: we judge assertions by their truth, and a writer's responsibility is to make true statements. But of course the simplicity dissolves as soon as we confront it with some actual assertions like these:

> Three feet make a yard.
> A *novella* is a short novel.
> Horses have manes.
> Churchill smoked cigars.
> These two are the most intelligent students in the class.
> More leisure leads to more contentment.
> Lemon pie tastes better than apple.
> Rousseau was a bad man.

Each of these assertions poses a different problem of verification, because they are unlike in several important ways. Some concern a whole class of objects; some are confined to particular members of a class. Some would appear to require very little in the way of verification; some would require a great deal. Some seem susceptible of almost certain proof; others are impossible to prove at all. And, finally, some appear to invite tests of validity; others, to warn that such tests are irrelevant. Because these assertions are different in so many ways, a writer commonly uses signals to warn his reader about the differences, signals ranging from parenthetical remarks ("without doubt," "to be sure," "so far as I can tell," "in my judgment," "from one point of view," and so on) to the development of an informative tone of voice in the paragraph (that, for instance, of reassurance, of decisiveness, of hesitancy, of cautious speculation, of skepticism). In general, these signals are intended to make the distinctions which we may indicate by the rough categories, *statements of convention, statements of fact, statements of opinion, and statements of preference.*

If we attempt to locate each of the sentences above in one or another of these four categories, we can get some notion of the issues involved. Clearly, the classification of any sentence is partly a judgment on it, particularly on its reliability or degree of certainty—certainty to the writer, certainty to the reader, and certainty irrespective of any one person. But certainty is primarily a matter of how we know, or how we would find out, whether an assertion is true or false. Hence the shortest way to the heart of our problem takes us directly to *verification.*

How would one set about to verify the assertion, "Three feet make a yard"? The question itself has an odd ring, for the assertion is so

patently true as scarcely to need verification at all. The certainty with
which we regard it issues, of course, from conventions—those conventions of measurement and of the English language. A yard, by definition, is three feet long; that is what the word *means*. It would be
ludicrous for anyone, asked about the truth of the statements, to begin
diligently measuring yardsticks to determine whether each of them
measured three feet. What could he measure them with except other
yardsticks or rulers? Likewise, no one would test the statement "A *novella* is a short novel" by counting the pages in actual *novellas*. Rather, if
he were uncertain about the truth of the assertion he would investigate
the linguistic practice of literary critics. Another way to understand the
force of statements of convention is to imagine rebutting the statement
"A *novella* is a long novel." The speaker has not made a mistake in fact,
but simply failed to understand the word *"novella,"* and the way to
correct his error is to explain the relevant convention. Assertions of this
type, in other words, depend for their truth upon rules, regularities of
usage, linguistic custom, and so on. One does not verify them through
an appeal to experience, other than experience of this limited sort. Para-
doxically, it is just because of this remoteness from experience that
statements of convention tend to seem more certain than any other kind,
for the other statements involve links between word and world, and such
links are often puzzling, even with the simplest statements of fact.

The statement "Horses have manes" would require for complete verification the examination of, or a reliable report on, all horses now living
and all that have ever lived or will do so; most of us would (and *must*)
settle for less, it is true, just as testers of all kinds now draw conclusions
from "sample populations." Whether or not we require reference to all
horses, we are satisfied that it takes only the simple tests of direct observation to determine the truth or falsity of the statement. And it is that
feeling of the simplicity or relative certainty of proof that leads us to
treat such a statement without qualification and to refer to it as though
it represented something about whose truth or falsity we could eventually
reach an unassailable decision. Statements of this kind we conventionally
call "statements of fact," meaning not that they are beyond doubt true
but that we are sure that their truth or falsity can be readily and finally
determined by reference to experience.

(In ordinary language, we occasionally distinguish between "factual
statements" and "statements of fact," meaning, by the former, statements
whose truth *or* falsity can readily be determined and, by the latter, those
which are true. In this discussion, the two terms are not distinguished:
a "statement of fact" may be either true or false, and it is different from
other statements primarily because of its high susceptibility to tests of
validity.)

If we treat "Horses have manes" as a statement of fact because we know that the proofs for establishing its truth or falsity are within our power to produce, we shall not hesitate to classify "Churchill smoked cigars" in the same group. Provided that we understand "smoked" to mean "sometimes smoked" or even "customarily smoked," we know that there are easy ways of finding out whether or not the statement is true. To be sure, the appeal to experience need not be direct; few were ever in a position to make *observations* of Churchill's smoking habits. But *reports* are easily accessible, reports just one step removed from observation. And even when the evidence consists of second-, third-, or tenth-hand reports, we still call an assertion a statement of fact if it has its origin in observation and if the reports come through reliable channels.

The statement "These two are the most intelligent students in the class" presents somewhat greater, but certainly no insuperable, difficulties. As soon as we get agreement on a means of measuring intelligence, we can proceed to test the truth of the statement. If the means agreed upon is a pencil-and-paper test, verification will be easy; if the means is a record of responses to all kinds of challenges and crises in actual experience, verification will be extremely difficult. Since by "intelligent" few people mean simply "good at tests," they are likely to think of the statement as one of opinion. The reason is in part our lack of confidence in actual tests; in part the complexity and unavailability of better tests; and in part the nature of the word "intelligent."

Obviously, "intelligent" is an ambiguous word; that is, it means different things to various people. What one will find adequate as the meaning of "intelligent," another will find inadequate or completely irrelevant. The more ambiguous the predication of a statement, the more difficult it will be to find generally acceptable tests of validity; the more difficult it is to find such tests, the more uncertain we are that any statement requiring them is sure to be found true or false by everyone. It is the increase of uncertainty that leads us to think of such statements as "statements of opinion" rather than as "statements of fact." There is no strictly logical difference between them: both kinds require reference to experience for verification. The difference lies either in the ambiguity of a term or in the difficulty of determining truth or falsity, or in both. Thus there can be little doubt that "More leisure leads to more contentment" is also a statement of opinion, for how is one to measure contentment? Certainly the tests would have to be complex, and probably unreliable to boot.

Another source of uncertainty in the classification of such statements is the connotative effect of words. For various reasons we respond favorably or unfavorably to certain words. Most words, indeed, besides directing us to consider something, influence us to take an attitude toward it as well. Suppose that a man regularly puts away all the money he earns except what he must spend on the necessities of life. Then consider these two statements about him:

He saves his money.
He hoards his money.

Whether we think of one as a statement of fact and of the other as a statement of opinion will depend partly on the denotation of the words "saves" and "hoards" but even more on their connotation, on the associations they raise in our minds. "Hoards" carries the sense of secret and greedy accumulation; testing the truth of the assertion which contains it would be difficult. Since "saves" means only "puts away," testing the truth of the statement is theoretically not hard at all, given access to the man's financial records and behavior. The connotative power of the key words may therefore lead us to place quite similar statements in different categories.

Within this class of assertions whose truth or falsity is determined by reference to experience, three subdivisions of some importance to the writer have so far been distinguished. The first, statements of convention, reflects the writer's certainty that no appeal to nonlinguistic experience could possibly overthrow his assertion. The second, statements of fact, represents the writer's feeling of assurance that the test of truth or falsity can be readily determined and that there is already general agreement about the truth of the statement itself. The third, statements of opinion, reflects the writer's uncertainty about the possibility of producing satisfactory proofs of soundness and his recognition that disagreement is more likely than not. This uncertainty sometimes is the result of the difficulty of the procedures necessary for testing, sometimes of the ambiguity of terms in the statement, sometimes of the connotative effect of terms in the statement. The progression, then, has been from relative certainty to considerable uncertainty.

To continue that progress is to move into another category common to everyday discourse about statements, that of statements of preference. In some ways, these are the most interesting statements of all to writer and reader. The medieval proverb, *De gustibus non est disputandum* ("There is no disputing about tastes"), reflects a popular view, shared by some philosophers, that the grounds of choice, being subjective, are neither logically defensible nor attackable. Yet, for the very reason that they are subjective, that is, that they refer not simply to the data presented to our senses but to our experience and judgment of it, we are likely to hold to statements of preference or taste with singular tenacity. At the same time, we recognize that there is no infallible means of testing the truth or falsity of such a statement as "Lemon pie tastes better than apple," and we do not try to do so. But if this statement is changed into "I like lemon pie better than apple pie," it then becomes an auto-biographical statement, and not very different, as far as proof is concerned, from "These two are the most intelligent students in the class." The tests which someone else would apply to determine the truth or falsity of our stated preference for lemon pie (seeing which kind we eat when we are given a choice, for example) are not different in kind from those he would apply to detect the intelligence of students in the class.

In its original form, however ("Lemon pie tastes better than apple"), the statement of preference means something more than "I like lemon pie better than apple." It either assumes agreement among people of "right" perception or it indicates that no agreement is expected and that the statement is really one about the condition of the stater rather than about lemon and apple pie. A proper feeling for the meanings of a statement of preference will often lead a writer to qualify it ("Connoisseurs agree that . . .") or to overstate deliberately in order to emphasize the limitedness of intention ("Every man who has ever put fork to pie crust knows that lemon pie tastes better than apple").

From the taste of apple pie to Rousseau's moral qualities is a long leap, but according to our criteria the assertion "Rousseau was a bad man" must also be called a statement of preference. Two men who both know all the facts of Rousseau's life may nonetheless disagree as to whether he was a bad man, and there is no final way to arbitrate the issue, for standards of goodness and badness differ. Thus *ethical statements,* as these are sometimes called, and *statements of obligation* ("Men ought to love their neighbors") are subcategories of statements of preference, along with *statements of taste* (the one about lemon and apple pie, for instance). But to make this classification is by no means to disqualify or undermine these assertions; in point of fact, they are among the most important in human discourse. And certainly the person who calls Rousseau a bad man does not merely mean that he dislikes Rousseau; nor would he be willing to concede, in all likelihood, that the issue is undecidable or meaningless. Rather, he probably assumes enough shared attitudes and moral standards among human beings to encourage considerable agreement about Rousseau, given the pertinent facts. The assumption is unjustified in this case; the argument about Rousseau's morality swirls on. But a great many ethical statements and statements of obligation do seem relatively certain: Hitler and Caligula were evil; St. Francis was good; men should be kind; they should not murder; and so on. Society would be impossible if most of us did not share such beliefs and the premises that support them. The writer need not shrink from statements of preference; on the contrary, they will often be his main justification for writing.

The writer's responsibility, rather than timidly sticking to what is certain, is to know what obligations he assumes by putting forth a given assertion. Who is in a *position* to write "Rousseau was a bad man," or "More leisure leads to more contentment"? And what kind of backing must he offer in either case? (That is, how can he "conduct himself appropriately afterward"? Rule F) If you think of an assertion not just as a parcel of truth or falsity, but as a dramatic move vis à vis an audience, you can more easily conceive what the assertion needs by way of accompaniment. The development of an essay is partly a matter of logic and order, but partly a matter too of staying on honest terms with the audience.

> • *Exercise 2.6:*   Classify the following assertions as statements of convention, fact, opinion, or preference. When the classification is difficult to make, analyze the source of difficulty.
>
>   a. Under a government which imprisons any unjustly, the true place for a just man is also in prison.
>   b. Birds are as subject as men to the emotion of jealousy.
>   c. No teetotaler drinks alcohol.
>   d. No woman sits on the Supreme Court.
>   e. No man is an island.
>   f. No good poem plays on stock responses.
>   g. The Spanish are a proud people.
>   h. Chemistry is a hard subject.
>   i. Pegasus was a winged horse.
>   j. Haste makes waste.
>   k. Inadequate discipline in the family causes juvenile delinquency.

4/   Other Ways of Judging Assertions

In the preceding sections we have said enough about judgments of truth and falsity to establish their central importance to the writer, as well as the importance of having satisfactory ways to tell whether this or that assertion is true or false. But our remarks may also have been disquieting to some. Not only does it prove impossible to label all statements with conviction as fact, opinion, and so forth: the very labels "true" and "false" are often difficult to apply. This is so partly because we simply lack information—no one knows (at this writing) whether the assertion "There is life on Mars" is true, although it is a plain statement of fact. But the more bothersome and interesting difficulties in determining the truth of statements have to do with the nature of statements themselves and of their relationship to experience. Words have multiple meanings and connotations; thus the assertions built from words often admit of several interpretations. And in any case, sentences do not match up to facts in neat one-to-one correspondences. So the truth or falsity of an assertion may be unclear. To complicate matters further, some statements are partly true and partly false ("France is a republic, but Italy is a monarchy"). In short, for a writer weighing assertions, the question "Is it true or false?" may be the begin-all, but it is scarcely the end-all.

And a little reflection will show that this question is not always the most illuminating one to ask. The writer who asserts, "Empiricism, more than any other science, causes reactionary developments," has obviously missed the mark, whatever that may have been. But to say that his statement is *false* is to deliver no insight whatever into the ways in which it goes amiss. Nor is it enough to call it *uncertain*. Truth and falsity, certainty and uncertainty: so far we have concentrated on these forms of evaluation. But assertions can be sick or healthy from other causes, too, and there is perhaps as much danger in overemphasizing truth as in slighting it. Philosophers, understandably, have always had an overmastering fondness for truth and falsity, but the writer needs more and sharper instruments of judgment in his critical workshop.

Fortunately, such criteria abound, and their use requires neither special technical training nor a recondite vocabulary. The assessment of statements is a common and necessary activity in daily life, and ordinary language has a rich supply of terms for this purpose. All we shall do is briefly mention a few of the most useful, to suggest the range of possibility.

MEANINGFUL AND MEANINGLESS

Before a statement can be judged either true or false it must qualify as meaningful; otherwise, of course, there will be no way to go about testing it. An assertion can be meaningless through grammatical disorder or through the inclusion of nonsense words. The most interesting examples, however, are statements in proper linguistic form which still somehow seem to defy verification, or even understanding. Two well-known examples are: "The Absolute enters into, but is itself incapable of, evolution and progress," and "Colorless green ideas sleep furiously." What predictions about experience could one make from either of these assertions? To be sure, context may give a kind of meaning to assertions that are in themselves meaningless. As a matter of fact the first of our examples comes from *Appearance and Reality,* by the philosopher F. H. Bradley, who undoubtedly thought he was saying something, given his use of "Absolute" and his whole philosophical system. The second—an example, devised by the linguist Noam Chomsky, of a grammatical but meaningless sentence—has been incorporated meaningfully in several poems. Moreover, the most empty assertion may be meaningful in other senses: it may have emotional significance, or suggest images. Still, there is an aura of futility in such assertions, and the writer will do well to avoid them.

Related terms: *significant, verifiable; nonsense.*

VAGUE AND CLEAR

Even though a statement is meaningful, it may be so loosely related to facts or experience that its truth is hard to assess. If a writer asserts, "Considerations of objective phenomena dictate modifications of certain aspects of the domestic posture," he may mean that the country needs new farm laws to deal with the crop failure, or that it is time to get up and have breakfast, or any one of a number of things. But who can tell? The statement is so vague as practically to defy interpretation, and no writer should permit himself to stray this far from clarity, even if context throws some light on the confusion. Vagueness disables an assertion for its main task, to communicate.

Related terms: *inexact, indefinite, abstract; precise.*

AMBIGUOUS

Vague assertions wallow in a morass of obscurity; ambiguous statements have clear meanings, but more than one. Ambiguity is often syntactical: "Flying planes can be dangerous." "The war broke out and there were numerous rebellions after the serfs were freed." Or it may stem from ambiguous words: "Oscar Wilde valued *sensual* experience"; "The Governor was criticized for the *execution.*" Context is a convenient antidote most of the time: "The Governor was criticized for the execution of his duties" (or "of the prisoner").

Related terms: *equivocal, indeterminate.*

MISLEADING

To call a statement meaningless, vague, or ambiguous is to say that its relation to the facts is unclear. The terms of evaluation to which we now turn point rather to *distortion* of the facts. The statement "During Eisenhower's administration there was an increase in serious crime" is both clear and true, but misleading in implying a causal connection. Assertions may also mislead by leaving out part of a complex truth: "Abraham Lincoln was a storekeeper." And indeed, the ways of misleading are plentiful and often subtle. No writer of integrity misleads intentionally, but in the grip of enthusiasm or affection for one's own thesis, it is easy to write assertions that angle in at the facts rather than meet them squarely.

Related terms: *slanted, deceptive.*

EXAGGERATED AND UNDERSTATED

One way of distorting the facts is to exaggerate, usually with the aid of words like "all," "never," "extremely," and "tremendous." For the statement "Women never reach the first rank in the arts" there is some basis in fact, and if it were limited to composing, painting, and sculpting, or if it read "do not generally" instead of "never," it would have strong claims. But it ignores Jane Austen, Sappho, Emily Dickinson, Jenny Lind, Sarah Bernhardt, and many others. The writer has marred a potentially valid point through overstatement. Likewise, "The League of Nations was a total and abject failure." As for understatement, it is not likely to offend so seriously, since it seems to proceed from caution rather than from flamboyance. Still, it, too, can lead to misrepresentation: the writer who refers to the Second World War as an "unpleasant skirmish" carries moderation to the point of euphemism, if not plain falsehood. Overstatement and understatement have their rhetorical uses, but the writer who employs them intentionally must make certain that his real purpose shows through the mask.

Related terms: *emphatic; hyperbole.*

OVERGENERAL

An exaggerated assertion describes the facts too strongly; an overgeneral one lays claim to more factual support than it actually has. Two examples will make the differences clear: "Asia is a primitive, agricultural continent" is an exaggeration; "Asian countries are not heavily industrial" is an overgeneralization, which could be saved by making an exception of Japan. (A writer may err in the direction of the specific, too, but when he does so he does not distort the facts; he simply wastes space or misses important generalizations.)

Related terms: *broad, loose, abstract.*

OVERSIMPLIFIED

An oversimplification is, of course, an assertion that pays too little heed to the intricacies of a situation—"Tragedy is a dead form in the twentieth century," for instance, or "Government spending causes inflation." Whatever the dangers of such assertions, they often prove necessary as a stage in inquiry or as a convenience. Many of the laws of science, not to mention those of the social sciences, are oversimplifications in that they leave out qualifications and exceptions for the sake of emphasizing a major principle. Every writer needs to oversimplify from time to time, and he may do so legitimately as long as he apprises the reader of his intention.

Related terms: *abbreviated, condensed.*

TRIVIAL

The faults we have considered so far all pervert the proper relationship between assertion and fact. Carried far enough, they can make an assertion *untrue*. The next two criticisms have little or no bearing on the truth of statements, but they are serious criticisms nonetheless. To call an assertion trivial is not to question its accuracy but, quite the contrary, to claim that it is so patently true as not to deserve mention. It may be trivial because the fact it refers to is minor ("The Nevada atomic testing grounds are closed to real estate development," in a paper on the evils of atomic weapons), or because it is obvious, unilluminating, or empty ("Children learn to talk by trial and error" as an explanation of language learning). With the notion of triviality we enter an area, of great importance to the writer, where truth and falsity have no place: namely that of emphasis, selection, and organization. An assertion is trivial, not in relation to the facts its describes, but in relation to *all* the facts and to the writer's purpose in treating them.

Related terms: *unimportant, obvious, insignificant.*

IRRELEVANT

To the argument that socialized medicine is wasteful and inefficient, the assertion "Both doctors and patients have a right to freedom" is simply not relevant. The charge of irrelevance is a grave one, for an assertion that is off the issue pulls no weight and may either confuse the reader or damage the argument. Even when there is no intent to deceive, irrelevance is a sign that the writer is not in full control of his material. This is not to say that digressions and asides are never permissible, but that the writer should understand that they are such, and clearly label them.

Related terms: *not germane, off the point.*

OBLIQUE

An oblique statement is one whose relationship to the facts depends on a special understanding between writer and reader about the use of words. Mention of obliqueness opens the whole Pandora's box of rhetorical figures, which belongs properly to a later section of this book, and here we shall only touch on the matter by listing the two main subdivisions of oblique assertions. In *metaphor,* the writer uses one or more words in a nonliteral sense: "A good editorial page is a court of justice before which public action stands trial daily." An *ironic* statement, on the other hand, calls upon the reader to reject the literal sense of the whole sentence, and substitute a contradictory one: "We can be grateful to the city fathers, whose judicious nonenforcement of fire regulations has so cheaply cleared our slums and so efficiently dealt with the problem of overpopulation." Needless to say, the fact that such assertions come at the truth by indirection does not necessarily count against them; so long as their force is clear, they can make an invaluable contribution to the persuasive power of expository prose.

Related terms: *indirect, figurative.*

TAUTOLOGICAL

Two criteria that have a more logical flavor conclude this catalogue. A statement is a tautology if part of it merely repeats another part, in the guise of adding information: "Penicillin cures because it has a therapeutic effect"; or "In my experience, every quadruped is a four-footed animal." To cure *is* to have a therapeutic effect, and the word "because" does not belong. Similarly, "quadruped" *means* "four-footed animal," and experience (except of language) has nothing to do with it. Notice that tautologies are rather like definitions, and if the writer offers them as such, he commits no sin. But when they masquerade as explanations or as discoveries about the world, they do not achieve what they claim.

Related terms: *redundant, circular, empty, analytic* (in a philosophical sense).

SELF-CONTRADICTORY

Precisely opposite to a tautology is a self-contradictory assertion—a statement of which one part conflicts with another, logically or otherwise. Statements of this kind are so obviously undesirable (consider "Iranians are mainly nomads, while Persians are mainly farmers") that we need say nothing more about them.

Related terms: *impossible, illogical, inconceivable.*

No mere primer of terms used in evaluating assertions can make it a mechanical task for the writer to decide when a given sentence is adequate to his purposes and to the facts. Sorting out truth from falsehood, clarity from obscurity, and distortion from precision is more complicated than separating good apples from bad. But even the novice at writing has a huge advantage on his side: since reaching the age of reason he has had constant practice in matching assertions up with experience, for on this activity the whole of rational thought and sane conduct depends. A list like the foregoing is no more than a codification of what intelligent speakers already know about the ground rules of statement. To apply this knowledge to writing should not be impossible.

- *Exercise 2.7:* What criticism(s) would you level against the following assertions? When possible, improve each through rewriting.

   a. It is not possible any longer to think anything out without a greater reality than one's self constantly pressing one's words in dramatic shape and unexpected meaning.
   b. The king had three cities taken.
   c. The atom bomb did some damage at Hiroshima.
   d. A veterinarian treats diseases.
   e. Hitler was responsible for the founding of Israel.
   f. American heavy industry was the creation of a few arrogant, ruthless, selfish men.
   g. Creativity is the handmaiden of art.
   h. Men differ from other species in having wide, flat fingernails.
   i. Some aspects of science militate against factors in education.
   j. All philosophy is footnotes to Plato.
   k. It took centuries for England to drive Ireland to rebellion, but it was worth it.
   l. The objective lies on the far side of the subjective.
   m. Disorders in the organism account for cancer.

5/ Assertions Keeping Company

Some of the criteria for weighing assertions led us away from the relationship between assertion and experience and toward that between assertion and assertion. There is a strong reason for giving more attention to this second relationship; the writer conceives what he has to say, not only against a background of facts, but in a context of other assertions, his own and those of other people. Therefore he had best understand clearly the possible connections between statements. This section and the two following ones will scan this crucial subject; the next chapter covers it even more extensively from another perspective.

The mention of self-contradictory assertions offers a starting point, for plainly this relationship can spread out to cover two separate statements. In the most elementary form of contradiction a simple "not" does the trick ("Life is good"; "Life is not good"). But such contradictions are less common and less interesting than those that involve different wording: "Alfalfa is a profitable crop" and "Among crops that bring little income to the farmer, alfalfa stands out," for instance. The example should make two things clear. First, two statements are *contradictory* if every state of affairs (say, high profits from alfalfa) that makes one true makes its partner false. And second, even direct contradictions often depend upon the interpretation of words—what one writer (or farmer) thinks of as a good profit may seem a small income to another. It is only common sense to say that the writer must have a keen sense of contradiction, both to know when he is contradicting an opponent and to avoid contradicting himself.

When two assertions do not meet each other in square, head-on opposition, but the truth of either one precludes the other's being true, they are often called *incompatible* rather than contradictory, and the distinction seems worth preserving. Thus the two assertions "Riggs is an orthodox Catholic" and "Riggs does not believe in life everlasting" are incompatible, though nothing in the sentences themselves (other than the name "Riggs") even suggests that they are about the same subject. Incompatibility depends upon what we know about the world outside of language—for instance, that orthodox Catholics believe in life everlasting. Another difference between incompatibles and contradictories is this: it is possible for two incompatible statements both to be false, but not so for contradictories (check this against our examples). In short, incompatibility is a rather looser relation than contradiction, but for this very reason it constitutes a greater danger to the careless writer, who may fail to notice that such and such a statement in the first paragraph is incapable of living in the same universe with the other one down near the end.

Two *compatible* statements, by contrast, may both be true. Notice that compatibility is an extremely weak relationship, for the two assertions in question may have no logical connection with each other whatsoever: "There is a fly on George's nose" is compatible with "Low tariffs stimulate trade"—but who cares? What we need is a slightly stronger rela-

tionship. One such is consistency; two statements are *consistent* with
each other if the truth of one might be suspected from the truth of the
other. If we know, for instance, that the assertion "Henderson likes abstract painting" is true, we know it is likely that "Henderson is an intellectual," for most people who like abstract painting are intellectuals (and
vice versa perhaps). Since one of the writer's main endeavors is to piece
together separate bits of information and fashion a coherent whole, the
relationship of consistency merits his attention. A still stronger type of
compatibility is inclusion. Assertion A is *included* in Assertion B (or
follows from it) if the facts upon which A depends for its truth are part
of those which make B true. Thus "Vermont has two senators" is included in "Every state has two senators," and "The Tasmanian devil is
a mammal" in "The Tasmanian devil is a marsupial." The included
assertion cannot be false if the other is true, though it may be true if the
other is false. Inclusion has special importance, obviously, for the writer
who is generalizing from particulars or deducing particulars from a
generalization.

Two compatible statements *may* both be true; two *equivalent* assertions *must* either both be true or both be false. That is, any conceivable state of affairs in the world will either justify both or defeat both.
Sometimes equivalence results from purely grammatical relationships:
"Wellington defeated Napoleon"; "Napoleon was defeated by Wellington." Sometimes the connection is a little harder to see: "Ferocity and
patience are qualities of the tiger"; "Tigers are ferocious, but not im-
patient." Equivalence does *not* entail exact sameness of meaning, as the
last example clearly shows, for language has more and subtler functions
than to unveil the truth. But the very fact that the writer is interested in
those subtler functions should turn his attention to equivalence, since he
cannot choose intelligently between alternate ways of saying the "same
thing" unless he knows whether they are actually equivalent and differ
only in rhetorical or emphatic features.

• *Exercise 2.8:*   What relationships hold between the following pairs of assertions?

  a. The theory of evolution is well substantiated.
      The theory of natural selection is probably false.
  b. Existence precedes essence.
      Essence precedes existence.
  c. A man cannot be both a liar and a good Christian.
      Either a man is honest, or he is not a good Christian.

d. Jones is irascible, and no irascible person should be a social worker.
    Jones should not be a social worker.

e. Every great advance in thought is the work of many minds.
    Einstein alone revolutionized our understanding of the physical world.

f. Character is destiny.
    A man of Lincoln's integrity was bound to influence the course of human
    events.

g. Conroy likes to play the horses.
    The Conroys are often in financial trouble.

If we shift our perspective a bit, we can discover another reason why relationships like inclusion and equivalence are of importance to the writer. When the truth of Assertion A hinges on the truth of B, the writer always has the option of leaving B unstated, especially if B states common knowledge or a widely shared principle. But B will lurk in the background as an *assumption,* even so. Statements of obligation, in particular, nearly always seem to lean on one or more assumptions. The statement "People in sedentary jobs should run a mile daily" probably assumes something like this: "Sedentary people should exercise," which in turn assumes that "exercise is good for sedentary people," and so on, back to some central principle such as "Men should maintain healthy bodies." Notice that the original assertion also has an assumption of another sort, namely that sedentary people *can* run a mile daily, a doubtful proposition at best. This assumption is subject to the usual tests of verifiability; the others are not. This statement of obligation, therefore, is a compound of the testable and nontestable, and most statements of obligation are of that kind. They are truly statements, or assertions (that is, they are true or false), but some part of them resists empirical verification and refers one to basic assumptions which cannot be "tested" at all.

The role that assumptions play in writing and reading extends far beyond statements of obligation. One way to describe assumptions would be to call them "what we take for granted" or "what we do not feel obliged to prove," or "what else must be true in order for this statement to be true." Certainly we "take for granted" fully as much as we make explicit in our writing. Most of the time we do not even give a thought to the assumptions from which we begin; we simply *assume* that others make the same assumptions as we do. When we do have any cause to doubt agreement, we may make the assumption explicit ("Assuming that legislative programs are to be judged by their enduring effects, the New Deal was largely a failure"). But very often writers assume agreement when there may not be any; in fact, they may make statements whose assumptions they neither have investigated nor would accept if they were to do so. To write in ignorance of one's own assumptions is to write irresponsibly.

The need to reckon with unstated assumptions does not usually arise with simple assertions like "Jefferson designed Monticello." When assertions are combined causally, however, the unstated assertion may be fully as important as any assertion explicitly stated. Consider this sentence:

> Jefferson was an extensive landowner and was therefore interested in securing the independence of the American colonies from England.

Underneath this sentence there is an unstated assumption to the effect that all landowners at that time and in that place were interested in securing the independence of the colonies. And behind that assumption there may well be another, more general, to the effect that all landowners everywhere and at all times are interested in securing the independence from foreign control of the political territory in which they hold land. The criteria for testing these assumptions are historical; if we apply such criteria, we shall have no difficulty in finding that the assumptions are false. We might say of the original sentence about Jefferson, then, that it is based on an *unwarranted assumption.* Such assumptions are a particular danger in expository writing, precisely because they remain behind the scenes; yet they deserve as much attention, both from the writer and from the reader, as explicit statements.

To talk about assumptions is to talk about the logical precedents of an assertion, about what must be true in order for that assertion to be true. Because it is a looking backward, a search for antecedent condition, the search for assumptions is not always easy: a particular statement may rest on many assumptions, each of which must be acknowledged if the writer is to feel secure about his statement. To appreciate the logical consequences, or *implications,* of an assertion is to ask, "If this assertion is true, then what other assertions are necessarily true?" If, for instance, someone says that maple trees always shed their leaves in winter and if he is able to demonstrate that the statement is true, then it is perfectly obvious that a particular maple tree in your front yard will shed its leaves when winter comes. The truth of the first assertion necessarily implies the truth of the second. This form of implication is the simplest of all, since the fact that a particular maple is part of the category of all maple trees makes the implication unmistakably clear.

In the ordinary course of reading and writing, however, implications do not appear so openly. Instead, they operate subtly, often by omission rather than by announcement. Frequently, they arise from a sudden or peculiar emphasis; sometimes juxtaposition produces them. In a recent political convention, one speaker praised by name all of the President's principal advisers except one, thereby implying by omission his disapproval or dislike of that one. Had he gone through the list and then made a pointedly offhand addition of that one name to his list, he would have achieved the same implication by emphasis. Or had he dealt with each name in ascending order of value and coupled the one name with others early in his list, in defiance of the man's actual status, he would have implied by juxtaposition what he actually did imply by omission. The use of implication is not confined, of course, to getting revenge on one's enemies; it is also a primary instrument of humor and of satire ("all the necessities of life—food, shelter, clothing, and a TV set"), and an important means of enlarging the significance of a statement without making it seem unnecessarily explicit.

"Enlarging the significance of a statement" points to an ampler meaning often given to the word "implication" in ordinary discourse, a meaning roughly synonymous with "suggestion." When Laborite Aneurin Bevan called an opponent "that Parliamentary doodlebug," he probably implied—in this loose sense of the word—that the opponent was unfit to hold office or was, at least, a fellow incapable of constructive action. Implication, in this sense, may reach to the furthest limits of association; in the stricter sense described above it includes only those additional statements logically entailed by the statement made.

Implications and assumptions really represent the gap between all that a man means and the language he uses to express it. Without them people would be required to lengthen their assertions almost endlessly, and they would be deprived, as well, of many of the artful devices by which they convey subtleties of understanding and feeling which lose some of their character when they are put into words. A considerable amount of the effectiveness of our language derives from the fact that people do not need to express explicitly everything they would have their readers or listeners understand. Were it not for assumptions and implications, a simple command like "Shut the door" would have to be elaborated in this fashion: "There is a door here, and it is now open, and you are able to shut it, and I want it shut; therefore, I order you to shut it; and I am treating you as a subordinate by omitting any polite form of request." And an exclamation like "Fire!" would require expansion to "There is a fire here; it is a dangerous fire; I advise everyone to get away from it as quickly as possible." There is no doubt, then, about the usefulness of this mode of saying less than we mean to have our listeners understand; it is only the matter of determining precisely what is meant in addition to what is explicitly asserted that makes a problem.

Every extended piece of serious discourse is made up of a series of assertions, however disguised. If a writer had to deal with each as elaborately as this book suggests, he would never get done. Yet, if he is responsible about his work, he cannot ignore the one consideration about asserting which underlies all that has been said here: *a writer must know the nature of the assertions he makes in order to understand what meanings they can convey and what responsibilities they impose upon him.* If that consideration becomes important to him, he has the kind of command over language that prepares him to represent honestly the world as he understands it.

• *Exercise 2.9:* What assumptions or implications do the following statements have?

a. Students who cut classes and neglect their work throw away their chance to earn a good income after graduation.

b. He smiled a lot, so he must have enjoyed the party.

c. Because D. H. Lawrence was a man of feeling, he deplored Bertrand Russell's rationality.

d. A fat paunch never breeds fine thoughts.

e. If a country's economy is sound, its people are happy; and the Poles are not happy.

f. The Lord protects drunkards, idiots, and Americans.

g. *Tropic of Cancer* is pornography, and should never have been published.

chapter three / *Proving*

An assertion can stand unsupported; many do. Consider "I'm hungry." Or consider the assertion "An assertion can stand unsupported." When the reader came upon it the first time he may have treated it in any one of a number of ways: pondered it, thought about something else, repeated it quietly to himself, accepted it implicitly, forgotten it immediately, written it down in his notebook, rejected it out of hand, analyzed its grammar, laughed aloud at it, translated it into German, been reminded of a story by it, discovered in it the way out of his dilemma, and so on. All of these responses, disagreeable though some would be to the authors, were within the reader's rights. And if he responded in one of these ways, the assertion was, for his purposes, sufficient in itself; he required no sequel. But if his response was to challenge it, or doubt it, or seek to test it for himself, then he raised issues that could only be settled by further assertions, assertions that would either confirm or refute the original one. That is, he was asking for proof: for although an assertion may *stand* by itself, it can hardly *prove* itself. Loud and repeated assertion may convince—witness the force of proverbs and superstitions—but in general, to assert is not to prove.

For the writer and the reader, proving has to do with relations between statements, with the effort to certify one assertion by linking it to another (or others) whose credentials are good. Another way of putting it is to say that a proof, when it works right, uses one or more pieces of certain, or familiar, or easily accessible information to get to a piece of previously uncertain, or new, or inaccessible information. The case is clearest in science, where much of our most valued knowledge—the existence of protons and electrons, the laws of heredity, the causes of disease—is such that investigators could not possibly have reached it by observation, nor in any way other than through proof. As man and scientist, Newton made a large number of observations, but he did not *observe* the laws of thermodynamics, nor did Harvey observe the blood circulating. Of course, the conclusion of a proof need not be new to the prover, but it had better be new to someone. A man who proves to you that you have two ears will, under normal circumstances, be wasting his and your time. Proving, then, is a matter of converting old knowledge into new, and, for the writer, of combining assertions so that one backs up another.

It need hardly be said that not every group of assertions will do, and not every arrangement of a proper group of assertions will do. That a woman swam the Bosphorus last Tuesday does not prove that life exists on Venus, and it is fruitless to argue that because all states are made up of counties and San Bernardino County is a county, San Bernardino County is smaller than all states (though *something* follows about San Bernardino County). Clearly, one of the problems facing a writer is what criteria distinguish sound proofs from those arrays of information or statement which are either bad proofs or no proofs at all.

But first it is well to point out that, although proving reaches its peaks of elegance and rigor in mathematics, logic, science, history, jurisprudence, and the like, everyone spends some of his time proving, and not always badly at that. Proving has its roots in the utterly commonplace activity of backing up assertions with other assertions—giving reasons. Take the following as instances:

1. I know there's a mouse in the room, because I can see its tail under the couch.
2. You *were* driving recklessly: you were on the wrong side of the double line.
3. Only members are allowed at the club's bar on Sundays, so we'll have to have our drink somewhere else.
4. You never see rattlesnakes around here; probably the climate is too cold for them.
5. If the bank is a ten-minute drive from here, and if it closes at three, you will be too late.
6. Whenever there's ragweed around he sneezes continuously, so I suppose he suffers from hay fever.
7. Since he suffers from hay fever, he'll sneeze continuously whenever there's ragweed around.
8. Most Irishmen are Catholics, so Mr. MacNamara will probably be going to mass at midnight.

Not a single one of these arguments would pass muster as a formal proof, yet each is adequate to its job—each is in perfectly good order, given an appropriate context. It would be absurd, in ordinary conversation, to challenge the speaker in (8) by saying "You haven't stated all your premises," or "Your proof is neither deductive nor inductive." The kind of objection one would expect, if any, is "But MacNamara is a Scot," a claim, in other words, that the original speaker was mistaken about part of the context. For everyday purposes (8) is a strong argument as it stands, provided the facts are what the speaker implies.

Moreover, there is little danger of logical deception in arguments like these. Suppose (3) had run, "Only members are allowed at the club's bar on Sunday, so if we go to Leary's Tavern for our drink we won't run into anyone from the club." The speaker's companion, if he were on his toes, would immediately have sensed the flaw in reasoning (a flaw strictly in *logic,* as it happens). Most educated people reason well enough for most purposes most of the time.

Nor is it sensible to create a mystique about logic or scientific method. The ground rules followed by logicians and scientists have their source in the ground rules followed by all intelligent men in candid and serious argument. At the same time, it is essential to recognize that there is a great difference in complexity and rigor between the methods of the man in the laboratory and those of the man in Leary's Tavern, and that, while the expository writer need not adopt the standards of the theoretical physicist or those of the logician, he can rarely settle for the standards of Leary's Tavern. Arguments (1) through (8) are in the main too ephemeral or too trivial even to find their way into written prose, but if they were to appear in an essay the reader would have a right to complain about some. In (4), for instance, an observation about rattlesnakes is offered in support of a tentative hypothesis. In order for the hypothesis to carry much conviction, the listener would have to know how many observers have failed to see rattlesnakes, and for how long, and whether they were looking in the right places. A critical thinker would also ask whether rattlesnakes thrive in equally cold climates elsewhere, and whether there are other factors—such as too much or too little water, a shortage of rattlesnake food, an abundance of natural enemies, or the presence of geographical barriers—which could account as well as the cold climate for the absence of rattlesnakes. Good answers to all these questions would make the argument a strong one, but the investigator could tighten it up still more by discovering features of the rattlesnake's physiology which prevent it from living in the cold. The original hypothesis may be a plausible one (and that is all the speaker claimed for it), but it is a long way from certain on the basis of the reason put forth.[1]

---

[1] In point of fact, some rattlesnakes flourish in climates as cold as that of the Canadian great plains.

It seems clear, then, that linked assertions which serve adequately as proofs in casual talk may fail to pull their load in reasoned prose. This is one reason why a student, however fluent he is in offhand argument, does well to familiarize himself with the sanctions that govern more formal reasoned discourse before proving his point on paper.

There is another reason, too. Notice that proofs (1) to (8) all have roughly the same shape. Sometimes, to be sure, the conclusion comes before its backing, and sometimes after; in some of the proofs the backing consists of two assertions rather than of one, and some lack logical connective. But all eight have an elementary structure something like this.

Backing assertion; therefore ———→ concluding assertion.

This is, indeed, the standard form for a casual argument. Yet even a cursory inspection of the eight proofs is enough to show how misleading this similarity is. Consider these special characteristics:

Backing

(1) offers, as backing for its conclusion, a single piece of conclusive evidence, but the backing in (6) sums up a number of past observations. The backing in (2) is not so much the evidence presented as an assumed partial *definition* of reckless driving. In (8) the backing is not evidence at all, but a general principle. In (5) the backing is not even stated as true.

Conclusion

The conclusion of (6) is an explanatory hypothesis, that of (1) a particular fact, that of (7) a confident prediction, that of (8) a statement of probability.

The connection between backing and conclusion

In (2) the conclusion follows inevitably from the backing, given the relevant traffic law, but in (4), as we have shown, a great deal more information is required before the backing will make the conclusion certain. Clearly (6) and (7) represent different types of proof; the conclusion of (6) is the backing of (7); and the observations of sneezing which constitute the backing of (6) turn up as predicted observations in the conclusion of (7).

The eight arguments also vary considerably in the number and kind of additional steps needed in order to make them formally complete. And of course the completed arguments would take a variety of forms.

In other words, beneath their simple external form, these proofs reveal a fair amount of complexity, and by no means the same kind of complexity in each case. And although this complexity need not emerge in casual talk—indeed, if it did, trivial worldly affairs would become both interminable and hopelessly dull—as soon as a *writer* undertakes to prove a point, the true shape of his argument becomes crucial. For, since the rules and conventions by which his argument will be judged sound or unsound depend on the submerged form of that argument, he can scarcely know whether he is talking sense or nonsense unless he has at least an intuitive grasp of the logic of his position. Now this is not to say that what he finally puts on paper must match up neatly with one or another fully expanded form of proof. On the contrary, he may well settle for the rudimentary form, Backing ———→ Conclusion. But if so, he must know what steps he is doing without; he must know that these steps are legitimate; and he must know that his *reader* will be able to fill them in and sense their legitimacy. Otherwise, his proof will fail to convince, and both he and the reader will be shortchanged. So if a writer wishes to combine assertions to make proofs, it behooves him to know something about the formal properties of arguments—in short, about logic.

> • *Exercise 3.1:* Expand and rework proofs (2) to (8) in such a way as to bring out their logical structures and make them qualify for relatively formal discourse.

1/ The Limits of Logic

Before we turn to the procedures of logic, however, two objections had better be anticipated. First, and most obviously, not all writing is argumentative. Granted. Description, narration, meditation, analysis, explanation, and many other types of prose can do their work flawlessly without a trace of overt argument. It would be difficult to find a proof in this piece of description:

> The bed-frame is not tall or at all ornate, as many iron frames are. Its former surface of hard white paint is worn almost entirely away to the bare, blue-brown iron. It is a three-quarter bed, which means a double bed so far as tenant usage is concerned.
>
> JAMES AGEE, *Let Us Now Praise Famous Men*

At the same time, even writers in these modes aim to *convince,* to capture the reader's assent; and when the reader's assent is at stake, the writer must always be concerned with the authority of his assertions. But the authority of his assertions depends upon the backing which might be adduced to support them, even if in fact it is not. And questions of backing are questions of proof. So it is wise to admit that argument lurks in more corners than might be suspected of harboring it, and that very little rational activity is altogether innocent of proof.

A passage written by the physiologist Walter B. Cannon will illustrate the point:

> Organisms, composed of material which is characterized by the utmost inconstancy and unsteadiness, have somehow learned the methods of maintaining constancy and keeping steady in the presence of conditions which might reasonably be expected to prove profoundly disturbing. Men may be exposed to dry heat at temperatures from 115 to 128 degrees Centigrade (239 to 257 degrees Fahrenheit) without an increase of their body temperature above normal. On the other hand arctic mammals, when exposed to cold as low as 35 degrees Centigrade below freezing (31 degrees below zero Fahrenheit) do not manifest any noteworthy fall of body temperature. Furthermore, in regions where the air is extremely dry the inhabitants have little difficulty in retaining their body fluids. And in these days of high ventures in mountain climbing and in airplanes human beings may be surrounded by a greatly reduced pressure of oxygen in the air without showing serious effects of oxygen want.
>
> *The Wisdom of the Body*

Although at first reading the passage looks to be simply a series of factual statements, clearly it is an argument: the last four sentences count as backing for the generalization of the first. Nor does the relevance of proving end there. Each of the supporting assertions is itself a generalization from, presumably, a large number of observations, and they will not have the impact they are intended to have unless the reader senses this. (Cannon's mention of precise temperatures assures the reader that the appropriate observations and experiments really have been made, as does his use of the verbs "manifest" and "showing.") Notice, too, that the four facts are chosen, not randomly, but for their argumentative force. The first shows that the body maintains constant temperature in extreme heat. But a reader might still wonder whether body temperature resists extreme cold, and the second fact stills that query. At this point, however, a reasonable hypothesis might be constructed to the effect that mammalian stability is merely *temperature-proof.* Cannon is pressing for a much more general hypothesis: he adds evidence about the body's independence of atmospheric dryness. Both dryness and temperature impinge mainly on the body's surface: wouldn't physiological steadiness be upset by a shortage of some essential substance that is taken *into* the body? The last fact dispels this conjecture. Not one of the four assertions is redundant; each one, in addition to supporting Cannon's generalization, reduces the number of competing hypotheses. Thus a passage presented as a bundle of information actually works for Cannon as a rather cleverly structured argument. If the submerged argument had been faulty, the passage would not have done its job. Hence, even when a writer describes, or states facts, or analyzes, he had better be aware that these activities are seldom hermetically sealed off from proving.

The second objection: not all efforts to convince depend on logic. Again, granted. The mystic's euphoria, the novelist's sense of pathos in daily existence, the poet's nostalgia for his childhood—these can be *transmitted,* and convincingly so, but hardly argued logically. And these are valuable things, central to richly human modes of life. Man is not inveterately, not even inherently, a logical creature: logic is his achievement rather than his inheritance. Beneath the subtle structure of logic which he has learned to erect lies a life of perceptions and emotions still largely uncharted. So to recommend logical procedure is not to ignore other valuable ways of knowing what is true ("The heart has its reasons," said Pascal); it is only to encourage the use of those procedures over which thoughtful men, in the course of two thousand years and more, have learned to exercise control and through which they have learned to reach useful conclusions and make viable judgments.

By and large it is not with the entirely unprovable that the writer has to deal. Twentieth-century discoveries in psychology, our philosophical love affair with "the absurd," and an increasing emphasis in the arts on irrational forces in human life have all conspired to produce a widespread suspicion of logic in our own day. However, to jettison logic altogether is to demean man's dignity and deprive him of the soundest way we know for him to comprehend his experience.

2/ Classical Deductive Proofs

It will be convenient to begin by making things look simpler than they are. Logicians have commonly divided proofs into two types, *deductive* and *inductive*.[2] This traditional division will serve as an introduction to

---

[2] Arguments of *probability* are sometimes presented as a third type in a no man's land between induction and deduction, and are sometimes assimilated to one or the other.

the subject, though the reader should keep in mind its artificiality when set against the profusion of forms taken by actual verbal arguments.

A deductive proof is one whose conclusion follows with absolute inevitability from its backing, provided that conclusion and backing are properly related, according to certain rules. Mathematical proofs and those of symbolic logic are deductive, as are many arguments in law and in virtually every field of human inquiry. Given this variety of users, it is not surprising that the rules of deduction have been framed in a number of different ways. Moreover, they have at times attained a tortuous complexity·and a degree of abstraction that are of little concern to the writer who argues in words. So in our limited space we shall barely hint at the technical elaborations of deductive reasoning, but shall seek mainly to establish its nature and its place as an instrument of thought.

Classical deductive logic, as developed by Aristotle, and perfected in the late Middle Ages, is built around a linking of at least three assertions (not *two,* as in most everyday proving) in such a way that the first two could not be true without also making the third one true.[3]

9. All Frenchmen understand love.   Backing
   All Roquefort cheese makers are Frenchmen.

   All Roquefort cheese makers understand love.   Conclusion

10. Only Frenchmen have understood love.   Backing
    Don Juan was not a Frenchman.

    Don Juan did not understand love.   Conclusion

11. Every man is either an amorous bungler or a Frenchman. Backing
    All Parisians are men.
    Some Parisians are amorous bunglers.

    Some Parisians are not Frenchmen.   Conclusion

However *silly* these proofs are, the reader can tell with a little scrutiny that if he is willing to concede the backing assertions, he can not, without contradiction, deny the conclusions. In other words, these are *valid* arguments, whatever their degree of soundness.

To see why they are valid, look at the matter in this way: each assertion can be thought of as saying something about the relationship between two *classes,* or between one or more individuals and a class. Thus the first assertion of (9) states that the class of Frenchmen is included in the class of people who understand love. A different way of putting it is to say that every member of the class of Frenchmen also belongs to the class

---

[3] Technically these arguments are called *syllogisms;* the backing assertions are *premises.*

of people who understand love. The relationship might be diagramed like this:

The second assertion has it that the class of Frenchmen includes the class of Roquefort cheese makers:

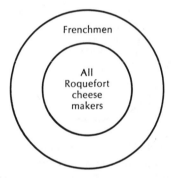

But if one class is part of a second class, which is in turn part of a third, then the first class must also be a part of the third; hence, the class of Roquefort cheese makers must also be included in the class of people who understand love:

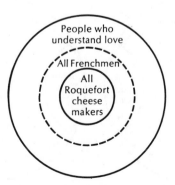

Class relationships being what they are, the argument is air-tight; just as, chronology being what it is, if Henry VIII antedates Cromwell, and Cromwell antedates Lloyd George, it follows inexorably that Henry VIII antedates Lloyd George.

Arguments (10) and (11) are a bit harder to translate into statements about classes. The first assertion of (10) might appear to have the same import as the first assertion of (9), but actually it reverses the class relationship. Rather than stating that the class "people who have understood love" *includes* the class "Frenchmen," it states that all people who have understood love *belong to* the class of Frenchmen. Clearly, if Don Juan did not belong to that class, he could not possibly have belonged to a *part* of that class:

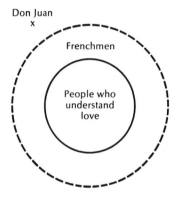

In (11), the first assertion states that the class of amorous bunglers and the class of Frenchmen include, between them, the entire class of men. So if the class of Parsians is included in the class of men, and if it has some members that also belong to the class of amorous bunglers, then naturally the class of Parisians has at least some members (these same ones) that are not members of the class of Frenchmen:

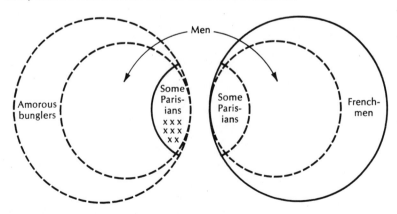

In like manner, any deductive argument of this sort can be converted into a group of statements about classes and their members.

Such analysis will also show, of course, when an argument is *in*valid. Take this one:

12. Only Frenchmen are good lovers.   Backing
    Every Roquefort cheese maker is a Frenchman.

    Every Roquefort cheese maker is a good lover.   Conclusion

The class of Roquefort cheese makers is contained in the class of Frenchmen, and so is the class of good lovers. But from this it does not follow that the cheese makers all belong to the class of good lovers, or even that a single cheese maker can court a woman skillfully. For the first assertion leaves open the possibility that a great many Frenchmen are *not* good lovers, and all the cheese makers might belong to that unhappy class of beings. So the following is a possible state of affairs, given the first two assertions:

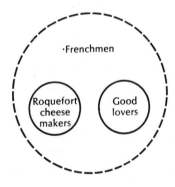

So, for that matter is this:

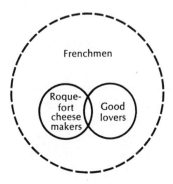

Or either of these:

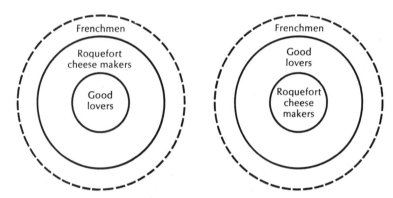

In short, the backing assertions prove nothing at all about the relationship between the two subclasses of Frenchmen, and so the argument fails.

Now the reader may have noticed that arguments (9) through (12), similar though they are in their general shape, contain assertions of various types. Such assertions can be positive or negative. They can speak of whole classes ("all," "only," "every"), of parts of classes ("some"), or of individuals ("Don Juan," "a," "the"). They can be unequivocal ("all men are") or equivocal ("all men are either *x* or *y*"). Moreover, they can be partly or wholly *hypothetical;* that is, (9) might be converted into

> 13. If any man is a Frenchman he understands love.   Backing
>   All Roquefort cheese makers are Frenchmen.
>
>   All Roquefort cheese makers understand love.   Conclusion

or

> 14. If any man is a Frenchman he understands love.   Backing
>   If any man is a Roquefort cheese maker he is a
>   Frenchman.
>
>   If any man is a Roquefort cheese maker he under-   Conclusion
>   stands love.

Since the conclusion one can draw from backing assertions varies with the form of those assertions, it is obvious both that the rules for classical deduction are fairly complex and that the legitimate manipulations are numerous. But there is no need for a writer who plans to *use* logic rather than *study* logic to learn all the rules and manipulations. He will have little difficulty with short arguments of this sort if he remembers that they can all be reduced to statements about class membership and class inclusion. His lifelong familiarity with the concept of classes will do the rest (aided, perhaps, by diagrams like those illustrated above). Perhaps it is possible to venture another definition at this point: a classical deductive argument is one in which two or more assertions about classes and members of classes precede an assertion which relates two of these classes, or one member and one class, in a new way.

> • *Exercise 3.2:* According to the rules of classical deductive logic, what conclusion (if any) follows from each of the following pairs of backing assertions?
>
> a. Some professional golfers are rich.
>   No rich man goes hungry.
> b. No car costs over $20,000 unless it is a Rolls Royce.
>   All the cars in my garage cost over $20,000.
> c. Every man is either a liberal or a conservative.
>   Some conservatives are Democrats.
> d. If any book came out before 1400, it was not printed.
>   Some printed books are prayer books.
> e. No monk is married.
>   Time waits for no bachelor.
> f. Some poets are fascists.
>   Only fascists scorn personal liberty.
> g. A coin collector is a numismatist.
>   Many students collect coins.
> h. A man who seeks fame is a fool.
>   If any man is a fool, he does not deserve fame.
> i. Keats was no philosopher.
>   No philosopher has solved the riddle of life.
> j. Where there's life there's hope.
>   There is no hope in Mexico today.
>
> (Notice that the only problem in most of these examples is getting the assertions into proper form—that is, expressing them in terms of classes. As we have said previously, deductive proving is mechanical once the argument is set up.)

3/ Validity and Truth

There are serious limitations on the value of deductive logic. For one thing, not all arguments lend themselves to the modes of analysis explicated here. How can anyone judge the recalcitrant proofs? Surely they are not all faulty. Even more disturbing, deductive proofs can function convincingly only if a good deal has already been proven. That is, the backing assertions must have their credentials in order, or there is no point in going on to the conclusion.

In other words there is an important distinction between *validity* and *truth*. Even though an argument is valid, its conclusion may be false unless its backing assertions are true. Consider:

> 15. All smokers have tuberculosis.   Backing
>   Everyone with tuberculosis is diseased.
>
>   All smokers are diseased.   Conclusion

Valid, but perfectly useless, because the first backing assertion introduces a falsehood that gets deposited in the conclusion in a different form. More puzzling still, it is possible to arrive validly at a true conclusion from totally false backing:

> 16. If Griggs is a normal man, he has three legs.   Backing
>   If Griggs has three legs, he has ten toes.
>
>   If Griggs is a normal man, he
>   has ten toes.   Conclusion

One might say that the end justifies the means, but no one is likely to be happy with this proof, notwithstanding its true conclusion and valid form.

The problem of truth is one that deduction cannot surmount by itself, yet deduction is inextricably bound up with truth in all practical matters, if not in all the examples of logicians. This difficulty has been so persistent that it has cast some philosophers into a state of disillusionment with formal deductions, even when those deductions are valid and true throughout. To be sure, they contend, it is easy to tell that since no American President before 1961 was a Catholic, and since Benjamin Harrison was President before 1961, Harrison was not a Catholic. But how was the truth of the backing generalization discovered? Presumably by knowing the religion of every President before 1961, Harrison among them. In that case, however, we already knew, and must have known, what the conclusion tells us. And why clutter up the argumentative scene with those other thirty-two Presidents? Here, as in most deductive proofs (including much less trivial ones), the more general, lawlike, and interesting assertions appear in the backing, not the conclusion. The proof simply *uses* them; they must have been *established* by other means.

It is best, therefore, to regard deductive forms as precisely that: *forms* into which the raw materials can be pressed, in order to give them maximum power and efficiency. Once they are there, the rest is mechanical. Deductive methods do not so much perform the labor of argument as reveal when that labor is done. Now this is an invaluable function; without it human reasoning would be crippled. But for the ultimate source of our knowledge about the world, other processes must be reviewed.

> • *Exercise 3.3:* Analyze the following proofs for truth and validity:
>
> a. Cats are animals, and all animals need food; therefore cats need food.
> b. Dogs are reptiles, and reptiles are warm-blooded; therefore dogs are warm-blooded.
> c. Fish are vegetarians, and vegetarians eat nothing but bread; therefore fish eat nothing but bread.
> d. Birds build nests, and sparrows build nests; therefore sparrows are birds.
> e. Snakes are harmful, and snakes are popular; therefore harmful things are popular.
> f. Horses are becoming stronger, and anything that is becoming stronger needs more to eat; therefore horses need more to eat.
> g. Whales are mammals, and mammals lay eggs; therefore whales' eggs are mammalian.

4/ Inductive Proofs

Of these processes, the most fundamental is of course perception. The child knows that his kitten's fur is soft by feeling it, and in similar ways he collects a vast amount of information about a large number of things. But even in moving from the single, momentary fragment of perceptual knowledge to a *collection* of *facts,* the child does something which has long baffled philosophers. For how can he know from having touched the cat five minutes ago that its fur is soft now? Well, probably he knows that physical things do not as a rule change their qualities abruptly and without cause. But how does he know *this?* Surely this rule is still farther from simple observation than the present softness of the cat's fur. So, too, the rules that all cat fur is soft, that if a dog frightens a cat the cat's fur will stand on end, and so on and on through the whole catalogue of what is considered knowledge. Almost none of the things people know at a given moment come from their sensory experience at that moment, and surprisingly few can even be said to come directly from memories of past sensory experience. Much of what people know, on the contrary, they know about things they could not possibly have come in sensory contact with (all cat fur, for instance, or what will happen tomorrow if a dog frightens a cat). Yet people do know these things. Indeed, such things and their ilk—generalizations, facts about the past, laws, certainties about the future—are absolutely crucial to our conduct and thinking. It is not surprising that the philosophical attempt to justify them has been massive and confusing, especially since the forceful attacks on the foundations of such knowledge by George Berkeley and David Hume in the eighteenth century.

This turbulent controversy is not of deep concern here. But since it bears directly on inductive argument—part of it is known as "the problem of induction"—a few remarks will be apposite, dogmatically though they must be offered. In the first place, even Hume at his most skeptical was well aware how foreign his philosophical doubts were to everyday experience. "I dine," he wrote,

> I play a game of back-gammon, I converse, and am merry with my friends; and when after three or four hours' amusement I wou'd return to these speculations, they appear so cold, and strain'd, and ridiculous, that I cannot find in my heart to enter into them any further

A Treatise of Human Nature, book I, part IV

Life goes on, however suspect philosophically our knowledge of causes, laws, and generalities. For dependence on such knowledge is profoundly natural to human beings, and even to lower animals. Somewhere between perception and thought there is an instinctive tendency to look for samenesses: this bundle of sensations and that one yesterday and that other one all mean "tomato," though of course no two tomatoes and no two sensings of the same tomato are exactly alike. And the word "tomato" is the same word each time we hear it, whether uttered fast or slow, soprano or bass—even printed on a page. To the very roots, men are categorizing animals. Moreover, we expect things of the same kind to behave alike, and to behave in the future as they have in the past. About these expectations not much can be said, except that human beings come with them as standard equipment, and that they pay off rather well on the whole. The findings of perception theorists in this matter are confirmed by the psychological study of learning. What a man or animal does once and is punished for, he will be less likely to do again; if he is rewarded he will be more likely to repeat. This process of "conditioning," in both elementary and more complex forms, accounts for much learning, though by no means for all. And its success compels the belief that organisms have an innate tendency to expect experience to repeat itself. Of course the fact that this expectation exists is no proof that the expectation is justified, but it does reduce to a certain hollowness the philosopher's cries of "no certainty."

If men must ask, in spite of the question's oddity, what justifies them in passing from limited experience to generalizations that go beyond it, and if "justify" is interpreted in a strict logical sense, the answer should probably be Hume's resounding "Nothing." But if the question is taken to mean, "How is it that some generalizations are reasonable and others not?" then the answer should be that a generalization is justifiable when it meets the standards by which generalizations are judged, exactly as a deduction is justified when it follows the rules for deduction. This answer may sound circular, as well as philosophically evasive, but it has the advantage of corresponding to the way people actually behave. Besides, it opens the door to a set of new questions far more relevant to the writer's problems of argumentations—questions about the several procedures of inductive proof and the requirements that such proofs must satisfy.

It is time to offer a definition: an inductive proof is one that moves either (a) from a group of assertions about *some* events, things, or situations of a certain class to an assertion about *all* such events, things, or situations, or (b) from assertions about miscellaneous things and events to an assertion which *explains* them in a relatively simple way. Types (a) and (b) belong together in the one definition because, logically speaking, type (a) is a variety of type (b), however different their conclusions may look. If one moves from "All the Hungarians I've met are intellectuals" to "All Hungarians are intellectuals," he does so precisely because the latter assertion (the generalization) seems the best explanation of the evidence described by the first. Notice that a different explanation may be better—if, for instance, the only Hungarians one has met were exchange professors at his university. In other words, the inference from some to all is justified only when the "some" are known to be a random selection. Thus inductions of type (a)—generalizations—are special cases of type (b)—explanations.

As will become increasingly clear later, this definition cuts some corners: the activities that go on under the heading of induction are too varied to submit to a description both neat and inclusive. But the main criteria are certainly the ones stated above: in an inductive argument the assertions are to the conclusion as parts to a whole or as facts to explanation.

Two examples should clarify the point:

  17. Disease X is unknown in northern Canada and
       Greenland.

It occurs rarely in New York State.

Epidemics of disease X have occurred in the
Mediterranean countries.

It is endemic to Central America.

It is fairly common in Burma.   Backing

Disease X thrives in all warm climates, and
only in warm climates.   Conclusion

18. Disease X thrives only in warm climates.

It never strikes where the temperature drops
below freezing in the summer.

It breaks out in seaports and passes to the in-
terior from here.

Epidemics occur in large cities, especially.

The disease is uncommon where the water supply is carefully purified.

The city poor are especially susceptible.

Rats always die in large numbers when there is
an epidemic.

Disease X is unknown in arid climates.   Backing

Disease X is caused by bacteria which flourish
in water, but die from exposure to the sun
or freezing. They are carried by rats, and
spread through contaminated water supplies
or from person to person.   Conclusion

Argument (17) takes several facts about the distribution of disease
X and converts them into a general statement. This is the simplest type
of induction, but even it presents some difficulties. Canada, Central
America, Burma, and so on are not the only places in the world, yet
the conclusion makes a claim about the whole world. From backing to
conclusion the prover of (17) has taken the so-called *inductive leap,* a
leap from partial evidence to a generalization that goes well beyond that
evidence. It might turn out, of course, that the very next piece of evidence acquired—for instance, that disease X is unknown in the Congo
—would upset the conclusion. And such things happen constantly:
philologists who were familiar mainly with European languages drew a
number of general conclusions about language which proved to be quite
false when more of the world's 3000 languages were described. Certainly
(17) makes too large an inductive leap to inspire much confidence.
Besides, the conclusion of (17) looks as if it were intended to apply to
the past and future, as well as to the present, so it poses in addition the
old problem of projecting past experience into the future. Still (17) has
a perfectly legitimate *form,* and if the data were three or four times as

bulky, and all favorable, few would be seriously disturbed by the proof.

Argument (18) differs in several important ways from (17). The conclusion, of course, does more than generalize from the backing assertions: it purports to explain them. Thus it is of a different type from them, in that it introduces the notion of cause. Moreover, it posits a factor, bacteria, which was nowhere mentioned in the backing. The same might seem to be true in (17), but actually the conclusion of (17) merely brings into the open a factor, climate, which was implicit in the backing. For these reasons it is harder to see the nature of the inductive leap in (18). The best way to do so is to ask what we would want to know in addition to the given information before we could feel relatively certain about the conclusion. Certainly it would be pertinent to know that a certain kind of bacteria were always found in the blood at some stage of disease X, that the same bacteria could be observed in the sick rats and in the water supply, that these bacteria attack the organism in a certain way to produce the symptoms of the disease, and so on. In other words, as it stands now, the conclusion of (18) is what we call an *hypothesis,* which needs further *confirmation.* The leap is from partial confirmation to all-inclusive hypothesis. Generalization and hypothesis shade into one another, but the distinction does have its usefulness in the classification of inductive arguments.

Another way to understand the nature of induction is by contrast with deduction. In a deductive proof the backing entails the conclusion; in an inductive proof the relationship is precisely the reverse: the conclusion entails the backing. Thus if disease X always thrives in warm climates and only in warm climates, it must necessarily be common in Central America, rare in New York state, and so on. This fact offers another perspective on the inductive leap. Even if the conclusion does in fact entail all the backing assertions, it may not be the right conclusion, for other ones may entail the very same assertions. In (17), for example, the evidence is also consistent with the conclusion that disease X occurs only in very *sunny* climates, or only in Catholic, Buddhist, Jewish and Moslem countries. One of the main problems in induction is choosing the best hypothesis or generalization. For another thing, the conclusion will usually entail many facts other than the ones used in getting to it. Hence a vital way of determining whether an hypothesis is the best one is by checking its additional consequences (and those of alternative hypotheses). If disease X turns out to be common in Ireland, that fact would count against the conclusion of (17), and in favor of the rather ludicrous alternative which links disease X with religion. An hypothesis, though it is the best one for certain data, may still turn out to be false, given further data.

The subject of hypotheses (and of *theories,* which are relatively well-confirmed hypotheses) is one of the most controversial in all philosophy. We shall not enter the fray beyond suggesting a few useful standards for evaluating hypotheses. We have already said that a good hypothesis should account for all the evidence; this much is obvious. But the difficulty comes in weighing hypotheses against each other, for no "good" hypothesis will be good enough unless it can outlast its competitors. A few decades ago American crime statistics clearly showed that more crimes were committed, proportionately, by foreign-born citizens than by natives. From this, many freely concluded that foreigners were inherently less law-abiding than natives. This hypothesis, though plausible, will not stand up against more serious scrutiny of the evidence. For of the foreign born, an unusually high proportion were men, belonged to low economic groups, had had little education, and so on. Now men commit more crimes than women, the poor than the rich, the ignorant than the educated. Therefore, all of these factors must be eliminated in any study of the criminal tendencies of foreigners. As it happens, once foreigners were matched up with natives according to level of education, sex, and the rest of the factors, it became obvious that people of foreign birth actually committed *fewer* crimes than like groups of native Americans. Hasty formation of hypotheses, without adequate attention to other possibilities, is perhaps the most common and most grievous flaw in ordinary argument, one responsible for untold quantities of prejudice, superstition, and shoddy thinking.

An hypothesis does not stand or fall only on its power to handle the available evidence. Often a number of hypotheses will do this much. How to choose among them? Three principles are worth mentioning here:

A. Other things being equal, the simpler of two hypotheses is to be preferred. Why this is so is hard to say, but here is an example. Assume there is a traffic jam a mile long before a major intersection at 6:00 P.M. on the third day of a holiday weekend. Is it better to guess that the traffic-regulating system at the intersection proved inadequate to the unusually heavy traffic, or that the local police have been bribed by Republican officials to create a jam and thereby embarrass the Democrats in their attempt to block the highway bill before the legislature, so that in the next local election the Main Street vote will go Republican?

B. An hypothesis never stands in isolation from what we know of the world in general. Even if it fits the evidence it is designed to explain, it will not hold up unless it jibes with the sum total of human knowledge, fact and theory. Thus the hypothesis that disease X is distributed along religious lines, although consistent with the facts at hand, goes against very general and well-founded notions both about religion and about disease, and will have a lot more against it from the start than an hypothesis which links disease and climate. Likewise the hypothesis of the scientist who, according to an old story, said "Jump" to a flea, which eventually jumped; then he pulled the hind legs off the flea, and said again, "Jump," but the flea did nothing, and the scientist concluded that when you amputate a flea's legs its hearing is impaired. Of the same sort, but more puzzling, is the hypothesis that the world was created last Tuesday, complete with fossils, memories, pregnant women and history books (to what assumptions about the world would one have to appeal in order to refute *this* hypothesis?). An interesting actual example from recent years is the reluctance of scientists and people generally to accept extrasensory perception as an hypothesis, although it is consistent with a good deal of experimental evidence. Inductive arguments depend on all sorts of unobtrusive assumptions about the way the world works, much as a deductive argument presupposes the rules of logic, and multiplication presupposes the axioms of arithmetic. Still, even when an hypothesis upsets the most cherished of received truths, it may eventually gain acceptance if it is powerful and cogent enough. After all, men came finally to believe that Copernicus was right, and think what a difference *his* hypothesis made in the structure of human belief!

C. An hypothesis will be more credible to the extent that it explains not only the facts that elicit it, but seemingly unrelated facts as well. Dalton hypothesized the atom to account for a few simple characteristics of chemical compounds, but the notion illuminated the whole field of chemistry, and explained various phenomena of radiation and spectroscopy. Moreover, it led to the discovery of new elements, and eventually made possible quantum mechanics, nuclear physics, and a whole range of new hypotheses and experiments. The great hypotheses of science have had this capacity to connect the previously unconnected, proliferate new hypotheses and uncover new facts, thus enlarging human knowledge far more than was the intent of their originators.

What we have said about the conclusions of inductive proofs can be summed up in a rather simplified scheme. Roughly, these conclusions are of four types. Some are *generalizations,* whose function is to describe or arrange the data and project the description outward to cover possible new data. ("Disease X thrives only in warm climates.") Some are *particular hypotheses,* designed to explain a unique group of circumstances. ("Norsemen must have landed on Cape Cod in the tenth century.") The other two types have more general importance for discovery and understanding. One, the *law,* establishes a causal connection between events or situations and specifies precisely their relationship. ("Ontogeny recapitulates phylogeny"; "wars are always followed by brief periods of economic prosperity.") Notice, by the way, that laws always imply predictions; they speak of regularities in past experience which are supposed to hold for the future as well. Conclusions of the fourth type might best be labeled *principles.* They are like laws, but of such sweeping generality that they leave particular observations or experiments far behind. ("$E = mc^2$"; "human nature never changes.") To repeat a warning, so multiform are the processes of induction that no simple classification will do justice to them. But this breakdown according to type of conclusion at least gives some idea of their range and scope.

- *Exercise 3.4:* How would you account for the following facts? In most American cities downtown areas have been declining for some years. Public transportation has diminished in scope and volume. Industry has increasingly settled in nearby rural areas. Highway building has proceeded at a great rate, but traffic problems continue to worsen. Suburban shopping centers flourish.

  What alternative hypotheses would you have to consider? What additional evidence would you need before settling for certain on an explanation? What additional facts will your hypothesis explain?

- *Exercise 3.5:* Produce three examples each of hypotheses, laws, and principles.

5/   Evidence

The discussion in the last several pages may have given the impression that induction is the preserve mainly of scientists. To be sure, the most full and rigorous uses of induction have been scientific, ever since Francis Bacon brushed away the cobwebs of *a priori* argument in the early seventeenth century. But of course induction is the servant of argument in every scholarly field, and in garden-variety proving too. The differences between scientific induction and more humble proving do not show so much in an analysis of conclusions as in an analysis of backing.

Most of the backing for scientific conclusions derives either from experiment (as in chemistry) or from highly skilled observation (as in botany), often aided by instruments (as in astronomy). But most of the inductive argument practiced by students in expository writing depends upon evidence considerably more accessible to the layman. For the purposes of this book, then, it is important to mention at least briefly some of the major types of backing. It is also important to remember that not all good arguments need be conducted on scientific models, and that what counts as good evidence will vary greatly from field to field and context to context.

In the humanities, in the social sciences, and in casual talk (as in science), the central type of evidence, from which all others derive, is *observation.* "I know there's a mouse in the room because I can see it" is still the prototype of a powerful argument. Not much need be said about observation, except the truisms that a trained eye is better than an untrained one, that a random mass of data is worth less than a few carefully selected observations, that even the senses are fallible, not to mention the memory, and that, since an observer's bias may color his observation, observations that compensate for such bias are better than observations that don't. Once these qualifications are recorded, it remains unarguable that the evidence of the senses is the best we have.

The difficulties multiply when an argument relies for its backing (as most do), not on the prover's observations, but on evidence gathered from other sources. In history, economics, social criticism, and the like, that evidence is most likely to come from *reports,* either of other people's observations or of still further reports which have a more remote origin in observation. Evaluating such reports is a major responsibility of the scholar, one that can be hinted at by a list of questions which he might wish to ask of a given book, article, or document:

SOURCE

What is the nature of the source? Is it one from which other reports have come? If so, what is their known reliability? Is the source of a kind that is likely to provide accurate transmission of data? Is it subject to inadvertent error? to distortion because of prejudice, ignorance, the situation or time in which it occurs, necessity to avoid or provide opposition, intention to conceal or deceive?

AUTHOR OR TRANSMITTER

Is the authorship certainly known? If so, is the author's reliability known from any other documents? What are the author's or transmitter's qualifications as a reporter? Did he have opportunity to observe directly the data he uses? Does he display sound knowledge of his subject and general intelligence on other sources? Is there any ground for thinking him susceptible to bias or pressures likely to cause him to alter or suppress data?

DATA

Are the data such as can be observed directly? If so, were they observed directly? With what degree of accuracy can they be recorded? Are they verifiable by others? Have they been so verified? Do they stand in conflict with other data? Are they complete, or only "representative"? If "representative," what were the grounds of selection? Are the methods of analysis used appropriate? Do the data actually support the conclusions drawn from them? Would they support alternative conclusions as well, or nearly as well?

A report that weathers such a line of questioning has a reasonable claim to reliability. Its solidity, even if all the questions are favorably answered, may never be beyond dispute, but in many fields of inquiry such a report counts as highly convincing evidence.

One step further removed from actual observation is evidence based on *authority*—that is, on opinions, judgments, generalizations, and principles voiced by people who should know. Since everyone lives in daily contact with complexities far beyond his comprehension, it is easy to understand why authority is such a popular ground for belief. As a shortcut to truth, the layman relies on the expert to tell him what happens to the economy after a tax cut, whether the text of *Macbeth* is corrupt, what effect a new drug has, or whether Moses was an actual historical figure. There is nothing wrong with this dependence; it is inevitable. But anyone conducting a serious argument should remember that some authorities are better than others, and that even the best authorities often disagree. Moreover, an authority in a particular field is not necessarily an authority in all matters that touch on that field: citizens listen to the general when he talks of military strategy, but his testimony on the social and political effects of military occupation is more vulnerable, and other authorities should be called in on these subjects. In the end, a certain skepticism about all authoritative judgments is warranted: it took a highly complicated study of radioactivity to prove the recency of the bones of Piltdown man, whose antiquity had been authenticated by many reputable scientists; but it took only an ingenious fanatic to fabricate them in the first place.

A similar type of backing consists of assertions whose credibility depends on *persistence.* If enough people believe something long enough it becomes part of a stock of "common knowledge" and will be used freely and uncritically in argument. Of course persistence by itself is usually a shaky foundation for belief. The history of knowledge is a drama in which hypotheses harden into received truth only to be altered or replaced by new hypotheses which themselves harden and are exploded. Everyone knew the world was flat, but that did not prevent Columbus from being right. Persistence does carry some weight when it represents a quantity of shared human experience—which is to say observation. Yet even farmers' rules of thumb are shot through with superstition, and it is an uncritical arguer who will rest his claims on persistence alone.

What, then, of *intuition,* the most ephemeral kind of evidence, the furthest removed from observation, and the most inaccessible to rigorous checking? The answer seems obvious, and yet we all rely on our intuitions from time to time—though probably not with such confidence as D. H. Lawrence, who told Aldous Huxley that he rejected the theory of evolution because he "did not feel it *here,*" meaning "here in the solar plexus." The trouble with Lawrence's method of demonstration was that the status quo in his solar plexus had rather little to do with the truth about evolution. There are fields of inquiry (psychology, for one) in which intuitions have some value as evidence: some powerful theories in descriptive linguistics depend partly upon the intuitions of native speakers. But in most fields the investigator had best regard his intuitions as no more than hints on which to proceed in the labor of experiment and rational argument. The intuition of an expert may incorporate a good deal of condensed wisdom and observation, but it is not likely to convince anyone else unless the wisdom and observation are made explicit.

On a different footing from all these types of evidence is backing based on *convention.* The speaker who concluded that his friend was driving recklessly because he was over the double line rested his case partly on a definition of reckless driving: one of the things *meant* by "reckless driving" is crossing the double line. This sort of gambit belongs more to deductive proving than to inductive, but it can and often should find employment at some stage of an essentially inductive proof. When the writer does call on convention (or stipulative definition) for support he stands on ground as solid as that of observation, provided that he reads the convention aright. And of course he must remember that convention is strictly a verbal matter and cannot prove anything about the way the world is. The fact that the sun "rises" does not prove that it orbits around the earth, nor is the whale cold-blooded because it is a "fish."

In cases like these the conventions of ordinary usage must yield to the discoveries of science and the conventions of scientific language. But the authority of common usage is sufficient for most argumentative purposes.

• *Exercise 3.6:*   Consider the hypothesis that the poet Yeats was a mystic, and suppose that the following evidence is available:

  a. There are well-documented reports that he was a disciple of Madame Blavatsky, the theosophist.
  b. He was seen at seances.
  c. In his book *A Vision,* he developed a mystical system, but said at one point that perhaps his symbols were just "metaphors for poetry."
  d. People often say that Yeats was a mystic.
  e. Professor X, a specialist in modern poetry, says that Yeats was a mystic.
  f. Some of his poems are impossible to understand without knowing the system of *A Vision.*
  g. Reading Yeats's poetry gives you a feeling that he was a mystic.
  h. He was active in Irish political affairs.
  i. You know a mystic who likes Yeats's poetry.
  j. A number of great poets are known to have been mystics.
  k. Yeats expressed in print belief in a "great soul" with which we are all in touch from time to time.

How would you evaluate each of these pieces of evidence? Apply tests for reliability, and assess the relevance or persuasiveness of each fact. (The point of this exercise is not to decide the issue, but to judge the evidence.)

6/   Forms and Strategies

So far, most of what we have said has encouraged a schematic view of proving. We have divided proofs into two fundamental types, deductive and inductive. We have developed two systems of deduction, each with its rules and conventions. We have classified inductive proofs according to their conclusions and backing, and have suggested some criteria for evaluating them. All of this apparatus has its use in the practical business of writing argumentatively, which, without some fixed points of reference or some ground rules, can too easily disintegrate into impressionism, smoke screening, and high dudgeon. But the system, as we have cautioned at intervals, is too neat; it is time to consider a somewhat looser approach, one capable of suggesting more richly the varieties of actual written argument.

That arguments can defy strict categorization is evident from such instances as this:

19. Both Napoleon's France and Hitler's Germany met defeat in attempting to expand eastward.

   Therefore, if China tries to conquer the West, it will probably fail.

It is unclear, to begin with, whether the argument is primarily inductive or deductive. Conceivably, it rests on a general principle to the effect that all great powers fare alike in similar undertakings. If so, additional backing assertions linking these three countries as great powers and their undertakings as similar would make the proof a deductive one of sorts. But perhaps its force is rather to *establish,* inductively, the principle that great powers fare alike in similar undertakings. From this principle the conclusion follows simply. In either case the word "probably" poses extra problems, for neither strict induction nor strict deduction, as we have explained them, allows for a sudden intrusion of probability in the concluding assertion.

Now the nature of this argument is obscure partly because so much is missing. But another cause of confusion is the gap, always present, between the actual language of proving and abstract logical *forms.* Proofs that are basically inductive or deductive may stray far from their prototypes without losing their essential character; a great many proofs blend induction and deduction; others seem to lack the features of either major type. Moreover, as already indicated, the major types branch out into a number of subtypes (and there are many more), so that simply calling a proof inductive or deductive says relatively little about its structure or about the standards to be used in evaluating it.

This complexity may seem untidy, but it is real, and the writer should reconcile himself to it. There is no automatic way to pour all arguments into logical molds without distorting some of them beyond recognition, and although the writer owes deference to logic, he has a still stronger obligation to the precise and sometimes unique intricacies of his own argument. The major forms of proof remain available as standards of rigor and clarity, by which a writer may measure his own argument, and to which he may sometimes wish to reduce it. But to require every proof to satisfy this or that set of formal criteria would be as arbitrary as to require everyone to be exactly this or that many inches tall, with no unseemly fractions left over. People argue in words, after all, and combinations of words are infinitely various.

To compress into a few pages a survey of the full range of proofs would be impossible. Instead, what follows is a brief outline of forms and procedures to serve as points of reference in the framing of actual arguments. We need not cover again the ground that we have been over; we shall merely summarize such matters.

A. DEDUCTIVE ARGUMENTS

  1. With classes:

     a) *Three-part arguments*
       The standard three-part proof of this type can take many, many forms; but these are amply suggested by proofs (9) to (14) above, excluding the invalid (12), of course. The precise shape of such an argument will depend upon whether its assertions contain "all _____" ("every _____ _____,"), "only _____," "some _____ _____," "no _____," "if," "either _____ _____ or _____," or reference to an individual member of a class.

     b) *Chain arguments*

       20. All residents of Pine Street are laborers.
           All laborers voted for Gurski.
           Everyone who voted for Gurski was paid off in cash.
           No one paid off in cash is dissatisfied.
           No resident of Pine Street is dissatisfied.

       Clearly the rules for the shorter arguments apply here, with appropriate modifications. Notice that the backing assertions lead to other conclusions too, such as the conclusion that all laborers were paid off in cash, but if this were the point of the argument, there would be no sense in having so many backing assertions.

     c) *Abbreviated arguments*
       Both of the following are truncated versions of the same three-part proof; each makes do without one backing assertion:

       21. Every alchemist is a charlatan, so Bruno must be a charlatan.
       22. Bruno is an alchemist, so he must be a charlatan.

       These are extremely common forms, in writing as in speech.

They escape the bulkiness of the full three-part proof and are perfectly adequate when the omitted assertion is a matter of universal knowledge, or has already been established. It remains in the background as an *assumption,* to use the language of the preceding chapter. The conclusion can also be left out:

23. Bruno is an alchemist, and every alchemist is a charlatan.

In this form, the argument may seem to work by insinuation, but it has a more honorable use in the hands of a writer who simply does not want to insult his reader by stating the thunderingly obvious.

d) *Proofs that depend on additional assumptions*
Given what we all know about relationships such as "taller than," "older than," "brother of," "similar to," "before," and "north of," it is possible to build arguments that are clearly deductive according to our definition, but that do not depend on relations between classes:

24. Diamond is harder than steel, so it must be harder than glass, which is not so hard as steel.

25. Oswald is George's only son, and he is a bachelor, so George has no daughters-in-law.

26. The congressman's future depends upon the vote upstate, and the weather on election day always affects the upstate vote, so the congressman's future hangs partly on the election day weather.

27. Since most ball games are nine innings long, and since most take under three hours, at least some nine-inning games take less than three hours.

Such arguments can be multiplied indefinitely, and the fact that they are not customarily treated in logic texts says nothing against their propriety, or their validity.

e) *Arguments of possibility*
Classical deduction has another offshoot in proofs which depend on the notion of "may" or "possible":

28. Some piano tuners have perfect pitch.
    Mr. Canelli is a piano tuner.

    Mr. Canelli may have perfect pitch.

Arguments like this one also have a firm place in ordinary usage, and must not be ruled out because they cannot be dealt with rigorously in the logic of classes.

f) *Arguments of assimilation*
The most notorious misuse of classical deductive logic is that represented by argument (12). In recent years it has burst into new prominence in politics: we know it as "guilt by association," in forms like this:

29. Some (all) communists take part in the peace movement. Some (all) world federalists take part in the peace movement.

    Therefore some (all) world federalists are communists.

Alternatively,

30. All traitors praise the Soviet Union.
    Professor Stone praises the Soviet Union.

    Professor Stone is a traitor.

Such proofs are as contemptible intellectually as they are crude politically, and one would like to write a stop to their infamous history. But it bears mentioning here that arguments rather similar to these do sometimes make good sense. From the fact that New Zealanders speak English and the fact that Virginians speak English, one cannot, to be sure, conclude that Virginians are New Zealanders—or even that a single New Zealander is a Virginian. But one *can* argue as follows:

31. New Zealanders speak English.
    Virginians speak English.

    Virginians and New Zealanders are similar in their linguistic and cultural heritages.

And, in general, if two people or groups of people share one important characteristic, they are likely to share others. Two men who have the same opinion of the Great Society will probably agree about censorship as well; and two Mexicans will probably be closer to each other in their eating habits than either of them is to a Swede. But such matters take us out of the province of deductive logic.

2. Deductive proofs involving the truth or falsity of statements: Arguments that can be formalized in terms of P's and Q's also come in many varieties, but these can all be handled within the framework of rules elaborated earlier in this chapter.

B. INDUCTIVE ARGUMENTS

1. From particulars to a generalization:

a) *With an inductive leap*

This argumentative pattern in its simplest form can cause little trouble, beyond that of the inductive leap, which was discussed previously. But generalization is often more intellectually taxing than the argument that, because every crow sighted to date is black, all crows must be black. Sometimes it is difficult to tell which generalization, out of many possible ones, is the appropriate one to make. Thus it may seem to be true of freshmen who flunk out of college X that they live in dormitories, that they are enrolled in English 100, that they come from east of the Mississippi, that they have domineering mothers, that they pledge fraternities, that they go away on weekends, and that they seldom enter the library. But some of these generalizations are obviously spurious (*all* freshmen take English 100), and others are of dubious relevance to the failure of the freshmen. In fact, it may be wrong in these circumstances to look for any single generalization to solve the dean's problem. Shoddy argument results as often from vacuous generalization as from faulty generalization or from excessive inductive leaping. In any case, this example makes it clear that generalization slips over into hypothesis, and that reaching useful generalizations is no trivial business.

b) *With no inductive leap*

Now and then it is worth while to generalize even when all the particulars are available. To prove that every one of Faulkner's novels contains Christian symbolism might well be valuable—more valuable, say, than knowing that most do and only suspecting that the others do. Such generalizations can often be incorporated, as backing assertions, in larger arguments. And they involve real problems: the problem, for instance, of deciding what is to count as an instance of Christian symbolism.

2. From facts to an hypothesis or theory:

a) *From miscellaneous facts to a particular hypothesis*
The great eighteenth-century philologist Sir William Jones, basing his conclusion on a wealth of knowledge about many languages, argued that the major European languages, plus Sanskrit, Persian, and a few others, exhibited similarities of structure and vocabulary too great to be a matter of chance, and that all these languages must have sprung from a common ancestor. There was nothing lawlike or general about Jones' hypothesis (which has been richly confirmed); it did not posit a general rule of linguistic development, or make predictions, or talk about repeated causal connections. It merely set up a unique train of historical events which made sense of multitudinous facts whose interconnectedness had not previously been noticed. A large amount of scientific proving is of this type; in history and in literary criticism it is probably the dominant type. (A critic who analyzes a poem seeks to discover a single principle of construction, or a theme, or a set of biographical facts about the poet which account for all the words in the poem, and their arrangement.) In this absolutely vital procedure, which takes innumerable forms, the hypothesis must meet the usual tests: it must actually illuminate all the evidence; it must do so as neatly as possible; and it must do so better than competing hypotheses.

b) *From facts to a law*
These arguments may be classified according to the relations stated in their conclusions.

JOINT-PRESENCE
32. Wherever there is poverty, there is disease.

SEQUENCE
33. After every war there is a period of moral laxity and experimentation.

EXCLUSION
34. No dictator can flourish where there is a free press.

CO-VARIATION
35. The larger the audience appealed to by a medium of communication, the lower the intellectual quality of its offerings.

CAUSATION
36. A deficiency of vitamin B causes beri-beri.

Observe that, as with most laws, these contain an element of *prediction;* in other words, they are timeless, approximating in this the model of scientific laws. As for *explanation,* some laws do more of it than others; but no law will be worth its salt unless the things it relates (whether causally or not) seem to have some *significant* connection with each other. Thus, although (36) as it stands does not explain disease, it does point to a condition importantly related to disease—a condition (for example) that any health-minded government should be concerned over. If (36) ran, "wherever there is architecture there is disease," its truth would be undeniable, but it could scarcely lay claim, as a law, to anyone's serious attention.

c) *From facts to a principle*
There is no clear line between laws and principles, but the difference is one of generality. A principle gathers in and accounts for a great range of data: the conduct of all men toward each other at all times, not just the conduct of soldiers in combat; the motions of all physical bodies, not just bodies in orbit. Needless to say, the successful establishing of principles is usually the work of learned and brilliant investigators, not of the apprentice researcher.
3. More complex procedures of induction:

a) *Choosing an hypothesis*
Often the facts are readily available, but not readily understood. Then the investigator's task may be one of eliminating inferior hypotheses and settling on the best one (or best combination). We all know there was a depression in the thirties; why did it happen? All normal children learn to talk: but how? An argument designed for such circumstances might be constructed like this:

37. Fact: American education proceeds at a slower pace than European education.

Possible Explanations:

   i)   Teachers' salaries are too low in America, and the most able young people go into other work.

   ii)   American education is dominated by the philosophy of John Dewey.

   iii) American parents expect less of their children.

   iv) Prosperity breeds slackness.

   v)   The American system rewards action rather than contemplation and knowledge.

   vi) Administrators have too much power, teachers too little in the American school.

   vii) American education is slowed down (but justifiably) by the democratic principle of equal education for all.
                    (And so on.)

Elimination of unsatisfactory hypotheses: They do not fit facts; they do not differentiate America from Europe; they do not get to the heart of the matter; and so forth.

Defense of the remaining hypothesis or combination of hypotheses.

• *Exercise 3.7:* From a *World Almanac,* get statistics on the growth in population of major American cities during the last fifty years. What generalization can you make about the correlation between geographical location and increase in size? Do any other generalizations suggest themselves?

The writer who pursues this path will, of course, be looking at his facts in new ways as he treats the various hypotheses; he may also find it necessary to look at some new facts. Hence this type of proof shares some features with another common one:

b) *Moving from facts to a tentative hypothesis, to new facts, to a final hypothesis*

   38. Facts: In factories A, B, C the workers were discontent and production was low. Teams of industrial sociologists studied working conditions and interviewed the employees, after which they recommended the institution of longer and more

frequent rest periods. Their advice was taken, the workers were happier, and in spite of the shortened working day, production went up.

Tentative hypothesis: Efficiency and morale in industrial plants depend on adequate rest periods.

Search for new facts to confirm or disprove the hypothesis: If the hypothesis is true, the workers in plants A, B, and C should stay happy and productive as long as the system of rest periods is in effect. In other factories with similar problems there should be no similar improvement without increases in work breaks. But actually, production fell off and morale declined in plants A, B, and C within months after the reform. In other plants similar surveys were undertaken, and other reforms instituted: more Coke machines, better lighting, more attractive lunch rooms, more recreation facilities, and so on. In each factory production and morale improved at first, but fell off later. Moreover, in some factories there were interviews and investigations, but no reforms. Even in those plants morale and production improved for a while.

Final hypothesis: *Any* attention to workers' complaints and needs will lead to more efficiency and better morale, but the effect is temporary.[4]

In inductive arguments the heaviest going often comes after the original data are in and the early hypotheses posed. Some ways of proceeding from this point are worth mentioning as arguments in themselves:

c) *Assuming that a favored hypothesis is right, determining what facts should follow from it, and checking it against these facts (as in 38)*

d) *Assuming the truth of a competing hypothesis, and showing that it does not suit the facts*

39. Facts: Prices of rare antiques, rare coins and stamps, rare paintings, and so on, increased fivefold to a hundredfold from 1950 to 1960, a period of general prosperity in the

---

[4] This case is imaginary, but it bears a close resemblance to actual cases.

United States. The rise in prices was steady. There were many new collectors from low and middle income brackets.

Hypothesis: People with a lot of extra money, much of it new money, forced the prices up by competing for rarities.

Competing hypothesis: The large numbers of new collectors forced prices up by increasing the relative scarcity of sought-after items.

Refutation of the competing hypothesis: If the price rise had been caused primarily by the new collectors, it would have been interrupted by the recessions of the decade, since people in low income brackets are hurt most by such economic setbacks. But the rise was steady; hence the hypothesis does not hold up.[5]

e) *Assuming that the favored hypothesis is* false, *and showing that such an assumption is incompatible with the facts, or leads to conceptual or logical absurdity*

40. Facts: Authorship of some of the Federalist papers is disputed, the two possibilities being Hamilton and Madison. Recent statistical analyses show that the incidence in these papers of many unimportant words and locutions ("upon," for instance, instead of "on") is very close to their frequency in writing known to be Madison's, and quite different from their frequency in Hamilton's prose.

Hypothesis: Madison wrote the disputed papers.

Supposition: If Madison did not write the papers, one of two things must be true: either Hamilton imitated Madison's style, or the statistical correlations are chance. But in order to imitate Madison's style with this degree of success, Hamilton would have to have known as much about the incidence of unimportant words as the statisticians have uncovered with the aid of computers. For a man without computers to get this data would take at least several lifetimes (not to mention the difficulty of approximating someone else's style after the data are in). And that the correlations are chance is almost unthinkable, for the odds against any

---

[5] Of course *both* hypotheses may be wrong, but this procedure at least leads to a decision between the two.

single correlation occurring by chance are thousands to one, and the total odds astronomical.

Conclusion: Madison wrote the disputed papers.

A final word about induction: clearly some of these arguments incorporate deductive methods. To decide what should *follow* from an hypothesis is to make deductions from it (remember the suggestion that induction is the inverse of deduction). It should also be clear by now that actual arguments can amalgamate the "pure" types and subtypes in an infinity of ways barely hinted at by our outline. At some point in the classification of proofs it becomes senseless to maintain the artificially simple distinction between induction and deduction. Be that as it may, in bringing our outline to a close, we shall purposely abandon the distinction, and consider briefly two species of proof which either straddle it or lie outside it.

• *Exercise 3.8:* Problem for investigation: what kind of college or university is most likely to produce famous graduates? Consult *Who's Who in America* and find out systematically (e.g., by covering the letters "B" and "C" or by taking every tenth name) where the people listed got their education. Then work out some schemes for classifying colleges—by type of institution, by location, by date of founding, by sex or sexes of students, and so on. Other relevant classifications should suggest themselves. Remember to allow for differences in size. When you have drawn your conclusions make sure to indicate the places at which your analysis may be weak.

C. ARGUMENTS OF PROBABILITY

Often the context of an argument neither warrants a firm deduction nor allows the passage, through induction, to a general hypothesis. Yet there are still conclusions to be drawn. Just as in ordinary talk, people hedge their bets by inserting "probably," "it is likely that," and so on, in more formal argument it is possible to retain soundness in the face of uncertainty, simply by building the uncertainty into the proof. Indeed, an important principle in the ethics of proving is that the writer should acknowledge, both to himself and to his audience, the loopholes in his argument. Sometimes he can do so only by the tentativeness of his presentation. But when he is dealing with relatively fixed uncertainties, with regular likelihoods, he can pay his respects to uncertainty and still achieve a measure of rigor. Such are the advantages that make arguments of probability attractive—so much so that a whole scientific field, that of statistics, has grown up around them. For the complexities of that discipline there is no place in this book; we can only list a few of the common-sense methods from which it springs.

1. From the whole to an individual

> 41. Most Democrats favor a tax cut.
> Burns is a Democrat.
>
> Therefore Burns probably favors a tax cut.

> 42. Since the suicide of a famous person generally leads to a rash of imitative suicides, and since Nola Roberts killed herself yesterday, there will probably be a number of suicide attempts soon.

2. From the whole to a precise estimate

> 43. Twins occur once in every 87 births. Therefore, the likelihood that any given pregnancy will result in twins is 1/87.

3. From an individual to a whole

> 44. The chances of rolling three with two dice are one in eighteen, so out of any ninety throws, about five will probably result in three.

4. From a sample to the whole

> 45. Out of a random sample of 10,000 citizens, 5621 disapprove of the present administration. It is probable, therefore, that about 56 percent of the whole population is against the administration.

The uncertainty contained in this conclusion by the word "probable" can be made quite precise by statistical methods. That is, statisticians could say how likely the figure 56 percent is, given the size of the sample and the size of the whole population. They could also specify the likelihood that the figure is 51 percent or 58 percent, and so on. But calculations are based on ideal cricumstances, and every observer of the pollsters knows how

often events belie their predictions. One reason is the extreme difficulty of obtaining a truly random sample. It will not do simply
to knock on every seventh door: the neighborhood may be unusually proadministration because it is wealthy or poor, because
most of the people there work in the oil industry, because a large
government project has brought money into the area, and so on.
The same problems beset anyone who tries to weigh the chances
of this or that occurrence, or attempts to generalize about the
composition of a whole group on the basis of limited past experience or a limited sample. But for all that, the assessment of
probabilities goes on, and goes on well enough on the whole to
justify the risk of error.

D. ARGUMENTS BY ANALOGY

As everyone knows, the fact that there are waves of water and waves
of light does not prove that if you stand in the sun you will get wet.
The analogy does not stretch that far. Still, it was useful to physicists
in developing a theory of light, and, later, in explaining that theory
to novices. Perhaps these are the two principal uses of analogy—to
assist in the initial groping for an hypothesis, and to clarify an argument or a description. In the service of these causes, an analogy can
be more graphic and economical than a direct attack on the problem.
Unfortunately, these virtues do not guarantee equal success to analogy in actual proofs. The fact that two things (situations, sets of
events, and so forth) are alike in some respects does not logically
entail their similarity in any further characteristics. Thus analogical
proofs are not valid, in the strict sense of the word. Yet they have
their cogency, particularly when the two things compared are of the
same general sort. At least three argumentative uses of analogy are
worth mention here.

1. To predict further similarities:

> 46. In many ways the social, economic, and political organiza-
> tion of human settlements resembles the plant and animal
> ecology of natural environments; the resemblance is espe-
> cially close in the delicate interdependencies of people, in
> the one case, and of plants and animals in the other. There-
> fore, just as the influx of a new species of insects is certain
> to have a profound impact on the ecology of a river basin, so
> a large and sudden immigration of a new race or class is
> bound to destroy the social equilibrium of a city and lead to
> a new system of balance.

Notice that the proof lacks final conviction: people are not insects. Certainly an investigator interested in the hypothesis would hope that he could finally rest his case on a thorough study of historical immigrations (that is, on induction). But the analogical proof does more than simply open up an avenue of research. So alike are ecology and social organization *in principle* (not just in a fanciful, metaphorical way), that what disrupts the one seems almost certain to disrupt the other. Analogy is most useful to an argument founded on likenesses of this sort.

2. To expose a fallacy:

>   47. Arguing that we should abolish surgery because some patients die on the operating table is like arguing that we should all stop eating because some people die of food poisoning. The two lines of reasoning are equally absurd.

Of course they are not *quite* equally absurd: without surgery the species would survive, but not without food. Yet the arguments are close enough in structure so that the analogy is telling, in spite of its rhetorical overstatement. This use of analogy depends, obviously, on similarities between arguments themselves, as well as between events, situations, and so forth.

3. To establish a classification:

A British pathologist has argued that the symptoms which Thucydides describes in victims of the famous plague of Athens (430 B.C.) are so like those of typhoid patients today that the Athenian pestilence must also have been typhoid fever. Similarly, students of myth classify the protagonist of a traditional story as a mythic hero if his life resembles the lives of other mythic heroes. Such characteristics as divine or semi-divine birth and a period of early obscurity determine the classification, even though the particular circumstances of birth and childhood vary greatly. The mythologists assume that the hero-myth, in its most general outlines, issues from universal patterns of human need and human imagination, and this assumption warrants classification by analogy even when the analogy might seem remote to a layman. Categories are essential to all thought; classification is usually necessary before induction or deduction can even begin. For this reason alone, the process of analogy, in spite of its abuses, deserves a place among the methods of argument.

It may be wise to conclude this survey with a reminder of what should by now be abundantly clear—that our outline is arbitrarily simplified, that the types of argument shade into one another, that they may be compounded in almost every conceivable way, and that there is no automatic way either of choosing the appropriate form, of translating logic into English, or of insuring soundness. None of this means that the writer concerned with argument (or for that matter, with truth) can afford to ignore the structures of formal and informal proof; for those structures represent a codification of sound thinking itself and constitute one of the signal achievements of rational man.

• *Exercise 3.9:* What steps would you take to test the truth of the following propositions?

    a. that women are superior to men
    b. that fluorine prevents tooth decay
    c. that God exists
    d. that international socialism is inevitable
    e. that air power was decisive in World War II
    f. that a religious revival is taking place in the colleges
    g. that smoking causes cancer
    h. that College Board scores have no predictive value
    i. that eighteen-year-olds should be allowed to vote
    j. that Caesar suffered from diabetes
    k. that Western civilization is dying
    l. that no man is an island
    m. that economic pressures were responsible for the American Revolution
    n. that Homer was a woman
    o. that the German character is militaristic

What form or forms of proof would recommend themselves in each case? Why?

7/ Refutation

When a writer rejects a competing hypothesis, as in (31), or discards a tentative hypothesis, as in (38), or assumes that his own hypothesis is false and demonstrates that such an assumption leads to absurdity, as in (40), he is engaged in *refutation*. As the preceding section shows, refutation can be a useful step in a proof, especially in an inductive proof. An inductive hypothesis is seldom absolutely certain, and one way to increase its relative credibility is to prove that others which have been proposed will not hold up, at least not so well as the one in question. When there are seemingly two or more hypotheses that can account for the data, refutation becomes a firm responsibility for the writer, since merely to show that *his* hypothesis accounts for the data is not to establish its superiority. And almost any essay that tries to prove something will have competing positions to deal with.

Moreover, it is often appropriate to refute an argument or an assertion even when the writer has nothing to offer in its place. No one knows for sure the identity of that "Junius" whose letters, during the reign of George III, revealed so many British state secrets and scandals, but it was of considerable importance to Edmund Burke and others accused of authorship to be able to refute the charges. Likewise, although neither Darwin nor anyone else has established the precise date of the earth's origin, Darwin's researches showed conclusively that the earth could *not* have been created in 4004 B.C., and that knowledge has its own value. The fact that refutation is a negative activity does not mean that it is a useless one: considering the amount of nonsense at large in the world, every successful refutation is a service to the cause of truth.

In treating the various forms of argument, we have already implied a good deal about refutation; to show that a proof deviates from acceptable form is to refute it. And the section on fallacies at the end of this chapter adds more information on the subject. But since refutation is often a separate activity with problems of its own, it will be well to state a few general principles here.

Most important is the distinction, often ignored, between refuting an argument and refuting an assertion. The validity of an argument depends upon its adherence to the standards of good form—deductive, inductive, or other—which govern it. In order to refute an argument, therefore, one must show that its procedure is somehow illegitimate. An attack on its *conclusion* is simply not to the point, for the argument may be valid though the conclusion is false, as in (15). Conversely, the writer who wishes to refute a conclusion must do so by attacking that assertion (as false, self-contradictory, and so on); to refute the argument that led to it is not sufficient, since there may be other arguments, sound ones, that legitimately support it. When Kant refuted St. Anselm's ontological proof of the existence of God, he did not intend to refute the conclusion, and in fact Kant himself believed in a divine being, though not in a conventional way. The writer must keep in mind the two types of refutation or risk irrelevance and confusion.

How, then, may an argument be refuted? By pointing to a fallacy in it. By exhibiting a flaw in its deductive logic. By showing its inductive leap to be unwarranted. By showing that it begs the question. By proving it inconclusive (showing, that is, that other conclusions follow equally well from its backing assertions). And so on. All of these methods are ways of attacking the move from backing assertions to conclusion. One may also attack the backing assertions themselves. To show that at least one of them is false or uncertain is to prove the argument *unsound,* though not invalid.

Refuting an assertion (whether or not it is the conclusion of an argument) calls for quite different stratagems. If the assertion is one of simple fact (Mrs. Jones has blue eyes), it may be refuted by direct appeal to experience or to reliable reports. But if it is a generalization, a law, or a principle, such an appeal will rarely suffice. Take the hypothesis, "Every child of blue-eyed parents has blue eyes." No one can examine the eyes of *all* such children; but notice that if the statement is intended literally, and not just as a rough approximation, the discovery of one brown-eyed child of blue-eyed parents refutes it. A single *counterexample,* that is to say, is enough to refute a rigid hypothesis, no matter how many supporting examples there are.

Even when no counterexample is available, it is often possible to refute a generalization or law. The most useful technique for doing so is known as *reductio ad absurdum:* the refuter assumes that the hypothesis he wants to defeat is true, and shows that intolerable consequences follow from such an assumption. In (40) there is an example of this procedure, when it is assumed that Madison did *not* write the disputed Federalist papers, in order to prove, eventually, that he *did.* Or consider the old puzzle of the three wise men, each with either a white or a black spot on his forehead, who are placed together in a mirrorless room, forbidden to talk to each other, and told that if any of them guesses the color of his spot he will be richly rewarded, that if he guesses wrong he will be executed, and that not all three spots are black. Wise man A solves the problem, after a time. He sees that both B and C have white spots. He suspects that his own spot is also white, but he assumes it to be black, and argues as follows: "B, then, would see a white spot and a black spot. But if so, it would be obvious to him that his own spot must be white, for otherwise C would see two black spots and know immediately that his own must be white. Since neither B nor C, wise as they both are, has hit upon this solution, my own spot must be white." Wise man A not only employs *reductio ad absurdum,* but imagines B as using it too. The example is fanciful, but the technique is invaluable for refutation.

Finally, one may challenge an assertion by showing it to fail through vagueness, meaninglessness, self-contradiction, and so on—the various shortcomings dealt with in the last chapter. In brief, an assertion, like a proof, must measure up to certain standards. Refutation is the invoking of those standards to point to inadequacies, and as such it is an essential technique, both of proving and of rational thought in general.

> • *Exercise 3.10:* This selection is from a speech by a leading English philosopher of the nineteenth century to an American audience. A comparison has already been made between the "spasmodic" energy of the savage and the "persistent industry" of the American.

> What I have seen and heard during my stay among you has forced on me the belief that this slow change from habitual inertness to persistent activity has reached an extreme from which there must begin a counterchange—a reaction. Everywhere I have been struck with the number of faces which told in strong lines of the burdens that had to be borne. I have been struck, too, with the large proportion of gray-haired men; and inquiries have brought out the fact, that with you the hair commonly begins to turn some ten years earlier than with us. Moreover, in every circle I have met men who had themselves suffered from nervous collapse due to stress of business, or named friends who had either killed themselves by overwork, or had been permanently incapacitated, or had wasted long periods in endeavors to recover health. I do but echo the opinion of all the observant persons I have spoken to, that immense injury is being done by this high-pressure life—the physique is being undermined. That subtle thinker and poet whom you have lately had to mourn, Emerson, says, in his essay on the Gentleman, that the first requisite is that he shall be a good animal. That requisite is a general one—it extends to the man, to the father, to the citizen. We hear a great deal about "the vile body"; and many are encouraged by the phrase to transgress the laws of health. But Nature quietly suppresses those who treat thus disrespectfully one of her highest products, and leaves the world to be peopled by the descendants of those who are not so foolish.

> HERBERT SPENCER, *Essays Scientific, Political and Speculative*

> Consider the passage with regard to sources of evidence, reliability of the sources, types of reasoning, and correctness of procedure. How might you undertake to refute it?

8/ Moral and Esthetic Arguments

Perhaps this is the best place for an aside about what happens to logic when it encounters the good and the beautiful, as well as the true. Philosophers, especially in this century, have been concerned with the rather special status of evaluative assertions (some of their conclusions are reflected in the previous chapter). It is not necessary to go into the controversies; it is enough simply to state our belief that, contrary to the positions of some philosophers, moral and esthetic judgments have as much claim to truth (or falsity) as other assertions, although the claim is based on complex sanctions. This being the case, there is no reason that a proof cannot legitimately arrive at the conclusion that such and such a course of action is good, or that this or that painting is beautiful. Indeed, moral issues probably give rise to more argument than issues of any other sort. And since people care as much about what is right as they do about what is true, sound moral conclusions are indispensable—to political and social thought, to philosophy, and to ordinary conduct. Thus it is comforting to know that moral arguments can be pursued logically, and that in general the same methods lead to soundness in both moral and esthetic proofs as in other types. But there is one additional requirement, which for moral arguments runs like this: no moral precept can be well grounded in argument unless the backing itself includes one or more assertions with ethical weight, or contains ethical assumptions. It might seem at first glance that the following reasonable argument violates this rule.

48. Slums usually breed disease, crime, and unhappiness.
    It is a duty of the moral society, therefore, to solve the problem of slums.

But clearly the proof *assumes* that disease, crime, and unhappiness are social evils, and that it is the duty of a moral society to attack social evils. The prover had best make such moral assumptions explicit, unless they are completely apparent and universally acceptable, for no field is more controverted than ethics.

Esthetic judgments, too, depend upon critical assumptions with evaluative content. That is why esthetic arguments about this or that artistic creation tend to open out into much larger arguments, which leave the particular work far behind. Suppose that two critics disagree about the value of Stravinsky's "The Rite of Spring." One considers it a frightful blare of sheer noise, and the other finds in it a stirring evocation of primitive emotions. This conflict will probably not be resolved by examining the data—the piece of music itself—for both critics are already acquainted with it at the outset. Rather, the argument will move to a higher level of generality: "Only traditional harmonies and consistent tempos can produce great music," claims the anti-Stravinskian, and his opponent counters vociferously. Finally the discussion is likely to reach a still more general level, that of ultimate esthetic values such as form, discipline, and power. If the two critics can agree at this level, perhaps they can work back down the scale to the music itself and achieve some measure of concord. If not, the argument is irresolvable—not, notice, a trivial difference in *taste,* but a significant difference in esthetic *principles.* Since critical assumptions vary widely, the writer should state his explicitly, or make them clear in other ways, to avoid fruitless confusion between disagreements on principle and disagreements about facts. Moreover, he will gain insight into his own deepest beliefs if, rather than contenting himself with particular judgments like "This novel fails because the hero is not lifelike," he seeks to discover the assumptions that lie beneath.

9/   Setting Up the Argument

Because even a highly abbreviated discussion of the procedures of proof is bound to be more or less technical, the relevance of those procedures to the actual processes of thinking and writing sometimes becomes obscured. Traveling from a problem, to a formalization of that problem, to a solution, and finally to a coherent essay is not always easy. But the passage becomes smoother with the aid of a few general rules.

First, it is important to frame the question properly in the beginning. To be sure, an argument sometimes germinates in a writer's mind, not with a question, but with evidence or backing assertions deductively linked. Most of the time, however, in science as in ordinary proving, the point of origin is a muddle, a problem, a paradox, a failure of understanding, an error. When it is, the investigator can simplify his task enormously by asking the right question, thereby making it clear to himself and his audience what procedures will lead most economically to an answer. He thus avoids both waste motion and further confusion. If he asks "What are the causes of unemployment?" instead of "What is the cause of unemployment?" he may escape a failure through oversimplification. On the other hand, he may be wise to limit the question more narrowly still, by asking "Is foreign competition a cause of the present unemployment?" In this way, he reduces the problem to manageable proportions in the hope of salvaging at least a small measure of certainty from the prevailing confusion. Or perhaps the prudent course is to begin by asking whether the present unemployment is even abnormally high—whether, that is, the analyst should look for a new and special cause, or try to find his answer in more permanent features of the economy. A move in the right direction at this point will not only save trouble later, but may well determine the very form of the proof.

Once the writer has posed his problem satisfactorily, he should assess it in order to decide what kind or kinds of proof are most pertinent, and which sections of the proof are likely to cause the most trouble. Some things he can assume without proof; others will require painstaking demonstration. To speak figuratively, each assertion lays an obligation on the writer: he must calculate the kind and amount of expansion necessary to make that assertion comprehensible and believable to his reader. To say that he must "calculate" the kind and amount is not to say that all his calculation is conscious. If he has a feeling for argument he will know without reflection how much explanation or proof an assertion requires and whether he has provided the right kind and amount. Lacking such an intuition, he should guard against disproportion by remembering the distinctions among assertions and kinds of proof suitable to each. He must keep alive his sensitivity to the difference between common knowledge and startling novelty, between the obvious and the paradoxical, between assertions that can stand by themselves and assertions that need backing up.

When he comes to the point of lining up his arguments, the writer should consider that not all backing assertions have equal weight or relevance. Since it is difficult to cast out one's hard-won knowledge, most students have a natural tendency to include all the evidence that they have uncovered, all the backing assertions that have passed across their minds; but the tendency must be resisted. In any proof some kinds of backing are crucial, others are trivial, and others are irrelevant. The writer will weaken his argument (logically and rhetorically) by giving undue emphasis to the trivial, or including the irrelevant. The danger is especially great in literary analysis. One word does not set the theme of a poem, nor one incident the theme of a novel. Tone, structure, and context are likely to be more important than isolated images or connotations, and it takes a keen sense of the work as a whole to prevent grotesque distortions of interpretation. The fact that Hamlet goes on a sea voyage is not enough to prove that Shakespeare's play is patterned after *The Odyssey*. In other kinds of argument, as in criticism, the value of any piece of evidence depends upon the shape of the entire problem, and slavish enumeration of "the facts" can only blur the lines of proof and destroy economy and elegance.

To put the matter more affirmatively, there is room for a good deal of ingenuity in the marshaling of data. Are campus riots and peace marches both evidence of undergraduate alienation from the status quo? Perhaps, but it will take perceptiveness and care to demonstrate the likeness (or the *absence* of likeness, for that matter). The process of sorting out backing assertions almost always goes beyond mechanical drudgery.

Much the same thing is true of the writer's handling of troublesome evidence. He can sometimes convert a seeming exception into a particularly compelling argument in favor of his case if he is alert to all the implications of his hypothesis. Nightmares seem, on the face of it, damaging to the hypothesis that all dreams are wish-fulfillment; but if the horror of the dreamer can be interpreted as a device for excusing him from the guilt that should accompany the wish, say, to murder his father, then the apparent exception actually strengthens the hypothesis. On the other hand, a law or generalization may be worth preserving even if it does have some exceptions—provided that the exceptions are relatively minor, and that the hypothesis simplifies most of the data so sweepingly that a few exceptions will barely tell against its usefulness. A Minneapolis bird watcher may sight a robin in December, but that in itself is not sufficient to make ornithologists give up the hypothesis of seasonal migration. Even if the writer cannot explain away the exceptions or relate them to a minor role, he owes it to integrity and completeness to deal with them. They may force him to adopt a tone of respectful tentativeness, but sometimes it is better to have a doubtful conclusion than no conclusion at all. And any proof will inspire more respect if the prover has faced all the difficulties openly.

As for the writing itself, no amount of logic can make cogent prose flow copiously from the pen. But more often than not the writer can use the patterns of proof as an aid to organization. The whole essay may fall into shape if he conceives it on the model of, say, facts to tentative hypothesis to new facts to final hypothesis, or of a deductive chain argument, whatever course he has followed to his conclusion in the prewriting stage. Paragraphs, too, can be made to cohere neatly around logical forms, and transitions become much less a problem. The literal transfer of logical procedures to expository discourse will, to be sure, produce nothing very lively or personal, and it is not recommended here as anything except a way of learning to manage what one has to say in an orderly and lucid manner. One must have something to say in the first place. But as with most things, genuine freedom in writing is greatest when the writer accepts firm boundaries. The power of invention is increased and the path to discovery shortened by the necessity to work within form, and not even the most imaginative writer can always afford to be liberated from the structures of argument, formal and informal. Rightly used, they will almost always enlarge a writer's powers, not constrict him.

10/ Postscript: Fallacies

A fallacy is a flaw in an argument, or a bogus argument, or an argument gone astray. Since the ethics of exposition and the writer's responsibility toward his assertions have been discussed in all three chapters, a number of fallacies have been mentioned already: persuasive definition, circularity, irrelevance, illicit use of authority, hasty generalization, and so on. There is no need to repeat here. Nor is it necessary to pursue the strictly logical fallacies, since the logical rules set forth in this chapter are sufficient guard against invalidity. The writer can spot a logical fallacy by noticing that this or that proof does not proceed according to the rules, and it matters little here what the various names are by which logicians have designated these fallacies. But there remains a residue of miscellaneous common fallacies, to be listed here with examples.

1. *Equivocation,* or shifting the sense of a word.

   49. "Through the past decade our various states have drawn together into one great political unit: Pomposia. Hence Pomposia stands united, ready to fight against foreign aggression."

       ("Pomposia" means a union of political districts the first time it occurs, but a cooperative union of people the second time. What is true of the first need not be true of the second.)

2. *Accident,* or treating as permanent a quality that may be only temporary.

   50. "Ten years ago Hubert Lutz was definitely shown to be a hopeless alcoholic. Today that same Hubert Lutz stands before us as a candidate for sheriff. Are we to have an alcoholic for our protector?"

       (Some people overcome alcoholism.)

3. *Smuggled connotation.*

   51. "We have overwhelming evidence that Lutz drinks wine daily and in large quantities. Shall we, by naming him sheriff, commit our safety to a wino?"

       (A wino is not simply a person who drinks wine voluminously; the word has extra connotations of dereliction and depravity, and the speaker has not shown that Lutz's case deserves those connotations.)

4. *Misuse of etymology.*

52. " 'Education' comes from the Latin roots 'e—' = (out) plus 'ducere' (lead, bring). Thus education is literally a bringing out of what is in the student, and the institution that attempts to impose knowledge from outside is perverting the aims of education."

("Education" means education, whatever the roots may have meant, and in any case, it is not possible to prove that practices in the nonverbal world are good or bad by analyzing the meanings of words. This fallacy is a special case of persuasive definition and is all too frequently used by writers who should know better.)

5. *Reification:* treating an abstract concept as a real entity.

53. "America became a great power because it was her destiny to do so."

(Is everything that ever happens caused by destiny? If so, destiny seems a superfluous concept, no different from the concept of *happening.* If not, what is this mysterious entity, destiny, that it should be able to cause large and significant events? This fallacy is closely related to circularity.)

The fallacies mentioned so far all involve, in one way or another, trickery with words. The next group, by contrast, achieve whatever plausibility they possess by perverting legitimate argumentative methods, mainly inductive.

6. *Post hoc, ergo propter hoc* (after the fact, therefore because of it).

54. "Both the French and the Russian revolutions were followed by periods of literary rebellion. Clearly political revolt causes revolt in the arts."

(And, by the same logic, the repeal of prohibition must have caused the Second World War. Perhaps literary and political rebellion are both caused by a third factor; perhaps there is no relationship other than chance. The facts presented do not in themselves allow any interesting conclusion at all.)

7. *Large numbers.*

55. "Fifteen million people suffer from mental illness in the United States. This is our main social problem."

(In a country of 200,000,000, still more people may suffer from other kinds of distress. And by what rule is the seriousness of social problems measured in sheer numbers? Almost everyone suffers from tooth decay, but tooth decay is not our main medical problem. Large numbers impress us too much; they should not be allowed to rout logic.)

8. *Composition:* assuming that what holds for each member of a class will hold for the class as a whole.

   56. "This must be a biased committee, since all of its members are biased."

   (Perhaps the indivdual biases cancel each other out.)

9. *Division:* the opposite fallacy.

   57. "If we increase our outlay for salaries by twenty percent, everyone will have twenty percent more to spend."

   (That depends on how the money is apportioned.)

10. *Genetic fallacy:* assuming that the present form of a thing reveals its origin, or vice versa.

    58. "The law is one of our most complex institutions; hence it must have arisen long after simple institutions like the family."

    (Societies don't always move from simple to complex. But more important, the only way to find out for sure whether the law or the family came first is to *find out*—through history, archaeology, and so on. Such things cannot be proven by rational speculation in an arm chair.)

    59. *"Kubla Khan* came to Coleridge in a dream, so it must lack rational structure."

    (No, it doesn't.)

11. *The call for perfection:* taking one objection (or a few) as decisive.

    60. "The automation of industry throws people out of work; therefore it is economically inadvisable."

    (The advantages may outweigh this disadvantage; or any alternative plan may have worse disadvantages. Objections exist to every plan, but that is no reason for leaving things as they are.)

12. *Begging the question,* or arguing in a circle.

> 61. "Lawyers are honest. Their integrity is vouched for by *Men and the Law,* a book praised unreservedly for its reliability by Professor Ryan; Professor Ryan is unquestionably trustworthy, for he is himself a prominent barrister."
>
> (The value of Professor Ryan's testimony, upon which the backing depends, is itself contingent upon the conclusion of the argument, namely that lawyers are honest. Such arguments can be highly deceptive when they are complex, and when their language subtly shifts—as from "lawyer" to "barrister.")

These fallacies twist arguments into invalid shapes. The ones that remain to be discussed detour arguments from their proper courses by evading issues, intruding red herrings, and so on. They would be beneath notice except that they are, a. ~ so common and often so effective.

13. *Proving the wrong conclusion.*

> 62. A writer sets out to show that the German people were responsible for the extermination of the Jews. He rests his case in a demonstration that most Germans disliked Jews, and that they were at least roughly aware of what was happening to the Jews.
>
> These are relevant points but not *the* point.

14. *Two wrongs make a right.*

> 63. "Harding is not to be blamed for Teapot Dome; other presidents have allowed worse scandals."
>
> (What the other presidents did has no bearing on the issue, unless the prover can show that they were not to be blamed either.)

15. *Diversion:* introducing an anecdote for humorous or rhetorical effect.

> 64. "The arguments of the American Medical Association against socialized medicine remind me of the fat wolf who proved with a great show of logic that it was in the nature of sheep to be eaten."
>
> (Very well; now let's get back to the arguments. Such diversions are harmless enough, to be sure, so long as they do not masquerade as proofs.)

16. *Damning the source,* or discrediting an argument because of its origin.

    65. "Let anyone who is tempted to believe in the efficacy of propaganda remember that Adolf Hitler was its first great spokesman."

    (If the devil himself first made the claim, it may still be true.)

17. *Ad hominem:* discrediting one's opponent.

    66. "You say that most policemen don't take bribes, but after all you're a policeman yourself—what else could you say?"

    (!)

One reminder: a fallacious argument may arrive at a true conclusion, but it will not have *proved* that conclusion. In proving, the end never justifies the means.[6]

---

[6] At this point we would like to acknowledge our indebtedness to several books. which we also recommend for further reading in the field of logic and critical thinking. As an introduction to formal logic we suggest Willard Van Orman Quine's *Methods of Logic.* P. F. Strawson's *Introduction to Logical Theory* and Stephen Toulmin's *The Uses of Argument* treat the subject more philosophically and less technically; both authors are concerned with the relationship between logic and ordinary language. Three works which deal with the whole field of proving are *An Introduction to Logic and Scientific Method,* by Morris R. Cohen and Ernest Nagel; *Critical Thinking,* by Max Black; and *Thinking Straight,* by Monroe C. Beardsley. The last two are more elementary than the first. Nelson Goodman's *Fact, Fiction, and Forecast* and S. F. Barker's *Induction and Hypothesis* focus on the theory of inductive logic. Finally, a useful and entertaining book on argumentative mishaps is *Fallacy—The Counterfeit of Argument,* by W. Ward Fearnside and William B. Holther. Any student who cares to pursue the subject of this chapter will find many other excellent books to help him.

1/ Strategies of Persuasion

At various points we have touched on the writer's consciousness of audience, but the principal emphasis has been on his private handling of percepts and concepts. It is time now to bring the party of the second part, as legal contracts put it, into the act.

INFLUENCING PEOPLE

A thug says to a hostage, "If you make a noise I'll kill you," and thus terrifies the hostage into silence. In answer to the question, "What did the thug do?" we could refer to his illocutionary act, and say, "He threatened the hostage." But there are other ways to answer the question, other ways to describe his act. We could also reply, "He said he would kill the hostage if the hostage made a noise." Then we would be describing his act with reference to linguistic conventions (he spoke a certain English sentence), but not to the conventions which distinguish a threat from a compliment or an invitation. We would have taken a narrower view of what the thug did, though still, of course, an accurate one. Let us call the act, seen this way, a *locutionary* act.

We might also take a wider view, incorporating the reaction of the hostage: "What did the thug do?" "He frightened the hostage." Or, "He made the hostage keep quiet." Either reply would describe what we shall call a *perlocutionary* act, an act accomplished *through* or *by* speech. Perlocutionary acts always include locutionary and illocutionary acts. In this case, the thug spoke the English sentence "If you make a noise I'll kill you" (locutionary act) in circumstances such that it counted as a threat (illocutionary act). By means of the threat, he accomplished the perlocutionary act of frightening the hostage. Here, in tabular form, is a similar analysis of Alexander Dubcek's act, referred to earlier:

| Locutionary act: | Saying that the Czech government would not take even a step back from the road it had set out on. |

Illocutionary acts: Affirming, and promising.

Perlocutionary acts: Angering the Soviet leaders; boosting the
                         morale of the Czech people; impressing
                         Western observers; etc.

Perlocutionary acts are what people consciously aim to perform, a good
deal of the time, in writing as well as in speech. Pleasing or angering
parents, deterring enemies, encouraging subordinates, teaching students,
impressing teachers, amusing friends, satisfying constituents—such en-
terprises make up the politics of every ordinary day, as well as the grand
politics of embassies and parliaments. The very learning of language is
bound up with perlocutionary acts to a significant but unknown extent,
for a child talks partly to affect adults and other children.

For all that, perlocutionary acts are not so simple to bring off as illocutionary acts, and the reasons are instructive. First, they depend on the
audience's cooperation, submission, or intuitive response in a way not
characteristic of illocutionary acts—or physical ones, for that matter.
Green can warn Brown, or promise him, tell, request, or ask him, with
no more help from Brown than listening. Likewise, he can push, pat, or
pummel an unwilling Brown, given strength enough. But if he wants to
convince, interest, or enrage Brown, he must accurately reckon a number
of things about the circumstances: Brown's makeup, his past history, and
so on. That is, he must take account of Brown as a particular man with
capabilities, experience, and character, not just as a member of a speech
community. (A large portion of people's humanity lies in their engage-
ment in perlocutionary acts—their freedom to be compliant or cranky,
literal or frivolous, brave or timid, responsive or stolid.)

The second reason is a corollary of the first: there are no conventions
for perlocutionary acts. Ritual exchanges and verbal formulas can in no
direct way bring about joy, depression, astonishment, or other perlocutionary effects. That is why, although many illocutionary acts can be
reduced to formal expressions ("I vote yea," "I hereby guarantee to . . .,"
"I defy you to . . .," "I forgive you"), the corresponding expressions for
perlocutionary acts are absurd, and would never be used except in jest:

> I hereby persuade you to . . .
> I console you
> You are hereby intimidated
> I humiliate you

It's true that some of the illocutionary rules seem almost to apply: a
general is perhaps better qualified than a private to fire up an army. But
a private can do so, and a general can fail. Again, circumstances have a

lot to do with perlocutionary acts, so that it's hard to amuse a man on
his way to the gallows. But not always impossible, and anyhow, the
barrier is psychological, not conventional. To bring off a perlocutionary
act, a speaker has to judge rightly his audience's emotional temper,
mood, and situation. (About humanity again: here are possibilities that
range all the way from compassion and empathy to manipulation and
brutality. Perlocutionary acts define one's relation to other people.)

In consequence, there's nothing certain about what perlocutionary
act(s) a speaker will accomplish by releasing a particular string of
words. A thug who says, "If you make a noise I'll kill you," in the proper
circumstances can be absolutely sure he has performed the illocutionary
act of threatening, but not the perlocutionary act of frightening. Suppose
the thug is frail, and pointing a water pistol, while the hostage is a heavy-
weight wrestler. The threat would still be a threat, but the hostage might
be more angry than frightened and more amused than either. (Think of
threats that could result in incredulity, patronizing superiority, willing
submission, impatience, even boredom.) Large audiences almost always
display the variety of response that makes perlocutionary acts undepend-
able: a politician says, "It is time to stop coddling looters and arsonists."
Loud cheers, equally loud boos, but also silent indifference, cynicism,
and a dozen other reactions.

> • *Exercise 4.1:* Study a few magazine ads or television commercials. What
> illocutionary acts do they perform? What seem to be their perlocutionary in-
> tentions? What perlocutionary acts do they in fact accomplish in your case?
> Through this kind of analysis, describe the difference between hard-sell and
> soft-sell. Are there other kinds of "sell"?

Not even the simple illocutionary act of stating is immune to variabil-
ity of perlocutionary effect. "No man with a genius for legislation has
appeared in America," wrote Thoreau, justifying his civil disobedience
by citing the fallibility of governments. Though debatable, his statement
seems to pass muster as a statement. What perlocutionary effect did he
intend? Perhaps to force to the reader's attention something he already
had grounds for knowing but had never particularly thought about,
and thus to surprise the reader, at the same time leaving him with a
sense of Thoreau's rightness, hence increasing the total credibility of
Thoreau's position. ("By George, he's got something, when you think of
it that way.") But of course the opposite reaction ("He's wrong—how
can I believe a man who talks so wildly?") is just one of many unwanted
responses that are perfectly natural. Some readers would be affronted by

the slight to Jefferson and Webster, some annoyed by the open-ended term "genius," some suspicious of Thoreau's personal stake in believing what he says, some amused at his lordly confidence. Some might close the book in disgust, some might go out and disobey forthwith. A good writer can build a context that will ward off many unwanted responses, but no one is complete master of his perlocutionary acts. The Sermon on the Mount probably left some of its hearers cold. (Thoreau's next sentence was "They are rare in the history of the world." How might this alter some of the responses we imagined to the first sentence?)

As with illocutionary acts, so with perlocutionary: bringing them off is trickier in writing than in speech. Spoken persuasion has on its side whatever bond exists between speaker and hearer, and in addition the speaker's ability to notice the responses of his audience and adjust to them by clearing up misunderstandings, adding extra reasons, defending his own motives, meeting objections, telling a joke, belittling himself, and a thousand other stratagems. A man writing must *imagine* his audience's state of mind and responses, using whatever leads he has.

Of course there is a kind of writing whose perlocutionary effects are highly predictable and "safe." We meet it in manuals:

> Breaking in a new engine is as important as breaking in a new car or truck. Run your engine for its first few minutes at one-third throttle. Increase speed to about half-throttle and run for a few minutes longer. Cut a few limbs or small logs at first. . . . Check your chain tension frequently and make frequent use of your chain oiler button.

The first sentence talks down to the reader and the others summarily tell him to do this or that. This sounds like a formula for antagonizing readers, but the situation neutralizes any such effect. The reader wants to learn how to use his new saw; the writer knows how. The main action is transmittal of information. Both writer and reader have their attention so wholly on the functioning of the machine that there is no room for taking offense or throwing up resistance. Here we do not have a person addressing a person, so much as a rule book addressing a blank page. The humanity of both is shrunken to the narrowest of roles, and it is quite irrelevant whether one is a capitalist and the other a socialist, one a mystic and the other a materialist, or whatnot. Given minimum intelligence and cooperation, the perlocutionary act of instruction will take place.

Purely pragmatic writing of this sort does a job; we needn't fuss about it. Its operational circumstance is exceedingly simple, and its perlocutionary maneuvers come off perfectly (provided that it is *clear*—how many manuals are mystifying just at the crucial point, thereby provoking such perlocutionary effects as would be quite unwelcome to the writer, were he on hand). The writing we're most interested in, the writing that shapes societies of men rather than of commodity-users, attempts perlocutionary acts that are riskier than this, more like Thoreau's.

Another essay on Thoreau's theme begins this way:

> Freedom means self-expression, and the secret of freedom is courage. No man ever remains free who acquiesces in what he knows to be wrong.
>
> — HAROLD LASKI, "The Dangers of Obedience"

To talk about this opener, it will help to use Burke's pentad for a while. The agency is the English sentences used. The act (illocutionary) is that of stating. The purpose (intended perlocutionary act) is perhaps to put the reader in his most libertarian frame of mind, rouse his sense of independence and integrity, prepare him to look kindly on civil disobedience. What might block this purpose? The answer is partly "the reader," of course. He may be too stupid to understand or too tired to care or too authoritarian to be shaken by such appeals—any of a number of fatal disabilities. But on the other hand, if he is persuadable but not persuaded, the difficulty may well lie in *agent* or *scene*.

We must use both of these terms a bit metaphorically. Literally, to be sure, the agent is Harold Laski, the English political thinker. But we don't know him, except by his work, nor do you (he died in 1950). His credentials are good, but in writing about personal freedom and obedience, a man's credentials will not take him far. Effectively, the agent is *created* by the very words he writes. It is from them that readers build a sense of the person they are dealing with. This particular agent—let's call him HL—defines himself first by freely using the word "freedom" and others like it: "courage," "wrong." He has no apparent qualms about the grand concepts. We mustn't expect him to be diffident about ideas. The definition he offers for "freedom" is unusual, but he neither qualifies nor explains, nor does he harbor doubts about *the* secret of freedom. The second sentence is just as uncompromising with its "no man" and "ever." And to HL it seems beyond argument that men can *know* right and wrong (what if I know something to be right that you know to be wrong?) HL is forthright, upstanding, and manly. Or is he cocksure, intellectually crude, and overbearing? Two reasonable readers, each open-minded at the start toward what Harold Laski is saying, could perceive HL in exactly opposite ways, and warm to his ideas or reject them accordingly. And such is the problem of agent. (Query: What kind of person do you suppose Laski wanted to reach? Would that kind of reader more likely admire or deplore HL?)

• *Exercise 4.2:* For each of the passages that follow, write a brief description of the "agent," then compare your descriptions with those offered by classmates. The differences should be as instructive as the separate analyses.

Those who maintain the insufficency of science . . . appeal to the fact that science has nothing to say about "values." This I admit, but when it is inferred that ethics contain truths which cannot be proved or disproved by science, I disagree. The matter is one on which it is not altogether easy to think clearly, and my own views on it are quite different from what they were thirty years ago. But it is necessary to be clear about it if we are to appraise such arguments as those in support of Cosmic Purpose. As there is no consensus of opinion about ethics, it must be understood that what follows is my personal belief, not the dictum of science.

BERTRAND RUSSELL, *Religion and Science*

I like a country where it's nobody's damned business what magazines anyone reads, what he thinks, whom he had cocktails with. I like a country where we do not have to stuff chimneys against listening ears and where what we say does not go into the FBI files along with a note from S-17 that I may have another wife in California.

BERNARD DE VOTO, "Due Notice to the FBI"

I ought not to conceal the fact that property and communism have been considered always the only possible forms of society. This deplorable error has been the life of property.

P. J. PROUDHON, *What Is Property?*

Adventure is the vitamizing element in histories, both individual and social. But its story is unsuitable for a Sabbath School prize book. Its adepts are rarely chaste, or merciful, or even law-abiding at all, and any moral peptonizing, or sugaring, takes out the interest, with the truth, of their lives.

WILLIAM BOLITHO, *Twelve Against the Gods*

• *Exercise 4.3:* Now try your hand at writing some opening paragraphs, two or three sentences long, in which you create a distinctive agent. Possible topics: equality of the sexes, pop art, life in Suburbia, motorcycling, student radicalism, police brutality.

Scene is as problematic as agent. Again, literally the scene is wherever the reader sits with Laski's essay before him, but another scene, an imaginary one, begins to take shape as the words come. Imagine HL speaking the two sentences, rather than writing them: what is the appropriate scene for such talk? Not, surely, a drinking party—the words are too serious. Not a lounge where a few friends sit and talk, for HL puts so much distance between himself and his audience that a friend, or anyone sitting close by, would rightly be miffed. These are public words, spoken in a forum or lecture hall where multitudes come to hear the rebel-sage speak his unconventional truths. And let's broaden this scene a bit, to include the kind of world that might contain such a forum. It is a world in which ideas have clean edges and men live by them, acting the part of heroes or cowards. Right and wrong are there to be known, and you can lose your freedom in a trice if you falter. There is no tolerance in this world for ambiguity, no place for "good Germans," who half-know that something is amiss, but, because evil comes mixed with good and fully reveals itself only after all the power is on its side, keep silent. In our *actual* world, there are pleas to be made on behalf of white liberals who live in the suburbs and contribute small amounts to the NAACP, but in HL's world they have sold their souls, quite simply. So the reader of HL's sentences is accepting a great deal if he accepts the scene they imply. Many readers won't. (Query: what difference might it make if these were the *last* two sentences of an essay, rather than the first?)

What to conclude from this dramatic analysis of Laski's sentences? Perlocutionary acts are fallible, inherently. Look at it one way, and this is a counsel of despair. ("If Thoreau and Laski can't control their speech acts, why should I be able to?") On the other hand, the awareness that complete success is impossible can be liberating. Since even the most timid, neutral, impersonal, or formal speech act will fall short of its purpose with some readers, you may just as well try for a more ambitious effect, a more natural or striking "agent," a "scene" that is vivid.

> • *Exercise 4.4:* Take the subject matter of Harold Laski's statement (we might
> call it "the secret of freedom"), assume that the agent is a precinct police-
> captain and the scene an induction ceremony for recruits to the police
> force. Write the opening sentences of the captain's remarks.

SEQUENCE

Speech and writing again: when people talk, no one person is likely to perform many perlocutionary acts in a row. The other fellow talks back. So speaker #1 gets acted upon in his turn, and responds to speaker #2's responses. In the process, he learns what success he is having in his own speech acts, and can change tactics accordingly.

The written form that most closely approximates this situation is the drama, especially when the playwright is generous with stage directions:

[MAJOR] SWINDON (*To* RICHARD, *sharply*).   Your name, sir?

RICHARD (*affable, but obstinate*).   Come: you don't mean to say that you've brought me here without knowing who I am?

SWINDON.   As a matter of form, sir, give your name.

RICHARD.   As a matter of form, then, my name is Anthony Anderson, Presbyterian minister in this town.

[GENERAL] BURGOYNE. (*Interested*).   Indeed! Pray, Mr. Anderson, what do you gentlemen believe?

RICHARD.   I shall be happy to explain if time is allowed me. I cannot undertake to complete your conversion in less than a fortnight.

SWINDON (*snubbing him*).   We are not here to discuss your views.

BURGOYNE (*with an elaborate bow to the unfortunate Swindon*).   I stand rebuked.

SWINDON (*embarrassed*).   Oh, not you, I as—

BURGOYNE.   Don't mention it. (*To* RICHARD, *very politely*) Any political views, Mr. Anderson?

RICHARD.   I understand that this is just what we are here to find out.

SWINDON (*severely*).   Do you mean to deny that you are a rebel?

RICHARD.   I am an American, sir.

SWINDON.   What do you expect me to think of that speech, Mr. Anderson?

RICHARD.   I never expect a soldier to think, sir.

BURGOYNE *is boundlessly delighted by this retort, which almost reconciles him to the loss of America.*

SWINDON (*whitening with anger*).   I advise you not to be insolent, prisoner.

RICHARD.   You can't help yourself, General. When you make up your mind to hang a man, you put yourself at a disadvantage with him. Why should I be civil to you? I may as well be hanged for a sheep as a lamb.

SWINDON.   You have no right to assume that the court has made up its mind without a fair trial. And you will please not address me as General. I am Major Swindon.

RICHARD.   A thousand pardons. I thought I had the honor of addressing Gentlemanly Johnny.

Sensation among the officers. The sergeant has a narrow escape from a guffaw.

BURGOYNE (*with extreme suavity*).   I believe I am Gentlemanly Johnny,
    sir, at your service. My more intimate friends call me General
    Burgoyne. (RICHARD *bows with perfect politeness.*) You will under-
    stand, sir, I hope, since you seem to be a gentleman and a man of
    some spirit in spite of your calling, that if we should have the mis-
    fortune to hang you, we shall do so as a mere matter of political
    necessity, without any personal ill-feeling.
RICHARD.   Oh, quite so. That makes all the difference in the world, of
    course.

• *Exercise 4.5:*   Trace the sequence of illocutionary and perlocutionary acts.
    How many failures are there? Write a short skit that builds upon misfires.

In continuous prose where there is only one agent, a kind of drama
takes place all the same. The writer conceives an audience and a scene,
as well as an agent who will serve as his voice, and an imaginary exchange begins. On it, the "feel" of the writing depends. Here, for instance, is Paine, in his pamphlet *The Crisis,* number 1. The literal scene
is winter, 1776, after Washington's forces had been routed by Howe in
the battle of Long Island:

> Quitting this class of men, I turn with the warm ardor of a friend
> to those who have nobly stood, and yet are determined to stand the
> matter out: call not upon a few, but upon all, not on *this* State or *that*
> State, but upon *every* State: up and help us, lay your shoulders to the
> wheel; better have too much force than too little, when so great an
> object is at stake. Let it be told to the future world, that in the depth
> of winter, when nothing but hope and virtue could survive, that the
> city and the country, alarmed at one common danger, came forth to
> meet and to repulse it. Say not that thousands are gone—turn out
> your tens of thousands; throw not the burden of the day upon Provi-
> dence, but *"show your faith by your works,"* that God may bless you.
> It matters not where you live, or what rank of life you hold, the evil
> or the blessing will reach you all. The far and the near, the home
> countries and the back, the rich and the poor, will suffer or rejoice
> alike. The heart that feels not now is dead; the blood of his children
> will curse his cowardice who shrinks back at a time when a little might
> have saved the whole and made *them* happy. I love the man that can
> smile in trouble, that can gather strength from distress and grow brave
> by reflection. It is the business of little minds to shrink; but he whose
> heart is firm, and whose conscience approves his conduct, will pursue
> his principles unto death.

Paine first invokes, and thus establishes, his audience. Then he proceeds through the illocutionary acts, roughly, of appealing, commanding, justifying ("better have too much force . . ."), exhorting, commanding, predicting ("the evil or blessing will reach you all"), and so on.

These acts do not occur in a vacuum, however: they form a chain, which is in part logical, but also and importantly in part dramatic. The purpose of the first independent clause, aside from singling out an audience, is to ingratiate Paine with that audience, both by direct appeal ("the warm ardor of a friend") and by praise ("who have nobly stood"). Paine moves immediately to his appeal and command ("I call . . ."). But he could hardly have done this with confidence unless the audience was on his side, and ready to acknowledge his comradeship and his authority. In effect, Paine has counted on the success of his first perlocutionary act as a condition for attempting his second and third—almost as if his audience of citizen-soldiers had turned physically toward him with respectful but urgent attention. Now he has given his command: "up and help us; lay your shoulders to the wheel." But this time he does not assume the immediate success of his act. Rather, the imagined audience has hesitated at the universal call to arms, and Paine follows it with an appeal to reason ("better have too much force"), to persuade the cautious. In the imagined drama, the appeal to reason works, but reason alone will not make men fight, so Paine adds a supplementary appeal, to pride and the sense of potential heroism that is in each man ("Let it be told . . ."). Now the audience almost audibly speaks: "Very well, but thousands have already gone to fight," and Paine is quick to put down such temporizing ("Say not . . ."). Follow for yourself the interchange between Paine and his audience from this point forward: why, for instance, does he shift from "The heart that feels not now is dead . . ." to "I love the man that can smile in trouble . . ."?

Paine wrote in the midst of rushing events; the actual scene was close indeed to the imagined one of his pamphlet. Washington had the pamphlet read aloud to every corporal's guard in his defeated army, and a few days later that army recrossed the Delaware, and won a great victory at Trenton. Few written words have so powerful a perlocutionary force within the flow of real events. But the imagined drama is always there. Each act generates its implied response, and that response helps bring about the next act.

So it is in this excerpt from *The Autobiography of Malcolm X,* although Malcolm has in mind a scene and audience much less specific— watch for the change that occurs before the last paragraph:

Human history's greatest crime was the traffic in black flesh when the devil white man went into Africa and murdered and kidnapped to bring to the West in chains, in slave ships, millions of black men, women, and children, who were worked and beaten and tortured as slaves.

The devil white man cut these black people off from all knowledge of their own kind, and cut them off from any knowledge of their own language, religion, and past culture, until the black man in America was the earth's only race of people who had absolutely no knowledge of his true identity.

In one generation, the black slave women in America had been raped by the slavemaster white man until there had begun to emerge a homemade, handmade, brainwashed race that was no longer even of its true color, that no longer knew its own family names. The slave-master forced his family name upon this rape-mixed race, which the slavemaster began to call "the Negro."

This "Negro" was taught of his native Africa that it was peopled by heathen, black savages, swinging like monkeys from trees. This "Negro" accepted this along with other teaching of the slavemaster that was designed to make him accept and obey and worship the white man.

And where the religion of every other people on earth taught its believers of a God with whom they could identify, a God who at least looked like one of their own kind, the slavemaster injected his Christian religion into his "Negro." This "Negro" was taught to worship an alien God having the same blond hair, pale skin, and blue eyes as the slavemaster.

This religion taught the "Negro" that black was a curse. It taught him to hate everything black, including himself. It taught him that everything white was good, to be admired, respected, and loved. It brainwashed this "Negro" to think he was superior if his complexion showed more of the white pollution of the slavemaster. This white man's Christian religion further deceived and brainwashed this "Negro" to always turn the other cheek, and grin, and scrape, and bow, and be humble, and to sing, and to pray, and to take whatever was dished out by the devilish white man; and to look for his pie in the sky, and for his heaven in the hereafter, while right here on earth the slavemaster white man enjoyed *his* heaven.

Many a time, I have looked back, trying to assess, just for myself, my first reactions to all this. Every instinct of the ghetto jungle streets, every hunting fox and criminal wolf instinct in me, which would have scoffed at and rejected anything else, was struck numb. It was as though all of that life merely was back there, without any remaining effect, or influence. I remember how, some time later, reading the Bible in the Norfolk Prison Colony library, I came upon, then I read, over and over, how Paul on the road to Damascus, upon hearing the voice of Christ, was so smitten that he was knocked off his horse, in a daze. I do not now, and I did not then, liken myself to Paul. But I do understand his experience.[1]

Even in the most dispassionate argument, a shadowy drama goes forward. Follow, for instance, the dramatic "plot" of this rather dry passage:

> There is no difficulty in showing that the ideally best form of government is that in which the sovereignty, or supreme controlling power in the last resort, is vested in the entire aggregate of the community, every citizen not only having a voice in the exercise of that ultimate sovereignty, but being, at least occasionally, called on to take an actual part in the government by the personal discharge of some public function, local or general.
>
> To test this proposition, it has to be examined in reference to the two branches into which, as pointed out in the last chapter, the inquiry into the goodness of a government conveniently divides itself, namely, how far it promotes the good management of the affairs of society by means of the existing faculties, moral, intellectual, and active, of its various members, and what is its effect in improving or deteriorating those faculties.
>
> The ideally best form of government, it is scarcely necessary to say, does not mean one which is practicable or eligible in all states of civilization, but the one which, in the circumstances in which it is practicable and eligible, is attended with the greatest amount of beneficial consequences, immediate and prospective. A completely popular government is the only polity which can make out any claim to this character. It is pre-eminent in both the departments between which the excellence of a political Constitution is divided. It is both more favorable to present good government, and promotes a better and higher form of national character than any other polity whatsoever.

JOHN STUART MILL, *Considerations on Representative Government*
(1861)

It may help to put each imagined response into words: What does Mill expect his audience to think at each juncture? And, by the way, what is the scene of this austere drama?

One moralistic word, in conclusion: there is no getting away from the imagined drama. You, as writer, may imagine it only unconsciously. But if you fail to imagine it at all, your writing will surely suffer from

---

[1] *The Autobiography of Malcolm X* with the assistance of Alex Haley. Copyright © 1964 by Alex Haley and Betty Shabazz. Published by Grove Press, Inc.

what we might call a "drama defect." The drama of act and response will still go on, but not under your control, and the result will be confusion or boredom. To put the matter more cheerfully, it is probably no exaggeration to say that the single most important cause of *good* writing is a lively dramatic sense, and the audible voice that goes with that sense.

2/   The Politics of Writing

As a perlocutionary chain lengthens, it draws writer and readers together in an implied community. At least, that is what the writer tries to do, except on those relatively rare occasions when his purpose is to flay his readers. In a sense, the writer is always inviting the reader to join one group or another. By the concepts and words he uses, he draws boundaries to the community he is creating: for instance, right now a writer will create very different alliances depending on whether he refers to urban riots as "civil disorders," "Black insurrections," or "crime in the streets." Or again, if he is arguing against the sterilization of Moroccan women (by American "teams" in a world-wide effort to control population), he can collect very different audience-communities around his goal by appealing to "natural and divine law," "human dignity," or "American imperialism."

But in another way, too, a speaker or writer creates a community. The illocutionary acts he performs locate his audience in a particular role, just as they imply a social role for the writer or speaker. He occupies a place in a social hierarchy, entitles his hearers to certain expectations, enters into tacit contracts. Similarly, the perlocutionary acts he attempts establish an ethic for this society—that is, they show what kind of persuasion or coercion or manipulation or respectful address is allowable in the community, what the ground rules are for one member's dealing with another.

• *Exercise 4.6:*   Consider the following passage:

But it is to you, ye Workers, who do already work, and are as grown men, noble and honourable in a sort, that the whole world calls for new work and nobleness. Subdue mutiny, discord, wide-spread despair, by manfulness, justice, mercy and wisdom. Chaos is dark, deep as Hell; let light be, and there is instead a green flowery World. Oh, it is great, and there is no other greatness. To make some nook of God's Creation a little fruitfuller,

better, more worthy of God; to make some human hearts a little wiser, man-
fuller, happier,—more blessed, less accursed! It is work for a God.

THOMAS CARLYLE, *Past and Present*

Carlyle is appealing to the working class of England in 1845: with what character and ideals does he endow them? What kind of community is implied
by his use of "nobleness," "manfulness," "greatness"? Of the capitalized
words? When he commands the workers to subdue mutiny, what role does
he assume? What is the perlocutionary goal behind "The whole world calls"?
In particular, examine the sentence beginning "Chaos is dark . . ." for its
illocutionary and perlocutionary forces, and try to say "who" Carlyle takes
himself to be in the imagined society. Then imagine yourself to be an English worker earning fifty cents a day, and write a short reply to Carlyle.

When friend speaks to friend, parent to child, employee to employer,
judge to prisoner, the contracts and entitlements of their speech acts take
effect within a community already established, and may alter its structure only the slightest bit. Presumably a wife who says to her husband,
"Get me a drink, dear," knows that their community will support this
command. She is not trying to *establish* her right to give an order—that
right already exists, and the community of two will continue much as
before. Such communities go through a continuous evolution, but a slow
one, except at those moments playwrights single out as material for
domestic tragedies and the like. For the most part, the communities
within which oral speech acts take place are stable ones. And through
all of human history except the last few hundred years, the overwhelming
majority of all speech acts must have taken place within such a social
framework.

The present situation in literate and technologically developed countries is radically different. When President Johnson said to millions of
television viewers, in March 1968, "I shall not seek and I will not accept
the nomination of my party," he acted, to be sure, within an established
social and political framework, but scarcely an intimate one. Few of his
hearers had so much as met the President. Moreover, close as they were
to his image on the screen, that closeness was entirely one-sided: they
had no way of responding, no way of completing the contract, no chance
of following up the event itself. The President himself could not sense
their reaction, or see whether the community was in fact as he estimated
it to be.

Even more different from the standard speech situation of a non-
technological culture is, for instance, that which obtained when Senator
Fulbright said in a press conference that the United States was losing the

War on Poverty and the war in Vietnam. He spoke to newsmen in his physical presence, but they were not his real audience. Really, he spoke through or around them, to the rest of us. Our relation to his speech act was that of *overhearing* it, acting as a shadow audience—and the community that results in such a situation is shadowy in consequence. The social relationship between speaker and reader is attenuated and weak, in spite of the way the hearer's life may be affected by what the speaker says and does.

Let's take one more step away from the face-to-face speech situation. An advertisement proclaims: "Now! Eat Mellowbits and keep slim." Who is speaking? Does he have the right to issue this command? Am I an appropriate audience for him to instruct in this fashion? Does he mean what he says about "and keep slim"? What responsibility has he for his implied claim? What thoughts and feelings should he have? How would he conduct himself appropriately by way of follow up? These questions are inherently unanswerable, for *no* prior community exists that incorporates him and me, and he is not present, or even inferrable, from his speech act itself. So, in order to participate in the act, I must do some inventing, posit a speaker and a situation, put myself in some relation to him. (And it must be a relation that permits him to say, later on, "Mellowbits are *better* than dessert," and "Here's happy news. Mellowbits now come in seven flavors." I am being *managed,* through imaginative reconstruction, urged into a particular social role, and a rather demeaning one at that.)

A great many of the speech acts that come our way approach close to this rather absurd extreme. We are constantly being dragged into communities in which we have no say, which we did not choose to join. Furthermore, in these communities the speaker is a stranger, is not addressing us directly, and often has no discernible identity. The inchoateness of the situation and the remoteness of the speaker conspire to unsettle the identity of the *hearer* as well, for how can he be all the things he is asked to be by the clamor of voices that address him? In a fluid social world such as this, one in which the media make it possible for anyone with money to corral an audience of strangers, the hearer/reader must constantly make choices of what person to be, what communities to join, what implied social structures to accept. In other words, his verbal environment is, for him, essentially *political*. And this probably is one reason why we have a New Left, dropouts and hippies, and rebelliousness among those who are not economically deprived, as well as among those who are.

Whatever the social consequences of this technological development (alienation, anomie, frustration, indifference), the consequences for the theory of communication are great. We are a long way from the situation in which the Athenians defined a viable political group as one small enough to encompass only those within the sound of a speaker's voice. Today that would take in the entire world's population, and we must assume that the rhetorical practices that worked for the Athenians simply may not work for us. It is not enough to say, as Marshall Mc-Luhan does, that "the medium is the message," but he is right in seeing that in the modern world both speaker and person-spoken-to have lost the sharp identity they had when Pericles harangued the crowds in Athens or even when Bryan stumped the country calling for "free silver."

The paradox of this political situation—immensely expanded communications resources and markedly diminished certainty that anything universally clear will be communicated—makes all the more important a writer's close attention to the specific writing acts he performs and to the means by which he makes them achieve what he intends. We have argued above that the most successful procedure in our time is for the writer to create, quite consciously whenever he writes, a drama, a piece of theater. In that drama he plays a role and he develops a role for his reader. There can be no avoiding the fact that this is manipulation, too, just as the advertising man's spiel about Mellowbits is manipulation. If it is manipulation with a difference, what does that difference amount to?

3/ The Ethics of Persuasion

Anything said about ethics by definition involves moralizing, and we therefore feel some embarrassment at this juncture. Who, after all, is entitled to tell someone else his position is a false one, his emotion merely sentimentality, his argument insincere? How, indeed, can a writer himself know whether or not he is being honest?

Two fairly safe tests do seem applicable, one for the matter, the other for the manner of speaking. Most statements have what we can call "truth-content," data or propositions or assumptions that can be measured against what is generally or specifically known to be so. The statement "Socialists are committed to preservation of the free-enterprise system" is false by definition. "Socialists control a majority of seats in the House of Representatives" is also false, but by head-count rather than definition. "Socialists are more likely to have sinus trouble than Republicans" raises no problem of definition and would be pretty hard to test by counting, but its truth-content looks low or nonexistent simply on the basis of common sense: what does political affiliation have to do with nasal passages? In general, if we take the trouble and resolutely refuse to be bamboozled by what simply sounds authoritative, we can come reasonably close to measuring the truth-content of a statement. If we find it low, we have reason to conclude that the stater is either ignorant or dishonest and to keep a wary eye on whatever else he has to tell us.

The second test, on the manner of speaking, is more difficult to apply but there are signs that help. As we noted above, speakers have somewhat greater latitude than writers in their manner simply because a gesture, a grin, a wink, or a particular tone of voice may signal the amount of credence to be given to a statement. Just as writers are somewhat more circumscribed, so readers must be more alert to nuance. A passage that is full of superlatives or absolute terms ("unique," "perfect") raises proper suspicion that the writer may be extending the force of his data or argument by exaggeration. There is some degree of fashionableness in such exaggerations, of course: "a fantastic amount," "the devastating decline" and similar phrases probably get a swift discounting today exactly because of their popularity, but even they call into question the reliability of the writer.

Like superlatives, and for the same reason, the constant use of general labels may point either to intellectual slovenliness or to dishonesty. Such labels are especially common in political argument, though they are not by any means confined to it. Broad ideological labels (conservative, radical, imperialist, isolationist) do indeed have some counterparts in reality and therefore some utility, but their perlocutionary intent is often unethical. The intent makes itself apparent either by context ("conservative" as associated with fiscal prudence or with personal greed; "radical" as associated with equitable distribution of wealth or with soak-the-rich tax programs) or by emotion-stirring epithets ("fat-cat conservatives," "wild-eyed radicals"). Careful definition of terms obviously goes out the window in such usage; the labels become bludgeons rather than knives meant to slice reality into reasonably accurate layers.

Another stylistic sign of unethical persuasion is misleading synonymy, the shift from a neutral label to one with flattering or denigrating overtones. The writer's first reference is to "anti-war critics," his next to "doves," and his next to "appeasers," all three apparently representing the same persons. This kind of synonymy often gets coupled with slogans: American businessmen abroad become "tools of the imperialists"; members of the American Communist Party become "red stooges." The equations are so blatant that they invite ready detection, but in the climate of impassioned oratory listeners and readers are more likely to become collaborators than detectives. It takes a cool head and a wary eye to call a halt when the labels come thick and fast.

The ethical problem posed by the strategies of persuasion is nothing new. Five centuries ago the French essayist Montaigne found it so disturbing that he argued for the elimination of all rhetoric:

> . . . Aristo wisely defines rhetoric as "a science to persuade the people"; Socrates and Plato as "the art of deceiving and flattering." And they who deny the general definition verify it throughout in their precepts.
>
> The Mohammedans forbade their children to be instructed in the art, on account of its usefulness.
>
> And the Athenians, having perceived how pernicious was the practice of it, though it was held in high esteem in their city, ordained that the principal part, the appeal to the passions, should be abolished, together with the exordiums and the perorations.
>
> It is a tool invented for handling and stirring up a mob and an unruly community; and it is a tool that is only employed for sick states, like medicine. . . .
>
> *Of the Vanity of Words*

Needless to say, neither the Athenians nor the Frenchman were successful, and there are two good reasons why. First, human nature makes as much room for wiliness as for honesty; secondly, explanations and arguments must be made through language, and most language is colored, loaded, freighted with associations that have emotional impact. Since there is no getting away from rhetoric, the only alternative is to understand it. The badness lies not in language or its deployment but in the character of those who use it. And any appeal to the ethics of persuasion becomes in the end a scrutiny of the character of the persuader. Since the scrutiny can only rarely be at first-hand, especially in a telecommunication age, it must resolve itself into a scrutiny of the instruments by which character expresses itself, notably the instrument of language.

Part 2

The writer who understands the game he is playing has still the game to play, and the gap between understanding and execution requires constant exercise if it is to be closed. The better he gets, the more time a writer spends not on large strategies but on detail—on the turn of phrase, the choice of a word that is exactly right, the structure of each sentence and the relation of each sentence to the ones that precede and follow. The second part of this book, earlier called the bread-and-butter section, deals with that kind of important detail.

Coleridge's formula—"the right words in the right order"— puts the matter in a nutshell if you know how to tell "right" from "wrong." Since the difference between right and wrong is not written in the heavens, there is no way to tell short of knowing the general conventions of the game and appreciating the possible variations and their likely effect. The exercises scattered through the first section of this book set you the problem of composing variations but provide no systematic rationale for them. In what follows we have attempted to put down, in an orderly fashion, the essential information for making that kind of practice a deliberate activity. We move from diction to syntax to structure, an order that has little to do with the way anyone actually writes but a great deal to do with the way everyone re-writes. If there is any single "secret" to the art of writing, re-writing—practice —is that secret.

chapter five / *Diction*

1/ Diction

Otto Jespersen, a great grammarian of the English language, is said to have remarked that the direction of change in a language is from ditch to castle. Since he made that remark (if he did) there have been many efforts by serious students of language to make sociological classifications of one kind or another. Thus, within the great classes of origin (Indo-European, and so on) and within the national and regional classes (French, Germanic, Arabic), additional classes have been sorted on the basis of characteristic vocabulary, syntax, and conformity to traditional or "approved" usages. Obviously these classes are of very different kind from the ones grounded on the historical development of linguistic forms, and they lack the neatness and reliability of those earlier classifications. Yet they have a particular interest for the writer because they attempt to distinguish, among the various patterns of speech in a given language, those patterns which are distinctive indicators of the economic status, the cultural experience, and the social position of the speaker. An analogy to this kind of classification can be found in the highbrow-middlebrow-lowbrow metaphor used a few years ago to describe social habits and tastes in clothing, cigarettes, movies, magazines, and alcohol.

People have undoubtedly made social distinctions about the forms of language since culture began. Attempts to teach young people to speak and write "correctly" imply established forms and corruptions of them, and the forms considered "established" are necessarily those which the teachers themselves are accustomed to using. If this were the complete story, however, there would be little difficulty in determining correct language: the language which the tradition bearers (teachers, priests, hereditary chieftains) learned from the tradition bearers who preceded them would continue to be the correct language. In isolated and strictly hierarchical societies, if there are any left, that may still be the case. But most societies have experienced frequent disruption of hierarchies and almost none are really isolated today. Certainly, as far as Western culture is concerned, it is not possible to consider any society of the past three thousand years as either rigidly hierarchical or culturally isolated. Wherever a society is at all mobile and flexible, its language will undergo change; and wherever language undergoes change, some of the changes that occur will develop in small groups and come to be identified with them. Quite naturally, those whose receive formal education in their youth will be exposed to the traditions of language-as-it-has-been-used, and those who do not will derive their norms of language from the speech they hear about them.

Now, although it is true that formal education often tends to perpetuate forms and distinctions that have lost currency even among educated people, it is also true that it preserves forms and distinctions which have developed in the language as aids to clarity, precision, and beauty. Given the fact that no absolute authority exists for distinguishing good from bad diction, right from wrong usage, our best recourse is to the spoken and written language of educated people. The obvious question, then, is this one: do educated people agree in matters of diction and usage? And the obvious answer is: Not always. Here it is important to note that the obvious answer is not a flat negative. A rough guess would be that ninety-nine out of a hundred expressions in any piece of writing by an educated person will go unchallenged by an educated reader. But the hundredth may be disputed vigorously.

A short time ago, the advertising writers for a cigarette manufacturer produced copy in which "like" figures as a conjunction. Indignant letters immediately began to pile up on editors' desks everywhere, protesting against debasement of the language, corruption of the young, countermand to the labors of schoolteachers, and so on. Sober consideration of what is at stake in a dispute of this kind will bring us close to the root of this whole business.

There can be no denying that "like" has often been used in the past by great writers exactly as it is being used in the advertisement. (There are examples in any historical dictionary.) This does not by itself mean that the usage is acceptable now, of course. Nor can there be any doubt that respectable writers so use it today, as the same dictionary will show. It does not seem possible, then, to discriminate on simple grounds of use. The next possibility is to quantify: do more use "like" as a conjunction than use "as"? There may be no way of getting a satisfactory answer to that question, but if there is, something further must be considered: is it better to do what most do or what few do? Another possibility is to qualify: do people I admire and wish to imitate use "like" as a conjunction? If that seems absurdly petty, the final possibility is to take the precise line: how does "like" compare to "as" in terms of precision, clarity, even euphony?

If all this speculation produces no certainty, why the fuss? We know that assertions of preference often arouse more fervor than those about which some common validation is possible. The same is true about a matter of this kind. It cannot be said that "as" is more precise than "like." It cannot be very convincingly shown that more educated people use one form than the other, and even if it could, something more is needed to make mere majority become the ground for action. There is really no alternative to this conclusion: that, in matters of disputed usage, it is a waste of time to argue about rightness and wrongness because it is a matter in which preference is the ground of arbitration, not fact.

This is not at all the same as saying that the choice between "like" and "as"—or any similar choice—does not matter. It matters a good deal, but it matters as a feature of style, of the conscious choices made by a writer, of his self-expressiveness, not as virtue or duty or moral goodness. When Fowler (*Modern English Usage*) describes some uses of the conjunctive "like" as evidence of a "slovenly parsimony of words," and divides the world into those who have an "instinctive objection" to the form and those who do not, he has in mind the style of a select group of writers whom he admires. Without arguing any superiority for "as," he prefers it to "like"—partly, no doubt, because he likes nice discriminations. Such a taste is not to be despised. Neither is it to be taken as adjunct to moral law.

Taste, then, is implicated in style, but taste is notoriously private even when, as in the matter just discussed, it has the weight of pedagogical consensus with it. No one can legislate taste; people cannot even talk helpfully about it without setting themselves up as arbiters of many specific literary forms for which there is neither clear historical sanction nor distinct rhetorical or semantic advantage. "Like" is used and has long been used as a conjunction by good writers; it is fully as serviceable as the alternate word "as"; these two facts argue for it. Against it is another fact: that most writers who pride themselves on propriety of expression do not use it. Given this knowledge, a writer chooses, and in choosing reveals something about himself. His choice affects his style, and his style suggests the grounds of choice.

There is, of course, no responsible choosing unless there is also knowledge. A writer steadily accumulates distinctions among words and phrases, and the distinctions most valuable to him are often those about which no dispute is useful. For his purposes, he prefers "behind" to "in back of" but uses "rest" and "remainder" interchangeably. Below the level of these distinctions, however, most writers recognize and respect a conventional body of usage. When they deviate from it, they deviate quite consciously in order to gain some rhetorical advantage. To knowledge of the convention and knowledge of variants, they bring specific intention and conscious judgment. They may choose unwisely, of course —in which case the meaning and effect of their work will not be what they intended—but at least they choose.

"STANDARD ENGLISH."   For better or for worse, "Standard English" is defined here as the English most educated users of the language commonly employ. There is some difference between standard *spoken* and standard *written* English. There is some difference between what is standard in Texas and what is standard in Vermont, and even more between what is standard in Chicago and what is standard in Leeds, England. But in the main the differences are not great, rarely cause confusion, and rather please than dismay. This book is written in Standard English, though some of its locutions are undoubtedly quite different from, even if not incongruous with, those of a history textbook. Its differences are differences of choice, therefore of style; the book has only one of the many possible styles in Standard English.

DIALECT.   Linguists use the term "dialect" to describe any of several coordinated language patterns commonly followed by groups for whom the language is native. "Standard English," as we define it above, is a dialect, one of several dialects of American English. The term "dialect," however, is more popularly thought of as language peculiar to a locality. It ranges from expressions used by all persons of the locality (like "He was graduated high school") to those used primarily in speech alone and retained for the most part by speakers of limited formal education ("a fur piece," meaning "a long distance" in rural localities all over the United States). It may be the special language of a cult, even a signal of recognition among members (as in the Beat "Like man I got this misery feeling from too much tea"). Dialect has considerable charm for the ear of the person to whom it is not native, and for that reason a writer may find it useful at times. He will not, however, expect to conduct much serious exposition in it. For purposes of humor, irony, surprise, emphasis, a writer may find dialect valuable as a supplement to standard diction. He will not find it useful as an alternative to standard diction.

VERNACULAR.   The basic meaning of "vernacular" is "native"; the vernacular tongue is to be distinguished from a foreign tongue which, for one reason or another, may be the official or prestigious language of one's country. In Dante's time, Latin was the proper language for the writing of learned and literary men; Dante's defense of Italian for such writing was a defense of the vernacular. When Chaucer wrote *The Canterbury Tales,* the language of the church was Latin, that of the court was French; Chaucer chose the vernacular, a hybrid of Romance and Saxon origins. Until the first World War, most Chinese writing was in Mandarin, though many vernacular dialects flourished for the ordinary purposes of life. During the War a vigorous program was initiated to displace Mandarin with a vernacular, both for purposes of communication and of education, and it is now fully established.

Because a conflict between the official tongue and that spoken and written by most of the populace is less and less common, the word "vernacular" has gradually taken on a slightly less specific meaning, though one that goes back to its Latin origin (*vernaculus,* born in one's house). When scholars speak of a poet of the vernacular today, for example, they have in mind someone who uses the language of the "common man," the man-at-home. Again, the use that is made of the vernacular, as defined in this sense, is a conscious choice of the folksy over the formal; it is justified if it serves a purpose.

COLLOQUIALISM.   The practical difference between colloquialism and the vernacular is likely not to be very great. "Colloquial" means "used in speech." It implies "used only in speech, not in writing." But, of course, speech is not thought of as colloquial; the term refers to written use of the vocabulary or syntax common to speech but not to writing. In modern prose, the distinctions are much less severe than they were a few decades ago. There has, indeed, been a conscious colloquializing of written prose in American English for over a hundred years. Still, the colloquial is uncommon enough to academic exposition, at least, so that its use there, like the use of dialect (though not so strongly), provokes attention and is therefore suitable mainly for emphasis and the like.

One effect of the colloquializing of our written language is the gradual assimilation of the second-person pronoun *you* to a third-person function, even in formal written prose. This use substitutes for the pronoun *one,* still more commonly used in England. (One has only to consider such a possibility; You have only to consider such a possibility). Another, more striking, is the notable reduction of connectives. Because speech can easily be fortified by gesture and intonation, it is possible to indicate many relationships with a few connectives (and, but, so, when, if). For a variety of reasons, some modern writers have tried to strip their prose to these few colloquial connectives, largely in order to deemphasize the presence of the writer's analytical and synthesizing mind.

Josephine was very sorry. It was not her fault. She was eating and a
dog slipped and a man was hurt. This has happened in Spain. Joseph
is so sorry. They told him they applauded him. He is not nervous. He
is easily hopeful. There was no use. The accident was hurtful. I remember Paul told me that it had happened and he remembered. Poor Joseph
he will be alright again but it is unfortunate.

GERTRUDE STEIN, *Painted Lace and Other Pieces*

The effect is a special one, certainly, and not one of great value to most
exposition, though something can be said for the objectivity gained by
such exaggeration of a colloquial practice.

SLANG. Slang has its natural habitat in colloquial language, but it
is not identical with it. Slang is the codification of exuberance. Like ginger
ale, exuberance begins to lose its fizz as soon as it is poured out, and
slang is for that reason short-lived. It either disappears completely (Would
anyone describe a dance as "mellow" today, and what would he mean if
he did?) or becomes idiomatic and is assimilated into the main current of
the language, colloquial, written, or both. "Beat" is a dialect word that
has become general slang. It may itself derive from another slang usage,
the past participial form "beat" meaning "exhausted." Right now, as an
adjective, the term is precise and respectable—"the beat generation."
Whether that usage will be recognizable a generation from now, it is hard
to say. It may become as archaic as "flapper," or it may assume some
midstation between colloquial and standard, as "deadbeat" has done, or
solidify its credentials with Standard English, like the verb ("He beats
every opponent he plays").

While it lasts, slang often has extraordinary power to make us see
matters in a new light. It exposes hidden properties, challenges fixed assumptions, and revitalizes words. But like this spring's hat, it looks
dowdy by summer and old-fashioned by fall. For that reason a writer
uses it sparingly and only when he believes the gain from freshness is
greater than the loss by tarnish.

IDIOM. Idiom is different from slang, though slang may become
idiom. The soundest definition is in this case the simplest. An idiomatic
expression is a construction of two or more words in which the sense of
the whole construction is not predictable from the meaning of its parts.
People say that they "catch cold" from sitting in a draft although the sense
of "catching" is not in their minds as it might well be in the expression
"catch your cold." Others talk of "getting by without effort," of "getting

on in business," of "getting at the job immediately," of "getting ourselves up for a party," of "getting out of town" and "of getting tired," in each instance indicating a shift of meaning for "get" by the preposition used with it. A cow "eats up" the grass, a girl "washes up" the dishes, and a driver "slows up" at an intersection; in each phrase a different meaning is given to "up."

Not all idioms involve prepositions, of course. In the sentence "We used to use the words we were used to," the first and third uses of the verb "to use" are idiomatic, the second is not. In such a phrase as "going the whole way," the idiom reflects a submerged metaphor both in verb and in noun; in "bearing up," a metaphor that is still potent works in both verbal and preposition. The use of idiom, more than any other matter of diction, requires sensitivity and memory: the former to detect nuance and the latter to record what even the best dictionaries cannot always capture. Good writing is alway idiomatic writing, for idiom is the living tissue of a language.

2/ Characteristics of Style

The brief accounts of kinds of diction given above are accompanied by a minimum of prescription. The main requirement is to be alert to the variety, to be interested in the possibilities it offers for expression, and to understand the grounds for choice when choice must be made. Even if a set of commandments could be drawn up on irreproachable premises, it would not serve half so well as the kind of self-education implicitly recommended above. In this matter of diction, there is simply no satisfactory shortcut for alertness and a lively interest in words.

About the general characteristics of style it may nonetheless be possible to make some helpful comment, even though that comment may entail a good deal of emphasis on what is commonly done wrong rather than on what is commonly done right. Some faults are so characteristic of amateur writing that the best way to deal with them is to face them openly, and that is what we do below.

REDUNDANCY. The English language inherited both from Romance and Anglo-Saxon sources the characteristics of repetition as a means of emphasis—repetition sometimes of a single word or phrase, sometimes of a meaning in different words. Thus, the conventional expression "wear and tear" indicates nothing more than "wear" but achieves a kind of reinforcement from the addition of "tear." Consciously used, repetition has great power, but there are kinds of repetition that come from no conscious use by the writer. They result rather from his ignorance of the full force of a word he uses or from inattention to what he is doing. Such ignorance or inattention produces what is called "redundancy" or "pleonasm."

> A hero is usually distinguished in bravery, fortitude, and courage.

The three nouns are not quite identical ("bravery" is derived from a word meaning "fierceness"; "fortitude," from a word meaning "strength"; "courage," from a word meaning "heart"). But the characteristic they refer to here is probably a single one. Unless the writer has a reputation for nuance, his reader will undoubtedly take this for mere wordiness.

> The deliberate, planned lie is generally less successful than the spontaneous one.

How are "deliberate" and "planned" other than synonymous here? It is conceivable that, in speech, a certain emphasis might be achieved by this repetition. If the same force is desired in writing, however, some change must be made. Such a simple change as this might do the trick: "The deliberate, the planned lie . . ."; or better: "The deliberate lie—planned with care and executed with calculation—is. . . ."

> He is an author contemporary with the modern time.

The verb is in the present tense, so there is no need that "contemporary" be reinforced by "with the modern time." "Contemporary" can, of course, be used with times other than modern: as in "St. Francis, the founder of medieval mystical piety, was a contemporary of St. Dominic, the founder of the Inquisition."

> Neither the big magnates of the corporations nor the specialized experts nor the trained technicians realize what is at stake.

By derivation, magnates are big; by necessity, experts are specialized; and by definition, technicians are trained. In this example, the writer doesn't seem to care that his reputation with his reader is also "at stake."

ELEGANT VARIATION.   Fear of repetition occasionally leads students to avoid it at too great cost. They escape the frying pan of monotony only to fall into the fire of overingeniousness and affectation. A right balance between repetition and variation is not a matter for prescription, but examples may help to suggest the nature of the disease and the character of a cure.

> *Prohibition* seems to be a stimulant to most people. Even if they have no inclination toward doing what is *forbidden,* they feel an urge to resist *proscription* for the sake of resistance; or they assume that what is *interdicted* must be worth investigating or it would not have been *disallowed* in the first place. And the more strict the *ban,* the more subtle will be their efforts to outwit it.

In this illustration, the effort to avoid repeating derivatives of "prohibit" is so noticeable that a reader is more likely to concentrate on the writer's ingenuity (or his capacity for using a book of synonyms) than on what he is saying. Such a laborious procedure is bad not only because it distracts the reader and lends an air of pomposity to the passage but because it fails to make effective use of the key word. The passage is better on all three counts if the writer shows moderation in the use of synonyms.

> *Prohibition* seems to be a stimulant to most people. Even if they have no inclination toward doing what is *forbidden,* they feel an urge to resist *prohibition* for the sake of resistance; for they assume that what is *prohibited* must be worth investigating or it would not have been *forbidden* in the first place. And the more strict the *prohibition,* the more subtle will be their efforts to outwit it.

Elegant variation may actually cause misunderstanding as well as distraction and annoyance, as in this example:

> *Power* is the basis of political action. Whether *control* is exerted by elected or self-appointed or hereditary officials, *authority* conditions and manipulates action at will.

Are we to understand the italicized words as synonyms, or is some distinction suggested? If the former, then surely the passage will be more effective if written thus:

> *Power* is the basis of political action. Whether *it is* exerted by elected or self-appointed or hereditary officials, *power* conditions and manipulates action at will.

It is not fair, however, to condemn a practice because of its abuse. Repetition is too valuable an aid in good expression to discard because the incompetent use it without discrimination. A better procedure is to look to the ideas; if *they* are not idly repeated, one need have little worry about the repetition of words. To see how effective sheer repetition may be, examine the following passage. It is the work of an author whose deliberate use of repetition consorted magnificently with his deliberate limitation of emphasis to a few great ideas and made his voice a dominant one in the culture of half a century.

> The pursuit of perfection, then, is the pursuit of sweetness and light. He who works for sweetness and light, works to make reason and the will of God prevail. He who works for machinery, he who works for hatred, works only for confusion. Culture looks beyond machinery, culture hates hatred; culture has one great passion, the passion for sweetness and light. It has one even yet greater!—the passion for making them *prevail*. It is not satisfied till we *all* come to a perfect man; it knows that the sweetness and light of the few must be imperfect until the raw and unkindled masses of humanity are touched with sweetness and light. If I have not shrunk from saying that we must work for sweetness and light, so neither have I shrunk from saying that we must have a broad basis, must have sweetness and light for as many as possible. Again and again I have insisted how those are the happy moments of humanity, how those are the marking epochs of a people's life, how those are the flowering times for literature and art and all the creative power of genius, when there is a *national* glow of life and thought, when the whole of society is in the fullest measure permeated by thought, sensible to beauty, intelligent and alive. Only it must be *real* thought and *real* beauty; *real* sweetness and *real* light. Plenty of people will try to give the masses, as they call them, an intellectual food prepared and adapted in the way they think proper for the actual condition of the masses. The ordinary popular literature is an example of this way of working on the masses. Plenty of people will try to indoctrinate the masses with the set of ideas and judgments constituting the creed of their own profession or party. Our religious and political organizations give an example of this way of working on the masses. I condemn neither way; but culture works differently. It does not try to teach down to the level of the inferior classes; it does not try to win them for this or that sect of its own, with ready-made judgments and watchwords: It seeks to do away with classes; to make the best that has been thought and known in the world current everywhere; to make all men live in an atmosphere of sweetness and light, where they may use ideas, as it uses them itself, freely—nourished, and not bound by them.

> MATTHEW ARNOLD, *Culture and Anarchy*

Both redundancy and elegant variation are failures in economy. The writer is guilty of wastage in both. When his language is redundant, it vitiates attention: why should a reader pay close attention if he can count on being told and retold? And it annoys the reader who has the habit of being attentive. When the writer resorts to elegant variation, he vitiates attention in another way, by sending the reader off on tangents rather than leading him to the point. The economy of a piece of writing need not be austere, as spare and dry as sea biscuit. It may, in fact, be luxuriant. But it is important that it be an economy—that is, a conscious management—not a thoughtless rattling on or a hyperfastidious avoidance of the obvious and useful.

VAGUENESS AND AMBIGUITY.   Most of the much-lampooned repetitiveness of legal language is the result of trying to make watertight statements. The danger of vagueness and ambiguity in legal documents is too obvious to need illustration. Perhaps it is only this life-and-liberty-saving importance that can make a writer hunt for ways of making perfectly clear whatever he has to say—unless pride in his craft is enough to impel him to do so. The authors of these sentences are certainly slipshod in their work:

1. This seems to be just inconsistency in American philosophy. (Is "just" adjectival or adverbial? It makes a great deal of difference.)
2. This word designates any person who acts in a civil way. ("In a civil, that is, courteous, manner" or "in his capacity as a citizen or employee of the government"?)
3. The ordinary man must act as a check on any usurpation of the expert's powers. ("Usurpation of power by the expert" or "usurpation by someone else of power rightly the expert's"?)
4. He says that since all Americans have equal rights, no one goes out of his way to get out of that class, and that the people who were out slowly descended back due to their own lack of ambition. (This one needs a complete rewriting: "He says that, since all social classes in America have equal rights, almost no one goes out of his way to get out of the class into which he was born, and that those few who, for one reason or another, do move out return gradually because the advantages prove not to be worth the effort.")
5. Humor is a very effective means for communicating discontent when used satirically, but when humorous analogies are applied to serious subjects, the humor becomes devoid of its purpose and indeed detracts from it. (Any reader patient enough to work over this sentence will finally discover that clearing up "its purpose" will do more than anything else to clear up the confusion in the sentence. "Its purpose" must be understood, apparently, to exclude satire. That makes the statement completely illogical, but at least it is no longer ambiguous.)

The corrective to vagueness and ambiguity is, in part, a taste for precision. This taste is not a natural one, and its acquisition is not easy. Nor is it invariably attractive. There are writers, and would-be writers, for whom precision is so important that they may engage in an infinite deal of haggling over a matter of little import. Henry James managed to make an art out of such haggling, though not an art unreservedly admired for that characteristic, as numerous parodies of it demonstrate. Precision seems to be compulsive for some people, and compulsiveness is always unattractive to the beholder. Yet there is too much virtue in exactness to allow abuse of it to demean its role in a writer's attitude. A writer cannot afford to ignore *le mot juste,* or a word as *juste* as he can manage without taking such pains that the effort rather than the meaning attracts attention.

A second corrective to vagueness and ambiguity is knowledge of the choices available, for they are not exclusively choices between the "right" and the "wrong" word. They may be choices between the concrete and the abstract, or choices along the spectrum from general to particular and along that from sensory to nonsensory.

> a. *Concrete and Abstract.* A concrete entity is one that has mass; an abstract entity one that does not. There is no shade of either, though some nouns may be used for both: "humanity," for example. "Appetite," "rigor," and "beauty" are abstract nouns; "chair" and "lead" are concrete. Despite the arguments advanced in many quarters, it is clear that abstract words are valuable and cannot readily be replaced by concrete ones. To begin with, abstract words are a convenient shorthand ("rigor" as a word summing up an attitude perhaps compounded of precision, punctuality, neatness, self-discipline, and sternness of demeanor —a great deal to make a word mean, as Humpty Dumpty remarked, but that's the way with abstractions). They also identify common properties (as "beauty" does whether the word is used of a horse, a rose, or a woman). It is true, however, that abstract words may increase vagueness unless they are coupled with concrete words as supplements:

> His life is rigor itself—up at five, at work within the half-hour, unremitted laboring until mid-afternoon, then off for a brisk walk and a quick swim before sitting down to a spare meal punctually at four.

Or they may be coupled with verbs that contain a strong sense of action:
Not "the composition in this painting is a reflection of . . ." but "the composition in this painting reflects. . . ."

b. *General and Particular.* There is a spectrum from general to particular, not a simple line of division between them. The most general word is the one that is most inclusive in its reference; the least general, or most particular, word is the one that refers to a single entity. The spectrum is valid not only for nouns but for verbs, adjectives, and adverbs as well. It is safe to say that writers run greater danger of vagueness and ambiguity at the general, rather than the particular, end of the scale, though there is, to be sure, the possibility of so much particularity that no general statement emerges at all where one is intended. An adjectival scale, from particular to general, might run: perfect, unexcelled, superb, excellent, good. Discrimination among such words stimulates a reader's confidence that the writer is taking care.

c. *Sensory and nonsensory.* Although the proportion of sensory to nonsensory language is necessarily a matter of taste, it is a simple fact of experience that appeal to sense increases the vividness of imagery and therefore the evocativeness of a word or phrase. "A rosy future" holds more promise than one that is only "promising."

INFLATION. The undisputed master of the inflated style is Dickens' Mr. Micawber.

> The blossom is blighted, the leaf is withered, the God of day goes down upon the dreary scene, and—in short you are ever floored. As I am!

It is funny in print; in life, it is often offensive and sometimes pathetic. There is a marked tendency among good prose writers today to write with as much simplicity as they can manage. But not all things can be said simply. And, more to the point, not all people want to say things simply. It is no heinous offense to write "Anyone who has a fair position in industry . . ." instead of "Anyone who has a decent job in industry . . ." but the inflation, the slight pomposity, is there all the same. This is more noticeably stiff: "Higher education of excellent quality can be had at very lenient terms at state universities." Coupling a passive verb with "at very lenient terms" marks this ineradicably for what it is—an attempt to make something simple sound imposing. Like "Those who uphold the negative side of this question," it represents a kind of shrinking away from rude contact with things-as-they-are.

It is a somewhat different psychological attitude that leads a writer to load his text with phrases which send up their echo from a previous century. He seems to know the rudeness of things-as-they-are but to have turned to a golden past for words with which to enhance their dignity. He never "uses" but "avails himself of"; for him, people are "wont" to do things. A third kind of inflation is that which seems to have no cause other than the love of abstractions for their own sake. Although it may be indicative of a potentiality in the writer, it is certainly as annoying to the reader as any device one can name. One example should be enough:

> The Editor claims that the two advantages of the proposal have since been rendered improbable, and, hence, the presence of the House Deans is *conducive to a feeling of surveillance.*

EUPHEMISM.   Euphemism is the use of a mild or vague or roundabout expression as a substitute for blunt precision or disagreeable truth. Some euphemisms are simply matters of propriety. (See H. L. Mencken's amusing remarks on "mortician" and on the invention of "ecdysiast" to meet the professional demands of a certain Miss Sothern, *The American Language, Supplement One,* pp. 569 ff. and 584 ff.) Probably most of the euphemisms that appear in students' papers, however, rise from hypersensitivity, a vain fastidiousness almost as repulsive as its counterpart, vulgarity. Hypersensitivity and vulgarity are both bad in writing because they keep the writer from making honest contact with his material, that is, they make him *insensitive* to its real character. The student who wrote "position" instead of "job" (see above, Inflation) has imputed to "job" certain unpleasant suggestions of meniality; he hopes to dignify by a name, feeling that there is a kind of magic power in words which can alter the objects to which they are attached. The hope is illusory, and the act pretentious. A salary is not made bigger or better by being called an emolument, nor is a luncheon made more delicious by being called a collation.

Another kind of euphemism, a vicious kind, is that which attempts to put a fair face on foul matter. "Liquidation of undesirable elements" is murder, plain and simple. A "deliberate defection from known truth" is a lie, nothing more or less. Such terms, unless used mockingly, are attempts to hide the facts, not reveal them, to complicate rather than simplify communication.

Both euphemism and inflation point to their own correction. Language that is direct and at the same time restrained bespeaks composure and control, not simply of language, but of attitude and character. Drawing back from unadorned and accurate expressions suggests a basic uneasiness in the writer's relationship with the world and with his reader. Inflation may stem from like uneasiness, but it adds a certain callousness and false energy to language that repels as much as euphemisms do.

JARGON. Of all the faults of style dealt with here, use of jargon is the most common one in the writing of college students. It is not hard to see why. For one thing, they inhabit a society in which imitation is not only hard to avoid but often rewarded. They sense that one way to sound well informed or learned is to use the language they take to be that of well-informed and learned people. They rarely take all of it and often seize only what is new to them; therefore, their shortcomings are not due to their environment alone. Every writer, young or old, experienced or not, is responsible for his choices, and choosing jargon is no exception.

The term itself has three meanings: (1) any outlandish and unintelligible speech (from its root, Fr. *jargon, gargon,* a chattering, warbling— *Webster's Collegiate*); (2) the specialized language of a trade or profession, of a special skill or science; (3) any hybrid language. What all three definitions have in common is unintelligibility from the point of view of the outsider. Specialists have a right to special language, among themselves at least, and jargon in the second sense (above) is therefore obviously useful. The vocabulary peculiar to printers, to doctors, to miners, whatever its origin, is a shorthand for them. "Galley" is one thing to a printer and another to a sailor, and each usage is a form of jargon. Moreover, jargon is a means, within a specialty, for controlling reference and avoiding ambiguity. "Party of the first part" is not simply legal unction.

It is when such specialized vocabulary is used by those outside the specialty or when it is abused, for purposes of show, by those inside it that jargon becomes offensive. Then it not only keeps the outsider out, it gives him a strong suspicion that he is being patronized or bamboozled. This example, from a book on business management, was picked out for spoofing in *The New Yorker:*

> The Golden Rule is another codification of considerations which should govern our choice of actions lest we end by suboptimizing in terms of our interpersonal objectives.

The New Yorker queries: "What would you say if we told you that we already *had?*" The jargon here is from the social sciences, and the question a reader raises about it is whether or not the distinctive vocabulary is necessary to what is being said. Does it sharpen definition? What is lost if the sentence is simplified?

> If we don't obey the Golden Rule, we may not get along with people
> as well as we'd like to.

The aura of science is lost, but what kind of science is it that depends
for its communication on aura? Jargon of this type is something very
close to the occult language of astrologers, medical quacks, and circus
spielers, surely.

A conscientious writer can test his own sentences for jargon in several
ways. If a considerable number of abstract words accumulate in any
passage he writes, especially polysyllabic and Latinate ones, he is probably flirting with jargon. If he *feels* superior about using this or that
word, if the word charms him by its suggestion of specialized knowledge, he is carrying on a full-fledged courtship. And if he has reached
the stage of writing what he himself cannot paraphrase succinctly, he is
already victim of the sirens and will need some rhetorical Odysseus to
reclaim him.

What can he do? The simplest corrective is to ask himself several
questions about each word or phrase: "Is this necessary?" Then: "Can
it be said more simply without losing accuracy and completeness?"
Finally: "Is the complexity or lack of complexity in the matter referred
to represented by the language used about it?"

Here is another example of jargon:

> To form a rule or formula so as to evaluate the causation of this bane
> of humanity, wars, one would have to evolve a psychometer, so to
> speak, with which the occurrences of certain attitudes and involved
> coordinating factors could be gauged, compared, and in the ultimate
> contrast made self-evident in a social-science general rule.

That sentence is from a student's paper. It shows how imitative use of
jargon (evaluate the causation, evolve, occurrences of attitudes, coordinating factors) not only muddles a statement but deprives it of clear
rhetorical effect. A reader cannot tell whether this sentence is meant to
be ironic (the invention of a psychometer suggests that it may be) or
solemn (as the final clause seems to indicate). Nor can a reader be
entirely clear about what is being proposed. A sentence like this one
would be no clearer to the full-fledged social scientist than to the outsider; it is probably not more than half-clear to the man who wrote it.

Jargon is more than an irritant to the reader. It is an insidious friend
to the writer, for it gives him a sense of power and facility that he has
not earned by thought. He can compose in jargon without reflection and
with almost no reference to reality. In doing so, he produces prose that
has everything but sense, as the final example will show.

The involute texture, the superb annealing tensions and interlocking ambiguities of this poem make a cloistral threnody in which overtone and undertone transfuse and permeate the whole. Symbolically, the paradoxical voice shields the meaning, sheds the half-light of ironic reflection—or deflection, to be more exact—over the argument, binding the velleities of rhetoric ineluctably with the sinuous evaluative renderings of thought. This is suspension of disbelief superbly collated with recollection in tranquillity, a shaping spirit of the secondary imagination.

In such a swell of language, writer and reader alike go under.

TRITENESS. An accomplice to jargon is triteness, the use of expressions so worn out that they produce no reaction in the average reader and only weariness in the person who is widely read. Moreover, like jargon, they close the eyes and numb the minds of those who use them. A person who writes as the author of the following passage did not only *sees* nothing and *thinks* nothing but *tells* nothing to his reader:

It was with a *feeling of awe* that I first entered Harvard Yard. *A mist came before my eyes* and I spoke *in hushed tones* to the man who had brought me with him, the *mentor* of my school football team. Before me the brick and stone buildings *reared their heads* proudly into *the wide blue yonder.*

Across the *velvet sward* moved *bright youth and gray-headed age.* From beyond the walls came the *busy hum* of traffic and of the *daily round of life* on the Square. Here all was *as silent as the dead.* My *heart caught in my throat* and I said *in muted tones,* "So this is Harvard Yard!"

Happily, so disastrously bad a piece is rare. Yet, the trite term—or cliché, as it is often called—is always a temptation to the writer because it relieves him of the responsibility to probe his consciousness for a more precise expression of his thought. The temptation is increased for the student by the fact that the cliché may be new to him and therefore, from his point of view, not really trite at all, an unfortunate situation admirably described by Fowler in these words:

The hackneyed phrases are counted by the hundred, & those registered below are a mere selection. Each of them comes to each of us at some moment in life with, for him, the freshness of novelty upon it; on that occasion it is a delight, & the wish to pass on that delight is amiable; but we forget that of an hundred persons for whom we attempt this

good office, though there may be one to whom our phrase is new &
bright, it is a stale offence to the ninety & nine.

Modern English Usage

If, as Fowler says, the trite phrase does not always sound trite to the
man who uses it, how is a writer to know what to do? The plain fact is
that no one escapes triteness entirely; we all live, in part, by clichés,
moving from one set to another more sophisticated set (which generally
means another set used by fewer people). Yet a conscientious writer
does have some check on himself. For one thing, he can watch for frequent recurrence of phrases in his own work and check them for aptness
and accuracy of reference. He can force himself to paraphrase. He can
keep an eye out for overuse of such "blanket words" as *field, aspect,
area, level, element, factor*. He can cock an ear at conversation around
him, for in it he is almost certain to hear stock phrases tumbling out to
suit the stock responses most people have to whatever situations they
meet. And he can watch particularly for the metaphorical expression that
has gained currency by its liveliness and is already well on the way
toward the dustbin of cant (like "keep an eye out" and "cock an ear,"
above).

chapter six / *Syntax*

In the past fifty years more and more people (linguists, then teachers, then their pupils) have come to regard grammar as a matter of record, not of rule. They speak of it as *descriptive* rather than *prescriptive,* and they have ample historical justification for doing so. Just as Aristotle's *Poetics* is an account of the drama *as it was* in his day (with observations by the author and some expression of preference), so grammar is generally considered today to be an account of what is acceptable and accepted in the language of contemporary society. It is a fact that a good many of the "rules" generally considered sacrosanct are themselves of recent origin. So it is with the "shall-will" distinction for the future tense, the distinction between "which" (to introduce non-restrictive clauses) and "that" (to introduce restrictive clauses), the distinction between "farther" and "further." But it must not be forgotten —and the defenders of the descriptive point of view sometimes do forget—that the questions of rules is a complicated one.

There are at least four ways in which rules enter into discussions of languages, and they should be kept distinct. First, people sometimes use "rule" in the sense of "regularity," the sense it has in the phrase "as a rule." Thus, one might say, "It is a rule in English that an adjective precedes the noun it modifies," which means simply: "Speakers of English regularly say 'terrible nuisance' and the like rather than 'nuisance terrible.' " There seems to be little harm in this use of "rule," though of course anyone rigorously studying language must prefer the plainly descriptive statement to the ambiguous one. The first statement is ambiguous because it might also mean something like this: "Any grammar that attempts systematically to specify the sentences of English, and distinguish them from nonsentences, will have to contain a rule saying that the adjective precedes the noun." This is the second sense of "rule": "rule in a descriptive grammar." In neither of these senses does "rule" have any prescriptive force; it simply points to ways in which people actually do talk. Rules of the third kind, by contrast, are patently prescriptive. They are in effect *legislation* by supposed authorities on the way people should talk—often in self-righteous defiance of the way the language in fact works. Such was the rule about "which" and "that" noted above, a rule which taxes the ingenuity of even such an authority as Fowler, author of *Modern English Usage*. Rules like that sometimes take hold, and become part of the language, but more often they do not, as Fowler himself remarked in the passage which introduces this chapter. (Both of the preceding two sentences violate the rule, but we venture a guess that most readers did not even notice the violations, much less sense them as ungrammatical.) Rules of this third kind are what make the linguist's gorge rise, and indeed the writer, like the grammarian, may safely ignore them except when they offer useful advice about *clear* writing and do not pretend to establish standards of *grammatical* writing. Nor, in general, will the writer need to learn rules of the first two kinds, for he already knows a great deal about how his native language actually works in daily conversation.

But there is a fourth kind of rule, one which does merit the writer's attention. Such rules begin as descriptive, but what they describe is the careful speech and writing of educated people, not the casual speech of the whole language community. And since a writer, when he takes up his pen in earnest, usually wishes to emulate fluent and respected writers, he must take such rules as having a certain prescriptive authority. In a formal essay he will write "it does not," in a less formal one "it doesn't"; but except in humor or mimicry he should never write "it don't," since to do so will mark him for his reader as one who does not know the rules of Standard Formal English. The blunder is not a moral one, not a logical one, nor even a sin against the English language. It is more like a social lapse: "it don't" is simply the wrong thing for the occasion, though it would do well enough in other circumstances. In a sense, every child, when he learns to read and write, begins learning a partially new dialect, and upon his eventual mastery of this formal dialect depends his admission into the fellowship of educated men.

Rules of the fourth kind, then, distinguish formal writing and speech from casual talk, and the writer must be acquainted with them if he is to perform adequately. For the most part he will have little difficulty with them; no reader of this book is likely to treat "he don't" as Formal English. Yet there is a large area of indeterminacy, for of course even Standard Formal English is not nearly so homogeneous as the label makes it sound.

Moreover, even the relatively firm rules of formal usage have a way of changing. James Boswell sometimes wrote (to himself) in his journals at the end of an exciting day, "You was the great man today." The use of "was" with the second person was common in the eighteenth century and served to separate the singular from the plural "you." Less than two hundred years later, however, a biographer of Walt Whitman reproached the poet with "a rather meager education" for writing, in a letter to his mother, "I wish you was here." What happened in those two centuries was that the intervention of grammarians fastened "was" to the first and third persons only. Very possibly another two centuries will make even "it don't" respectable. Some of the currently popular (but not standard) forms will take longer to come into formal usage or may never get there at all. The prejudice against "ain't" and against such double negatives as "can't hardly" is so great that there is little likelihood of their early absorption. The point to be made is that forms of language alter. Changes usually come first in speech; they make their way into personal letters and diaries, then into creative expression (the dialogue of realistic drama and fiction, for example), and later into more somber studies and documents. The proliferation of ephemeral printed material in news-papers and popular periodicals hastens change; so also do the unceasing flood of words from radio and television and the constant mixing of cultures that results from easy, fast transportation. Formal education retards the process, yet even in a country like ours, which boasts of universal education, change goes on. There are new words constantly pushing into general use, old forms disappearing (and, curiously enough, reappearing), a vast unchartable mutation delightful to lexicographers and infinitely upsetting to the native learner, the foreign visitor, and the lover of things as they are.

Where, then, is the student to turn for guidance when in doubt? The answer is not an easy one. On the other hand, it is not nearly so complex as the last two paragraphs may lead him to fear. In the first place, he can always play safe, that is, observe the "rules" in any good handbook. His language may seem stiff at times, but it will always be acceptable and even respected. The one danger in this strict adherence to the guide books of language is the development of a kind of linguistic snobbery, a "purism" that too often leads the adherer to make essentially moral judgments on his fellows based solely on the degree of their respect for what are, after all, matters not necessarily of character or of conscience. If the student chooses this "safe" way, the history of language obligates him not to be unduly proud of his choice: he has picked the conservative gray flannel, knowing that it will serve him for most occasions, in pref-erence to a garment somewhat less adaptable but more self-expressive.

If he adopts a purely descriptive standard, if he determines that any form now in use is good enough by virtue of its existence, he will find his sensitivity to nuance dulled and his capacity to communicate markedly diminished. By this extremism, he impairs the power language has to sharpen his own intellectual processes and he impairs the power it has to provide communication with the thoughts and actions of others. If he is intellectually curious and naturally inventive and adventurous, he may, however, wish to free himself somewhat from the kind of minimum standard that a handbook provides. In that case, his course will be risky though exhilarating. Much of the richness of language lies beyond the rules, and it is there that this combination of historical knowledge and intelligent respect for current standards occurs. But the student who chooses this way must know more, not less, than the handbooks tell. Fortunately, the student ambitious enough to want such an acquaintance with language has today many good sources at hand. The *Oxford English Dictionary* traces changes in form and meaning, providing dates and examples in profusion. H. L. Mencken's *The American Language* is packed with information about the development of English in this country. Its style is at times witty, at times indignant and scornful, but its learning is generally sound, and its scope broad. Margaret Nicholson's *A Dictionary of American English Usage,* though sometimes finical, Eric Partridge's *Usage and Abusage,* and Bergen and Cornelia Evans's *A Dictionary of Contemporary American Usage* are volumes that every student should have on his desk alongside his dictionary. With these reliable resources at hand, almost any student with enough diligence to turn pages and enough interest to watch for the questionable spots in his own writing can venture with confidence into what someone on the staff of the *New Yorker* has called "the brier patch of English usage."

1/   Saying Things in English

The most remarkable achievement of human beings—speaking and understanding a language—is one that most people scarcely notice, so natural does it seem. Perhaps that's because they achieve it early and easily. No one teaches a child to speak: he simply learns, much as he learns to walk without going to a walking school. And he does so mainly before he is six years old. By that time he has mastered all the basic, yet incredibly complex, structures of his language, and from then on he lives "in" language as he lives in air—totally dependent on it, but rarely conscious of its presence.

There are many sides to his accomplishment (for example, his skill in speech acts, which we glanced at in Chapter Two), but the one that concerns us here is the ability to put sentences together when speaking or writing, and to understand their structure when someone else is speaking

or writing. Every normal child of ten can speak and understand an un-
limited number of sentences. He has, then, a creative capacity that is
literally infinite. Moreover, most of the sentences he produces or encounters are new to him. (Look back over the last twenty sentences in
this text, and think how unlikely it is that you ever saw or heard any one
of them before; yet you had no trouble recognizing them as sentences or
understanding them.) These facts show that human beings could not
possibly learn language sentence by sentence. Evidently they learn a
somewhat abstract set of rules which equip them to use language in
novel situations, to say and understand novel things. These are rules
in the second sense mentioned above—purely descriptive rules—and it
should now be clear that what they describe, taken as a group, is a
speaker's linguistic competence. To speak only a bit metaphorically,
each speaker has a grammar "in his head"; and the grammarian's task
is to discover the rules of that grammar.

So complex are the rules of English (and every natural language)
that no grammarian has succeeded in this. But the outlines of an adequate grammar are fairly clear, and we shall sketch them here very
roughly. We do so, of course, not in order to reveal which are the well-
formed sentences of English—you already know that, by and large—but
to point to some of the main structures of English that offer the writer a
choice of expressive means, and to discuss the consequences of some
of these choices.

The rules are of two kinds, called *phrase structure* and *transformational*. Phrase structure rules account for the basic simple structures
of a language, and they work in a way quite similar to the phrasing or
diagraming of school grammar. Hence the first rule of an English grammar is

Sentence ——→ Noun Phrase + Predicate

which reads, "a sentence is composed of a subject and a predicate." Let
us continue with a few more:

Noun Phrase ——→ Article + Noun
Pred ——→ Verb Phrase + Time
Verb Phrase ——→ Verb + Noun Phrase
Article ——→ the, a
Noun ——→ boy, soldiers, secretary, etc.
Verb ——→ believed, contradicted, respected, etc.
Time ——→ yesterday, today, then, etc.

These rules are equivalent to the following diagram:

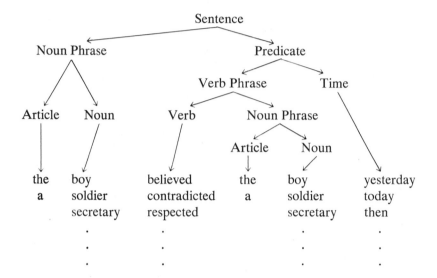

Reading across the bottom, you can see that the rules account for sentences like "A soldier respected the boy yesterday" and "The secretary believed the boy then," and, of course, many others that could be produced by adding new vocabulary items. All these are of one basic type, one structure.

Alternative rules produce other structures and other sentence types. For instance, another form for the Predicate is Verb[1] + Place. Subsequent rules:

> Verb[1] ⟶ sat, ran, stopped
> Place ⟶ Preposition + Noun Phrase[1]
> Preposition ⟶ in, at, etc.
> Noun Phrase[1] ⟶ Article + Noun[1]
> Noun[1] ⟶ park, school, hotel, etc.

Such rules gives us sentences like "The secretary stopped in a park" and "A soldier sat at a hotel." Other basic sentence types, like

> The chef has a cold,
> That animal is a wolverine,
> The movie was tedious,

are produced by similar rules that can be easily imagined.

For a variety of reasons, unimportant to this discussion, it is impossible to account for all the sentences of English by such rules. Apparently the grammar that speakers learn also contains rules—transformations —for altering and combining the elementary structures, thus producing more complex ones. One kind of transformation simply rearranges the elements of a given structure (and perhaps adds or deletes some). The passive transformation, for instance, can be expressed this way:

Noun Phrase[1] + Verb + Noun Phrase[2] ⇒
   Noun Phrase[2] + Was + Verb + By + Noun Phrase[1]

or, to apply the rule to one of our examples:

The soldier contradicted the secretary (yesterday) ⇒
   The secretary was contradicted by the soldier (yesterday).

We have given the rule in simplified form; it would have to be modified slightly (in obvious ways) to deal with verbs in other tenses. But if precisely stated, the passive transformation accounts for all passive sentences in English, by relating them to parallel active sentences. The economy is significant, since without the transformation, all the passive sentences would have to be built up by separate phrase structure rules. Of course this is a *mental* economy for the speaker, too: for any particular active sentence, he knows the appropriate passive, without "storing" it separately.

Other transformations of the same sort are responsible for "yes-no" questions—

The movie was tedious ⇒ Was the movie tedious? —

for "Wh" questions—

That animal is a wolverine ⇒ What is that animal?—

and imperatives—

You will leave this room ⇒ Leave this room.

- *Exercise 6.1:* Write a rule for each of these three transformations. Then see if you can write a more general rule for "Wh" questions, bearing in mind such varieties as the following:

The boy believed the soldier ⟹ Who believed the soldier?

The boy believed the soldier ⟹ Who(m) did the boy believe?
The boy believes the soldier ⟹ Who(m) does the boy believe?
The boy will believe the soldier ⟹ Who(m) will the boy believe?

The cat is eating a mouse ⟹ What is the cat eating?
The secretary stopped in a park ⟹ Where did the secretary stop?

(You will have to divide the verb into at least two parts: the main verb and an auxiliary.)

Many other transformations alter single structures, and thus contribute to the variety of English. But most of the complexity comes from another sort of transformation which combines two or more basic structures. What follows is a list of some of the most important of these.

CONJUNCTION.   When two basic structures are in part identical, they can be combined into one, with the identical part stated only once, and the nonidentical parts joined by *and*.

The child was pale
The child was sickly   ⟹ The child was pale and sickly.

The man tanned the skins
The boy tanned the skins   ⟹ The man and boy tanned the skins.

The man cured the skins
The boy cured the skins   ⟹ The man and the boy cured the skins.

The man and the boy cured the skins   ⟹ The man and the boy
The man and the boy tanned the skins   tanned and cured
                                              the skins.

And two structures not in part identical may be joined by *and,* preserving all their parts:

It started to rain
Edith ate a peach   ⟹ It started to rain, and Edith ate a peach.

NOMINALIZATION.   By a number of different transformations, one structure may be *embedded* in another, and serve the function of a noun phrase, usually after being somewhat altered.

I believe (something)
Tom went home   ⟹ I believe that Tom went home.

(Something) puzzled Bill ⎫
John failed   ⎬ ⇒ John's failing puzzled Bill.

I looked into (something)   ⎫ ⇒ I looked into his decision to
He decided to oppose the Governor ⎬   oppose the Governor.

(Someone) runs   ⎫
(Someone) is tired ⎬ ⇒ The runner is tired.

There are many other kinds of nominalizations; examine a few hundred words of prose from any source to see how many structures you can find that are acting as noun phrases but seem to be derived from underlying sentence-like structures.

VERBALIZATION. A basic structure can be made part of the verb—a "complement," as it is usually called.

I wanted (complement) ⎫
I (would) excel   ⎬ ⇒ I wanted to excel.

I wanted (complement) ⎫
Jane (would) excel   ⎬ ⇒ I wanted Jane to excel.

(Notice that the embedded structures are not noun phrases acting as direct objects; if they were, the passive transformation would apply, but "To excel was wanted by me" and "Jane to excel was wanted by me" are not sentences.)

He designed (complement) the building ⎫
The building (would) house 75 people ⎬ ⇒

*He designed to hold 75 people the building ⇒
He designed the building to hold 75 people

ADJECTIVE FORMATION. Most embedded structures that function as adjectives derive from a series of connected transformations. Here is a typical series:

The man was shouting ⎫
The man was furious   ⎬ ⇒ The man who was shouting was furious ⇒
The man shouting was furious ⇒
The shouting man was furious

Each successive transformation yields a well-formed sentence with an

---

* The asterisk indicates a sequence of words that does not form a sentence.

embedded adjectival structure. That is not quite true if we embed the second basic structure in the first, instead of vice versa:

The man who was furious was shouting =▶

*The man furious was shouting =▶

The furious man was shouting

In this sequence, the last transformation is obligatory, just as it was obligatory to change the order of "He designed to house 75 people the building."

• *Exercise 6.2:* In each of the sentences listed here, the italicized word or words are an imbedded structure serving as an adjective. Show how each sentence might have been derived from two basic structures, by a process similar to that sketched above:

The car *that I drive* is red.
The car *I prefer* is the Jaguar.
The man *sitting on the desk* is a millionaire.
The speaker, *an idealist,* convinced few people.
The *girl* bride was pitiable.
He found a church *destroyed by vandals.*
The *ruined* church overlooked the valley.

(Note: to derive the last two sentences, you will need to apply the passive transformation to one of the basic structures before embedding it.)

ADVERB FORMATION.   Adverbial structures answer questions such as "where?," "when?," "why?," and "how?." Many of them are transformationally derived.

I found it (there)   ⎱
George left it (somewhere)   ⎰ =▶ I found it where George left it.

I left (then)   ⎱   =▶ I left when she came =▶
She came (then)   ⎰   When she came, I left

I left (cause) ⎱   =▶ I left because she came =▶
She came   ⎰   Because she came, I left

He annoyed her (by some means) ⎱ =▶ He annoyed her by wagging
He wagged his finger   ⎰   his finger.

Adverbial clauses are mobile; they can often appear at any of several points in a sentence:

After paying her respects, the Duchess refused to speak to anyone there.

The Duchess, *after paying her respects,* refused to speak to anyone there.

The Duchess refused, *after paying her respects,* to speak to anyone there.

The Duchess refused to speak, *after paying her respects,* to anyone there.

The Duchess refused to speak to anyone there, *after paying her respects.*

Even from such a condensed presentation as this, it should not be hard to see how sentences of great complexity are built from extremely simple basic structures. For transformations can be compounded, one upon the other, until something like this is achieved:

. . . failed overseers, one-armed tinkers, bankrupt country store-keepers, reformed drunks, God-maddened paralytics, they were a bleak and undone brotherhood of true believers with scarcely a dollar to divide among them and only the hope of the soul's rescue through total immersion to preserve them and their goiterous women and pale, straw-haired, worm-infested children from absolute disintegration.

—WILLIAM STYRON, *The Confessions of Nat Turner*

Here the main underlying structure,

(the men) were a brotherhood of true believers.

has a great many others embedded in it, via a number of simple steps. For example, the phrase, "God-maddened paralytics" has its roots in two structures:

1. (the men) were paralytics
2. God had maddened the paralytics

The second of these goes through the passive transformation, to produce

the paralytics had been maddened by God,

to which the transformation that makes relative clauses applies:

the paralytics who had been maddened by God.

Then "who" and "had been" are deleted:

the paralytics maddened by God,

and finally, a transformation that reverses the noun and the participle and drops out "by" applies:

the God-maddened paralytics.

At this point, the phrase is embedded in structure (1) above:

(the men) were God-maddened paralytics.

This structure is in turn combined, by conjunction, with a number of others derived in various ways from base structures, to produce

(the men) were failed overseers, one-armed tinkers, . . .
    God-maddened paralytics.

Then this composite phrase itself goes through the relative clause transformation, and the transformation that deletes "who" and "were," and the result is embedded in the main underlying structure:

(the men), failed overseers, one-armed tinkers, . . .
God-maddened paralytics, were a brotherhood of true believers.

Another transformation replaces "the men" by the pronoun "they," another series embeds the adjective "bleak" and the adjectival "undone," and the first half of the sentence is in its final form.

• *Exercise 6.3:*   Sketch a derivation for the second half of the sentence, beginning with these underlying structures:

    the true believers had (complement) scarcely a dollar
    the true believers (would) divide the dollar among the true believers
    the true believers had (complement) (something)
    (something) (would) preserve the true believers from (something)
    (something) (would) preserve their children from (something)
    their women were goiterous
    their children were pale
    their children were (adjective)

worms infested their children
the true believers (would) disintegrate absolutely
their women (would) disintegrate absolutely
the true believers hoped (for something)
something would rescue the soul through (some means)
(someone) (would) immerse (someone) totally

2/ Structure and Choice

Back at the beginning of the chapter we remarked on the ability of human beings to understand (and produce) an infinite number of sentences which for the most part they have never heard or spoken before. For instance, unless you had read *The Confessions of Nat Turner* it is highly unlikely that you had ever encountered the sentence about the brotherhood of true believers, or any other sentence that is like it in a superficial way. Yet presumably you had little trouble recognizing it as an English sentence, or understanding it. The foregoing sketch of English structure indicates why Styron's sentence, like all complex ones, has a structure like this:

Phrase structure rules
↓
underlying structures
↓
transformations
↓
final form

There are a limited and manageable number of phrase structure rules and transformations; because these can combine in an endless variety of ways, there is an infinite number of final sentence forms. Yet the mind can relate any of those final forms to the simple underlying structures, and so to the relationships between word and word that the phrase structure rules represent.

Another way to look at the matter: there are relatively few basic ways to get an experience or fact or situation into English words and structures:

The woman read a novel
the cat slept
the beer is in the refrigerator
the road is long
the thief has a limp

And so on. Forms like these (built up by phrase structure rules) offer the only way we have to represent our thought and experience in language. Forms like these also make up the underlying structures of all English sentences. So it is fair to say that the underlying structure of a sentence carries all of its basic meaning—all of its meaning which can be put in *propositions*. However many transformations an underlying structure goes through, the meaning it embraces is still conveyed by the sentence in final form. For instance, the phrase "God-maddened paralytics," from Styron's sentence, conveys to a reader the same meaning as its underlying structure, "God had maddened the paralytics," even though "God-maddened" works as an adjective, while in the underlying structure "God" is a noun and "maddened" is a verb.

On the other hand, the final form of a sentence does convey meaning of a different kind—shading, emphasis, angle of vision, attitude: in short, the speaker's or writer's personal way of looking at things. For instance, consider the difference between

> The overseers had failed. The tinkers had one arm. The country storekeepers were bankrupt. The drunks had reformed. God had maddened the paralytics.

and

> failed overseers, one-armed tinkers, bankrupt country storekeepers, reformed drunks, God-maddened paralytics

The two versions communicate the same information. The first one, however, seems to emphasize the individual calamities that afflict the men, while the second makes the men seem all of a type, sharers of a general disaster. This effect the second version owes to the two main ways in which its underlying structures are altered and combined. The varying predicates ("had failed," "had one arm," "were bankrupt," and so on) have all been transformed into modifiers, and placed in identical positions before their nouns. Functioning as adjectives, they make the disasters seem almost like innate qualities of the men. And, since the modifiers are all in the same form, they suggest that the overseers, tinkers, drunks, and the rest are all pretty much in the same fix. The other transformation that collaborates in this effect is conjunction, which coordinates all the nouns, and so implies that all the men are more or less alike. We can say, then, that the two versions convey exactly the same information, but do so with quite different inflections because of the different relationships between underlying structure and final form.

All this adds up to something important for the writer, if he is interested in his style, and in the overtones of what he is writing. Suppose that he knows roughly what information he wants to include; that is to say, that he knows what propositions are to form the base of what he writes. In effect, then, he has in mind his underlying structures. But not the final form of his sentences. So an enormous range of choices is open to him—choices of structure and arrangement which are also choices of emphasis, point of view, and the rest. Naturally, the writer does not—no writer could—first get clearly in mind all his underlying structures, and then run them through a series of transformations. (Transformations are not mental processes, simply rules.) But he can make himself aware of choices open to him, and of the consequences that follow one choice or another. "Playing" with the grammatical possibilities for style and rhetoric helps build this kind of awareness.

Here, for an example, is a list of basic propositions, which we can take, roughly, as underlying structures (their subject is William Jennings Bryan):

I confess something
  People talk of sincerity
  The talk fatigues me
The fellow may have been sincere
Then P. T. Barnum was sincere
Such uses disgrace the word
  The word is "sincere"
Such uses degrade the word
In fact Bryan was a charlatan
In fact Bryan was a mountebank
In fact Bryan was a zany
Bryan had no sense
Bryan had no dignity
Bryan had a career
  The career brought Bryan into contact with the first men of his time
Bryan preferred the company of ignoramuses
  The ignoramuses were rustic
I watched Bryan at Dayton
  Something was hard to believe
Bryan had traveled
People had received Bryan in societies
  The societies were civilized
Bryan had been a high officer of state
Bryan seemed only a poor clod like those clods
  Those clods were around him
A theology deluded Bryan
  The theology was childish

     Bryan was full of hatred
       The hatred was almost pathological
     Bryan hated all learning
     Bryan hated all human dignity
     Bryan hated all beauty
     Bryan hated all things
       The things were fine
       The things were noble
     Bryan was a peasant
       The peasant had come home to the barnyard

Choosing these units of content determines what will be said about
Bryan, and to some extent determines the tone (it would not be easy to
achieve an amiable or flattering tone with this material). But a wide
range of expressive possibilities remains open.

Suppose, for instance, that the writer wants to achieve a swift, continuous rhythm, and a sense that all the content is closely connected, of a
piece. He might produce a version like this one, which relies heavily on
the conjunction and relative clause transformations:

1. This talk of sincerity fatigues me, and I confess it, for if the fellow
    was sincere, then P. T. Barnum was sincere, and such uses de-
    grade and disgrace the word "sincere," but in fact Bryan was a
    charlatan, a mountebank, and a zany, who had no sense and no
    dignity, and though his career brought him into contact with the
    first men of his time, he preferred the company of rustic ignor-
    amuses. I watched him at Dayton, and it was hard to believe that
    he had traveled, and that people had received him in civilized
    societies, and that he had been a high officer of state, for he
    seemed only a poor clod like those who were around him, and
    he was deluded by a theology that was childish, and he was full of
    a hatred that was almost pathological, of all learning and all
    human dignity and all beauty and all things that were fine and
    noble, and he was a peasant who had come home to the barnyard.

This style seems to blend all the material together, as if the writer is
caught in a flow of ideas, but is unwilling or unable to sort them out.
And of course sharp emphasis is absent.

For an almost opposite style—one that puts great emphasis on each
new item, word, or phrase, one might try deleting connectives and unnecessary phrases wherever possible, actually stripping down the underlying structures and leaving them pretty much separate:

2. I confess. This talk fatigues me—talk of sincerity. If the fellow

was sincere, so was P. T. Barnum. Sincere! Such uses disgrace the word. Degrade it.

In fact Bryan was a charlatan. A mountebank. A zany. He had no sense, no dignity.

He had a career. It brought him into contact with the first men of his time. He preferred the company of ignoramuses. Rustic ignoramuses. I watched him at Dayton. Hard to believe: he had traveled; people had received him in civilized societies. A high officer of state.

He seemed only a poor clod. Like those around him.

A childish theology deluded him. He was full of hatred. Almost pathological hatred. Of all learning. Of all human dignity, beauty, fine and noble things.

A peasant. A peasant come home to the barnyard.

Here the mind of the writer seems stunned by each new fact or idea; he offers each in its turn as if it spoke for itself, and needed no interpretation. Here, too, the tone is very different from that of version (1). The author seems much more indignant and superior.

Another way to render the material is to rely as heavily as possible on embedded adverbial structures of cause, time, and so on:

3. This talk of sincerity fatigues me, I confess, because such uses degrade and disgrace the word. If the fellow was sincere, then so was P. T. Barnum. Having no sense and no dignity, Bryan was a charlatan, a mountebank, and a zany, and thus, although his career had brought him into contact with the first men of his time, he preferred the company of rustic ignoramuses. Since he seemed only a poor clod like those around him, it was hard to believe, watching him at Dayton, that he had been a high officer of state, and that, traveling, he had been received in civilized societies. Because he was deluded by a childish theology, he was full of an almost pathological hatred of all learning, human dignity, beauty, fine and noble things. He was a peasant who had come home to the barnyard.

The writer of this version is doing what neither of the others did—connecting the bits of content intellectually, seeing relationships and causes. The view of Bryan that results is also different: the man's character seems more rationally comprehensible, more subject to analysis and explanation, than in the first two versions, where Bryan appeared almost as a freak.

Versions (4) and (5) are a contrasting pair. (4) gets through the main business of each sentence—subject and verb—rather quickly, and appends "extra" material in structures that follow the noun they modify. (Recall that such moʊifiers are created by the relative clause transformation and its successor.) Version (5) amasses clauses and phrases *before* the main underlying structure, building what are traditionally called "periodic" sentences. (Analyze the transformation used in (5) and try to characterize the effects of both versions.)

4. I confess myself fatigued by this talk of sincerity. If the fellow was sincere, P. T. Barnum was sincere—the word disgraced and degraded by such uses. Neither sense nor dignity had Bryan, a charlatan, a mountebank, a zany. He had a career that brought him into contact with the first men of his time; he preferred the company of rustic ignoramuses. It was hard to believe, watching him at Dayton, that Bryan, a high officer of state, a traveler, had been received in societies that were civilized. He seemed only a poor clod, like those around him. Bryan, full of an almost pathological hatred, hating all learning, all human dignity, all beauty, and all things fine and noble, deluded by a childish theology was a peasant come home to the barnyard.

5. That this talk of sincerity fatigues me, I confess. If the fellow was sincere, if P. T. Barnum was sincere, the word "sincere" is disgraced and degraded. A charlatan, a mountebank, a zany with no sense and no dignity, brought by his career into contract with the first men of his time, Bryan preferred the company of rustic ignoramuses. That he had traveled, that he had been received in civilized societies, that he had been a high officer of state, was hard to believe, watching him at Dayton. Like those around him, full of an almost pathological hatred of all learning, all human dignity, all beauty, all fine and noble things, Bryan was a peasant come home to the barnyard.

• *Exercise 6.4:* Here are five more versions. Try to determine the transformational origins of each, and analyze the kind of tone, emphasis, and point of view that each achieves. Then try a version or two of your own.

6. I am fatigued, I confess, by this talk, disgracing and degrading the word, of sincerity. The fellow may, perhaps, have been sincere, but so, then, was P. T. Barnum. Bryan, in fact, was a charlatan— he had no dignity; a zany—he had no sense; a mountebank. He preferred, though his career had brought him into contact with the first men of this time, the company of ignoramuses. It was hard, watching him at Dayton, to believe that he had traveled, that he had been a high officer of state, for he seemed, like those around

him, only a poor clod. A theology, a childish one, deluded him, and a hatred almost pathological, filled him. All learning, all human dignity, all beauty he hated, and all fine, all noble, things. He had come, a peasant, home to the barnyard.

7.   When sincerity is talked of, I am fatigued, I confess. If the fellow was sincere, then so was P. T. Barnum. The word "sincere" is disgraced and degraded by such uses. It may be asserted that Bryan was a charlatan, a mountebank, and a zany with no sense or dignity. By his career he was brought into contact with the first men of his time. The company of rustic ignoramuses was preferred.

Bryan was watched by me at Dayton, and it was not easily believed that he had traveled, had been received in societies that were civilized, had been a high officer of state. He seemed only a poor clod like those around him. He was deluded by a childish theology, and full of an almost pathological hatred. All learning, human dignity, and beauty were hated by Bryan. All fine and noble things were hated, too. He was a peasant who had come home to the barnyard.

8.   People talk of sincerity. I confess something. This talk fatigues me. The fellow may have been sincere. Then so was P. T. Barnum. Such uses disgrace the word. They degrade it. In fact, Bryan was a charlatan. He was a mountebank. He was a zany. Bryan had no sense. He had no dignity. His career brought him into contact with the first men of his time. Bryan preferred the company of rustic ignoramuses.

He had traveled. He had been received in civilized societies. He had been a high officer of state. I watched him at Dayton, and this was hard to believe. There were poor clods around Bryan. Bryan was like them.

A theology deluded Bryan. The theology was childish. He was full of hatred. The hatred was almost pathological. Bryan hated all learning. He hated all human dignity. He hated all beauty. He hated all fine and noble things.

Bryan was a peasant. The peasant had come home to the barnyard.

9.   I confess: this talk of sincerity fatigues me. Was the fellow sincere? Then so was P. T. Barnum. Such uses degrade and disgrace the word "sincere." In fact, Bryan was a charlatan, a mountebank, a zany. Did he have any sense or dignity? No. His career brought him into contact with the first men of his time, did he not prefer the company of rustic ignoramuses? I watched

Bryan at Dayton. It was hard to believe: he had traveled, been received in civilized societies, been a high officer of state. A poor clod, like those around him, was what he seemed. He was deluded by a theology, a childish one. The hatred he was full of was almost pathological. Did he not hate all learning? Did he not hate all human dignity? All beauty? All fine and noble things? A peasant, surely, come home to the barnyard.

10. My confession is that this talk of sincerity fatigues me. If the fellow possessed sincerity, then so did P. T. Barnum. Such uses of the word are a disgrace and a degradation. Bryan's having no sense or dignity was a fact, as was his being a charlatan, a mountebank, and a zany. His career brought him into contact with the first men of his time, but his preference was for the company of rustic ignoramuses. Watching him at Dayton, it was hard to believe: his having traveled, his having been received in civilized societies, his having been a high officer of state. He seemed only a poor clod like those around him. A childish theology deluded him. He was full of an almost pathological hatred: a hatred of all learning, of all human dignity, of all beauty and all fine and noble things. He was a peasant who had come home to the barnyard.

Finally, here is the passage the way H. L. Mencken originally wrote it, in an essay called "In Memoriam: W. J. B."

This talk of sincerity, I confess, fatigues me. If the fellow was sincere, then so was P. T. Barnum. The word is disgraced and degraded by such uses. He was, in fact, a charlatan, a mountebank, a zany without sense or dignity. His career brought him into contact with the first men of his time; he preferred the company of rustic ignoramuses. It was hard to believe, watching him at Dayton, that he had traveled, that he had been received in civilized societies, that he had been a high officer of state. He seemed only a poor clod like those around him, deluded by a childish theology, full of an almost pathological hatred of all learning, all human dignity, all beauty, all fine and noble things. He was a peasant come home to the barnyard.

Having worked through ten versions of the same passage, you may be interested in how Mencken himself continued it:

Imagine a gentleman, and you have imagined everything that he was not. What animated him from end to end of his grotesque career was simply ambition—the ambition of a common man to get his hand upon the collar of his superiors, or, failing that, to get his thumb into their eyes. He was born with a roaring voice, and it had the trick of inflaming half-wits. His whole career was devoted to raising those half-wits against their betters that he himself might shine.

It should be easy to see the same marks of style here that characterize the previous section of the passage. (How does Mencken achieve the epigrammatic quality of his prose? How would the writers of versions 1–3 have rendered this second part?)

The ten versions of Mencken presented here are only ten out of an enormous number of possibilities. For all practical purposes, the writer has an infinite number of ways in which he can render any extended set of ideas or observations. If he were actually to view his task as that of scanning all the possibilities before choosing one, he would quickly lose all sense of style, and grind to a stop. But it is a good idea to keep in mind the constant availability of choices, so that you do not become a prisoner of just one habitual style. And conscious practice, of the sort urged here, can help a good deal to keep choices open, and even to turn up some unexpected ones.

3/ Phrases

We have just been insisting that a good part of sentence construction is a matter of choice. Some part is not—not, at least, for the writer who wants to be clear and consistent. In this section and the next we offer specific advice on points of this sort.

PARTICIPIAL PHRASES

Some phrases are transformationally derived. These include participial phrases, as we have seen. Their form causes little difficulty, but their placement in the main underlying structure can be troublesome.

Probably more students are familiar with the classic blunder in the use of participial phrases than with the particular effects achievable by correct use of them. To move from the familiar to the unfamiliar, then, is to begin with that cardinal error, the *dangling participle*. Considering the prominence it has in most handbooks of grammar, it is remarkable how persistently it continues to disgrace the writing not only of students but of others who might reasonably be expected to avoid it. Part of the persistence is due, no doubt, to its innocence and convenience. Only in such "boners" as

Wearing a red shirt, the bull attacked the unfortunate man

does it offend and amuse the general reader. And were it not for the confusion a dangling participle often causes, it would not deserve further attention. That it does cause confusion is evident in a sentence like this:

> Defending liberty with such vigor, my opinion is that Milton in his *Areopagitica* is the leading libertarian of his time.

Who or what is "defending"? The answer can be solved, of course, but one writes to inform a reader, not to puzzle him. The construction of such a sentence is, therefore, indefensible. Such confusion can usually be avoided by keeping a simple rule in mind: the participial modifier should come as close as possible to the word it modifies. Not:

> Having no grounds for his argument, it seems to me that Alcibiades decided to rely on rhetoric in order to defend his position.

But this:

> It seems to me that, having no grounds for his argument, Alcibiades decided to rely on rhetoric in order to defend his position.

Wherever possible it is wise to avoid separating subject and predicate verb by the participial expression:

> Alcibiades, having no grounds for his argument, decided to rely on rhetoric in order to defend his position.

> CORRECTED: Having no grounds for his argument, Alcibiades decided to rely on rhetoric in order to defend his position.

The earlier sentence about Milton is so awkward that relief can be found only in complete revision:

> Milton's vigorous defense of freedom in the *Areopagitica* makes him, in my opinion, the leading libertarian of his time.

So much for the abuse of the participle. What of its effective use? The principal utility of the participle seems to lie in its power to create a sense of *simultaneity*.

> Cassius spoke cautiously to Brutus, measured each word with care, and increased his fervor at each sign of impatience in Brutus' face.

CORRECTED: Cassius spoke cautiously to Brutus, measuring each word with care and increasing his fervor at each sign of impatience in Brutus' face.

In these examples, "spoke" indicates an action which *includes* the other verbs. Turning "measured" and "increased" into participles makes the inclusion clear and gives the reader an almost graphic realization that the actions of measuring and increasing go on during the speaking and are a part of it.

Moreover, participles make it possible to establish clearly the relationship of two periods of time within a single sentence:

Although he tried repeatedly to do so, Coleridge could never recapture the vision of "Kubla Khan" which came to him in a dream that was interrupted by the untimely intrusion of a visitor.

CORRECTED: Although he tried repeatedly to do so, Coleridge could never recapture the vision of "Kubla Khan," the product of a dream interrupted by the untimely intrusion of a visitor.

Participles, present and past, also serve as instruments of *unification*. In this sentence

The sighting of the new star, which was later named Pluto, was made possible only by the development of a more powerful telescope.

improvement might be made by reducing the dependent clause to a participial phrase:

The sighting of the new star, later named Pluto, was made possible only by. . . .

Such use of the participial phrase is almost too common to warrant mention, and its abuses—largely those of misplacement—are relatively infrequent. The use of the participle in so-called "absolute" constructions, however, is less common though fully as useful as a unifying device:

He climbed out of the ring, his ears nearly deafened by the roar of the crowd around him.

Its oars rising and falling rhythmically, the first shell swept around the bend of the river and into the final stretch.

Here the participial constructions attach relevant information to the main clauses and thus unify the action described in them.

PREPOSITIONAL PHRASES

Mention has already been made of the important role which the position of words plays in conveying the meaning of a sentence. The need for a considerable fixity of position in English is obvious, for without it the relationships between the various nouns in a sentence and between the nouns and verbs would quickly become obscure. If position were all that English could rely on to establish relationship, however, it would be a very inflexible language. That it is not falls partly to the credit of the preposition. Although position is principally responsible for our understanding the relationships in a sentence like this

> He gave the girl the money.

it is through prepositions that relationships are conveyed in sentences like this

> The girl in the bank put her pen on the counter.

A simple test of the importance of prepositions is to block out all of them in a brief passage of prose and then try to understand the meaning without them:

> Genuine crises are rare. Various times, civil and religious disputes have filled the air lasting and deafening clamor, yet leading vital transformations. The political and social foundations State were never shaken or even called question. Hence they cannot be regarded genuine crises. We find examples this firstly the Wars the Roses England, which the people trooped one two factions nobility and the Court, and secondly the French Wars Religion, where actual fact the main issue lay the followers two noble houses, and the question was whether the King would maintain his position independently either, or which he would join.

While it is possible to guess at the prepositions omitted in many places, especially where idioms are involved ("called *in* question," for instance), the nature of the relationship between nouns and between nouns and verbs becomes ambiguous in many others. It is those relationships that the preposition clarifies when it is properly and accurately used.

As its name implies, the preposition is not used alone; it always has an object which is, grammatically, a noun or a pronoun or some word acting as surrogate for a noun or pronoun:

We are going *to his house.*

He delights *in singing.*

He came *from New York.*

Where did he come *from?*

This combination, known as the prepositional phrase, is generally used as a modifier (adjectival or adverbial) within the sentence:

The man *on the horse* is a polo player. (adjectival)

He strikes the ball *with a mallet.* (adverbial)

Its use as subject or object of the verb is either elliptic or awkward or both:

In the air is better than *on the ground.*

At my house will be satisfactory.

Considering the many functions of the prepositional phrase in its adjectival and adverbial roles, it seems wise, therefore, to separate it entirely from the subject-object functions, and formal writing generally respects that separation.

As modifiers, prepositional phrases act like one-word adjectives and adverbs. They name attributes of nouns (the girl *in blue*) when they are adjectival. When they are adverbial, they express one of the usual adverbial relationships: those of time, place, direction, derivation, condition, consequence, exclusion or inclusion, means, manner, or agency. Like one-word adverbs they usually precede the adjectives they modify and may either precede or follow the verbs they modify. The word "usually" is needed for any statement about the placement of prepositional phrases: because they are supplements to the "main line" of the sentence—subject-verb-object—they are relatively instable and quite susceptible to the demands of emphasis, rhythm, and euphony as well as to those of logical relationship.

The difference between the two following sentences is one of emphasis:

He put down his knapsack in the middle of the room.

In the middle of the room he put down his knapsack.

The difference between these is one of clarity:

> They poured the syrup which they had spent all afternoon boiling out of the bucket.

> They poured out of the bucket the syrup which they had spent all afternoon boiling.

And between the sentence immediately above and the one below the difference is one of rhythm and euphony:

> The syrup which they had spent all afternoon boiling they now poured out of the bucket.

Problems of placement do not yield readily to solutions by rule. A writer has to be alert to detect the possibilities of confusion from bad placement and sensitive to the sound of language to detect those placements which offend the natural rhythm of English or throw emphasis where it is not wanted. Although the same alertness and sensitivity would certainly prevent other abuses of the prepositional phrase, it is possible to make concrete suggestions for a few, not as a substitute for alertness and sensitivity, but as an aid where they may not be sufficiently acute to be a guide.

A. There are much worse sins than leaving a preposition at the end of a sentence. In speech even the most fastidious users of language are likely to do so on occasion; in formal writing, however, the preposition is usually joined firmly to its object. Some of the uses objected to by the overly cautious are not really abuses of prepositional unity at all but are simply emphatic placements of adverbs so closely attached to the verbs they modify that they constitute a part of the verb: "That is treatment he is not willing to *put up with*." It was a secretary's correction of such a locution that is said to have led Winston Churchill to write in the margin, "This is the kind of nonsense up with which I will not put."

B. Much worse than the "dangling" preposition is the overuse of compound prepositions, especially of those whose metaphorical ground has been obscured by time: *on the basis that, in terms of, in consideration of the fact that,* and so on. A paragraph full of such prepositional structures so far divorces the active words of the sentence that a kind of miasma begins to rise from it, covering its movement and its meaning:

> In respect to the terms of the agreement made on the basis of a consideration of the factors in the case, we are of the opinion that to act in the sense of the terms in this instance without more examination concerning the possible effects on the ground of damage to other parties in the situation would not be in the interests of anyone.

C. Any *succession* of prepositional phrases is likely to confuse a reader because it presents a string of qualifiers separated from the words they qualify. Even when the meaning is not obscured by such a succession, the elegance of the sentence may be injured.

D. Occasionally the practice of separating a preposition from its object leads a writer to repeat it unintentionally:

> The shrubs along the road *in* which he had for the last two hours been crouching *in* were thick enough to conceal him completely.

To expose such a repetition is to condemn it.

E. The most serious misuse of prepositional phrases, and probably the most common, is that arising from indifference to meaning. "With," for instance, has become a jack-of-all-prepositional-trades; "in" and "into" are carelessly interchanged; "by" is used to mean "beside"; "off of" is substituted for "off" in defiance of logic. There is nothing harder for a foreigner to get used to than the prepositions in our language when they are correctly used; considering the cavalier treatment some of them habitually receive, it is not surprising that they are frequently confusing even to natives. Only a laborious catalogue would make it possible to establish the significance of each English preposition, and a complete catalogue, if it included all current usages, would undoubtedly show so much overlapping that most distinctions would become questionable. The best single piece of advice may be this: since prepositions are relational in their function, it is wise to think, whenever possible, about their relational intention in physical terms to prevent misuse. It ought certainly to eliminate such sentences as these:

> *With* such people all you can do is hope they will change.

> He sings *with* a high voice.

> If you want to succeed *with* some other means, you are free to try.

> He came back to the house *with* his hat lost.

> He earns his living *with* the sweat of his brow.

INFINITIVE AND GERUND PHRASES

The infinitive phrase is a convenient but not very flexible structure. Its most natural use is as object of a verb or as appositive:

> He wants *to spend his vacation in Bermuda.*

> His plan *to do so* was foiled by an accident.

As subject of the verb, the infinitive phrase is rather formal and not common to speech, in which it is likely to be replaced by a gerund.

> *To see* is to believe. (*Seeing* is believing.)

The gerund, or verbal noun, is used as nouns are most commonly used—as subject or object of a verb, as object of a preposition:

> *Climbing* the mountain is more fun than *descending* it.
>
> He thinks his success comes from *waiting*.
>
> They tried *running* in pairs but soon gave up *trying*.

Both the infinitive phrase and the gerund phrase provide ways of maintaining the vitality and movement implicit in a verb. At the same time, they make the action figure as the thing talked about in the sentence. Their grammatical peculiarities cause little difficulty except in connection with the agent of the action they imply. Despite the fact that they function as nouns, they retain some of their verbal character, grammatically speaking. Thus, although they may themselves be subjects or objects of a verb, they also have subjects and objects; and the form of their subjects is often mishandled. The logic of the distinctions may be omitted here, but the distinctions themselves need brief mention:

A. The subject of an infinitive is in the objective case:

> She wants *him* to go alone.

B. The subject of the action implied in a gerund is in the possessive:

> She approves *his* trying to go alone.
>
> They like Mary's singing.

The so-called dangling or detached infinitive—

> To treat first matters first, the ship is too slow for our needs.

—is frowned upon by some, but its only disadvantage seems to lie in the possibility of confusion. In the example given above, no one is likely to think that the infinitive phrase modifies "ship"; in the one that follows the construction is less defensible because it does create some ambiguity:

> This is a means, to do him justice, by which some good may be accomplished.

This section began with simplification. The English sentence, it stated, is basically a simple structure. It then discussed and demonstrated some of the structural variety and the complexities possible within it. Both may be summed up in another simplistic formula that may prove useful:

who (what)? + does (is)? what   [+ to whom (what)?]

Here, the emphasis is not on form but on the meaning of the sentence. The usefulness of such a formula will become apparent in the next chapter, where paragraph and whole essay are considered. At this point, it is mentioned only because it is one of those handy devices for testing prose already written and now ready for revision. If any of the three questions (the third is not always relevant, of course, as in "The sun shines") cannot readily and clearly be answered in the words of the sentence under examination, something is wrong. If the answer those words give, taken by itself, sounds indefinite or confused, clarification is in order. The metaphor of action which the formula uses makes a reviser sensitive to unnecessary abstractness and abstruseness. If he has it in mind, he will not in conscience be able to retain a sentence like this one:

> The motivational components of the action of collectivities are organized systems of the motivation of the relevant individual actors.

4/ Consistency in Viewpoint

Consistency in viewpoint may be examined under five separate headings.

Person. There are, grammatically speaking, three persons in English: the first person (speaker), the second person (person spoken to), and the third person (person spoken about). Consistency demands that there be no unmeaningful shifts in person, and that sentences be so constructed as to eliminate ambiguity of person. To write

> Everyone likes pleasure, but you shouldn't be its slave

is to move, for no adequate reason, from the third person ("Everyone") to the second ("you"). A proper choice of pronoun for the second clause not only corrects the grammatical error but improves the rhetorical quality of the sentence:

> Everyone likes pleasure, but no one should be its slave.

The phrase above "for no adequate reason," is meant to catch the eye. As a matter of fact, there is *a* reason for the shift in the illustrative sentence, even though it is not an "adequate" reason. Modern English actually uses *two* persons for the indefinite pronoun rather than the traditional *one*. In colloquial speech we commonly use "you" to indicate the indefinite, saying, "When you try to figure out a problem like this, you invariably discover the depth of your ignorance." The "you" of this sentence is not the person-spoken-to but the person-spoken-about. Actually, the person-spoken-about in this situation seems to make a more intimate inclusion of the speaker himself and of the person-spoken-to than does the indefinite "one." In more formal discourse, we adopt a generic noun ("a man," "a person") or an indefinite pronoun ("anyone," "someone"); more and more rarely, in American English, does the once-traditional form "one" appear. No matter which form is used, however, the rule of consistency stands; it is bad to shift persons unmeaningfully.

Number. Like shifts in person, shifts in number generally stem either from carelessness or from the confusion that still marks the activity of the indefinite pronouns in English. That a student, after years of the study of English, should write

> The practice of simony, like that of gaining indulgences, were common in the medieval church

is inexcusable; that one should get tripped up in a sentence like

> Everyone has their own way of doing things

is, considering the double suggestion in "everyone," not entirely surprising. A careful grammarian would point out that "one" is singular and is so considered by the writer since he employs a singular form of the verb; pragmatists point out that "every-" obviously implies more than one and has good cause to assert its plurality in the adjective "their" even if it does not do so in the verb. The debate about these pronouns rages wherever English is taught, and differences in use occur wherever it is spoken. But the practice of treating what the textbooks consider to be singular pronouns as though they are plural if the sense of plurality can be inferred appears to be increasing and now occurs even in the speech of educated people. It is not, however, commonly encountered in the serious writing of those people, and it is on such ground that a stand affirming the rightness of the singular concept of the indefinite pronouns *everyone, anyone, no one* must rest:

> Everyone has his own way of doing things.

Maintaining consistency in number is necessary not only within the sentence but also in the sequence of sentences. If not absolutely wrong, it is at least confusing to write:

> *Soldiers* highly trained in the convention of traditional warfare *are* often terrified by the irregular. *The soldier* cannot accommodate *himself* to the tactic which *he has* never encountered. So it was with the Roman *troops* when *they* faced the unorthodox attacks of the barbarians from the North.

Tense. Consistency in the use of tenses does not limit the writer to the use of a single tense within a sentence or passage, but it does limit him to a sequence. The most common errors in tense found on students' papers come from failure to understand the relationships indicated in this grouping.

I		II	
present tense		past tense	
perfect tense		past perfect tense	
future tense		conditional tense	
auxiliaries:	may	auxiliaries:	might
	can		could
	shall, will		should, would
	has, have		had

Crossing the tenses of one group with the other may disturb the time balance in a sentence:

> If Arnold *has not used* the phrase "sweetness and light" so frequently, the importance he *attaches* to it *would be* less apparent than he *wanted* it to be.

> CORRECTED: If Arnold *had not used* the phrase "sweetness and light" so frequently, the importance he *attached* to it *would have been* less apparent than he *wanted* it to be.

The ramifications of tense order are many but the little chart above is a simple and handy guide for the most common perplexities of this sort.

One further note about tense is relevant here. The present tense is a particularly lively one in English. It not only indicates current action:

> I *see* your books are new

and habitual action:

> I *hear* the opera every Christmas

and future action:

> He *goes* to Paris next spring

but is also useful in animating the past, particularly in narrative passages:

> Lincoln *strides* into the committee room, his face rigid with anger

and in presenting textual analysis:

> In this episode, Homer *introduces* the goddess who is to watch over the fortunes of Telemachus and Odysseus throughout their adventures.

The use of the present tense in textual analysis is so important to the writer of critical essays that it deserves emphasis. If he is referring to a source and his interest is in the content of the source, not the historical situation in which it appeared, he should use the present tense:

> Professor Wilson *suggests* that "solid" is actually a misreading for *"sordid"* in Hamlet's famous lament, "O that this too too solid flesh would melt!"

This use of the present tense is proper whether or not the author is still alive:

> Goethe's interest in Faust-the-man *is* greatest of all in the last act of Part II, where care overwhelms the proud humanitarian Faust has become.

Both of these illustrations use the present tense because emphasis is on the text and the text is, in some sense, always alive.

Where emphasis is on the author and the historical situation in which statements are made, the situation changes:

> A few months ago, Professor Wilson *suggested,* in an article in *PMLA,* that. . . .

> As he grew older Goethe's interest in Faust-the-man *deepened.*

The historical situation and the textual analysis may, and frequently will, occur together:

Crèvecœur *was* the first to attempt a definition of the independent spirt of the colonists. His popular book *depicts* the emergence of . . .

Mood. Traditional textbooks list three moods for English: the indicative, the subjunctive, the imperative. These they distinguish as referring to definite action (indicative), probable or desired or predicted action, or action contrary to fact (subjunctive), and command (imperative). The indicative and imperative moods are firmly fixed in the language:

> According to report, Carlyle *rewrote* his history of the French revolution from memory after the manuscript was accidentally destroyed. (indicative)

> Bertrand Russell's advice is this: in matters of thought *distrust* all authority. (imperative)

Of the subjunctive, however, there seem to be only vestigial remains. The contrary-to-fact condition still exerts influence on the verb *to be,* as in

> If Ptolemy *were* right, there would be no way to account for the behavior of heavenly bodies in galaxies distinct from our own

but, even there, ordinarily only in the past tense. The action denoting probability or wish or prediction may be subjunctive, but there is today very little use of the "subjunctive" form of the verb, save as that term is applied to the use of certain auxiliaries (as in *"may be* subjunctive" in this sentence).

The demise of the subjunctive need not concern us here. The one point to be made is that undiscriminating shift of mood within a sentence is a troubling matter to the reader because it requires him to follow a shift in attitude-toward-action for which he is not prepared. Such shifts are particularly annoying when they are from the imperative to either of the other moods. This sentence is bad for that reason:

> It *may be* that Toynbee *is* right about repetition in history, but *take* the similar idea of Spengler and you *will see* how different the conclusions from such an idea *can be.*

> CORRECTED: It *may be* that Toynbee is right about repetition in history, but Spengler *had* a similar idea and *reached* a very different conclusion.

Voice. Some modern grammarians are as dubious about there being two "voices" in English as about there being a "subjunctive," and they prefer to talk of a "passive construction" rather than a "passive voice," since the verbs used for such a construction do not alter their form. Whichever term one chooses, it is clear that there are two patterns in our language which differ in the relationship of their grammatical subject to the predicate verb.

In the active voice, the grammatical subject performs the action:

James I created a new dynasty in England.

In the passive voice, the grammatical subject receives the action:

Charles I was beheaded in 1649.

Both voices have their usefulness, naturally, or they would not exist. Here, for example, is an order produced by the Office of Price Stabilization for display in restaurants and stores during World War II:

Quality and Quantity Are Required To Be Maintained.

The reason for the passive construction in that order is obvious enough. *Who* requires? No one is named, but the downrightness of "Required" indicates that it is Someone or, more likely, SOMEONE. Such impersonality has its uses, but it can readily become a device for making matters seem more important or imperative than they really are.

The problems of *person* and *voice* often combine to annoy the writer of expository prose. If he is describing or explaining an activity or condition in which human participation is implicit, he has these choices: (1) to create a semifictitious personage to whom he can refer ("the writer" is the one often used in his book); (2) to reify abstractions, making them the subjects of active verbs ("Such an analysis requires careful examination . . ."); (3) to use the "editorial *we*" ("If we examine this analysis carefully, we see that . . ."); (4) to avoid "we" by using "one" ("If one examines this analysis carefully, one sees that . . ."); (5) to employ direct address ("You must examine such an analysis . . ."); (6) to resort to impersonal constructions ("From an examination of such an analysis it becomes apparent that . . ."; or (7) to use the passive voice ("If such an analysis is carefully examined . . ."). There is no rule of thumb for deciding among them, and within a long piece of prose a writer will ordinarily use several. Such differences as are discernible alter from context to context, and generalizations about them are likely therefore to be somewhat misleading. Nonetheless, a few recommendations are warrantable to accompany the choices just listed.

1.   A semifictitious *persona* often becomes a trap for the writer sim-

ply because he has no real existence as a flesh-and-blood being, even in the writer's imagination. Gradually he is transformed from a generalized being into a prototype to which all vices or virtues can with impunity be attributed. The reader, meeting this bloodless character on page after page, develops an independence from him rather than the identification with him which was the author's aim in introducing him in the first place.

2. Making abstractions act as vital agents in a sentence is, on the whole, a good practice, principally because it is forceful and economical. The active verbs brighten and give movement to matter which might otherwise be heavy and static. The danger in this procedure is that the abstractions will become so independent that they obscure their derivation from separate events, that is, from the "facts" which are their ground and reason for being.

3., 4. The "editorial *we*" and the formal "one" are both such obvious conveniences that they have little vital juice in them. "We," particularly, is a convention which has lost much of its original weight. The true "editorial *we*," like the "royal *we*," is meant to convey the power of concerted action. The critical essay which uses "we" to mean "the author" is probably making the best of a bad situation: the writer wants to avoid the intrusion of himself-as-a-person which takes place if he uses the pronoun "I," and he wants also to avoid the awkwardness and heaviness of passive and impersonal constructions. There is one "we" which seems to have a better argument for existence, that which a writer uses when he *joins* the reader in speculation. If misused, however, it is likely to sound patronizing ("We don't want to make that sort of error, do we?"), but judiciously and honestly used it helps to strengthen the communication between writer and reader.

5. Direct address is proper for commands but likely to be annoyingly avuncular or magisterial when it is used to point out the application of statement to the reader's own life. When "you" is a substitute for the third-person indefinite pronoun, it does not carry those overtones, but it is still rather colloquial for formal expository prose.

6., 7. Impersonal constructions and the passive voice depend on the static verbs of equivalence (copulative verbs) and therefore have a certain rigidity about them. Moreover, as noted above, they tend to obscure the *real* agent of whatever relationships are predicated. Certainly they are not always to be avoided; neither are they to be preferred if alternatives readily present themselves.

The grammar and rhetoric of the sentence are, of course, to some extent also the grammar and rhetoric of the paragraph and of the essay or book. Increased dimension raises additional problems for the writer, however, and at the same time offers him scope for more complex effects. Those problems and effects are the subject of the following chapter.

chapter seven / *Structure*

The paragraph may best be described as Dr. Johnson described a woman preacher: the triumph of art over nature. There are no paragraphs in nature. They are the product of art, though—as Polixenes remarks in *The Winter's Tale* about cultivated flowers—it is "an art that nature makes."

The best way to consider the paragraph is to think of it as the result of deliberate arrangement, a calculated disposition of parts. Paragraphs are not often written that way; but that is the way they have to be re-written, and the sooner a writer learns to bring some of the discipline of revision to the original process of writing, the better off he will be. A risk is involved, of course, and sometimes the risk is greater than the possible gain. In the full flood of inspiration or of overpowering conviction, restraint may be unwise or even futile. The result is likely to be greater need for revision later, but that may not matter. When, however, the mind is not so much fired to the job of writing as set to it—a condition more ordinary, by far—skill at order is not only a saver of time and energy but an important provoker of thought.

Typographically, a paragraph is simply several lines of type, the first of which usually begins some distance to the right of the margin. Logically, it is a coordination of related assertions. Rhetorically, it is a series of sentences so ordered as to achieve a single major effect. The range is from fact to hope, of course, but it is with the ideal that we must grapple to make any progress at all. We shall not worry about typography, but as elsewhere logic and rhetoric claim our attention. If a paragraph is a progression of sentences, how can the separate claims of logic and of rhetoric most efficiently be realized?

What is needed here is some governing metaphor, and the one we propose is theatrical. The paragraph is a scene from a play. As a separate scene, it has characters and action; as one of many scenes in the play, it has some meaning and function beyond itself. The writer is playwright. His concern is to make the scene-paragraph represent something that is happening. That means distinguishing actor from action from acted-upon. It means supplying sufficient matter to give the action appropriate size; it means providing motivation and sequence and result. It means forecasting and concluding and connecting. And, perhaps most of all, it means keeping the actor in focus throughout—a matter that will be discussed quite specifically later, under the heading of "Coherence."

The metaphor may seem fanciful, but it is far from that. These are the central matters of structure and development (the thesis statement or topic sentence, devices of expansion, systems of arrangement, opening and closing and connecting strategies, coherence). And the writer with a sound sense of craft is constantly aware as he writes not only of what he is saying but of what he is doing. He deploys sentences, which is precisely what the playwright does with characters.

1/ The Topic Sentence

The topic sentence (or thesis statement, as it is sometimes called) is a more or less fictitious entity. It does sometimes make an appearance in so many words, of course, but fully as often it is not something written but what is meant by what has been written. That is, the topic sentence is something a reader extracts from a paragraph and something a writer has in mind as the unity he wants to achieve. The schoolboy notion of a topic sentence as the big firecracker from which a string of little firecrackers is suspended, each due to go off with a tiny "pop" when the big one is ignited, has little relationship to the truth. An accomplished writer of prose is much too well aware of the weaving required for a good representation of his thought to lay it out, thread by thread, with no regard for the original design. But accomplished writers no longer need to read analyses of this kind, so it is wise to consider, even in half-fictional terms, the problems of those who do.

Paragraphs can be written of course, in firecracker order. For some purposes, that may be their best order. An explanation of process, for example, is most efficient if the steps of the process are chronologically catalogued:

> An omelet requires strictly fresh ingredients and a skilled hand. The yolks and whites of the eggs are separated first and the yolks beaten slightly with a fork until they are well blended. To the blended yolks is then added. . . .

Even in this simple process, a strategy is apparent, and a part of that strategy is the opening sentence which serves as a kind of warning and summary-in-advance.

A more helpful view of the topic sentence comes from thinking of it, not necessarily as some single grammatically complete utterance in a paragraph, but as a central proposition which it is the business of the paragraph to develop. It is, in this view, a succinct summary of the paragraph; or, to return to the metaphor introduced above, it is the meaning of the scene.

Consider, for example, the uncomplicated sentence that follows as the "core" or "topic" to be developed:

> The battlement speech in *Macbeth* expresses perfectly the despair that follows discovery in a tragedy.

As discussion will show, there is plenty of matter in this sentence for more than a paragraph, but at this point we can examine its possibilities for expansion without concern for the eventual product. Simple grammatical analysis will give us a start.

SUBJECT	The battlement speech in *Macbeth*
VERB	expresses perfectly
OBJECT	the despair that follows discovery in a tragedy.

Now the subject of a sentence is always the "given" of the proposition. It is the thing of which something is to be predicated and is therefore above suspicion, so to speak, for the moment. Its being above suspicion does not mean, however, that it is necessarily self-explanatory, and a certain amount of information may be needed in this example to identify the speech, as a preliminary to satisfaction of other obligations implicit in the sentence. The verb makes the first step beyond what is to be taken for granted in the proposition, and in this instance that step is a big one. The meaning of "expresses" as it is used here must be explained and, one would expect, illustrated as well; but it cannot be adequately elaborated apart from its object, which requires some attention to the statement that despair follows discovery in a tragedy as well as clarification of the terms "despair," "tragedy," and particularly "discovery." Since verb and object are both, as parts of a proposition, that which is "to be proved," they can be linked in the single term "predicate" and the sentence redivided in this fashion:

SUBJECT	The battlement speech in *Macbeth*
PREDICATE	expresses perfectly the despair that follows discovery in a tragedy.

Now what is gained by this division? Simply a separation of two distinct obligations which the writer takes upon himself when he writes the sentence: (1) to explain the subject, and (2) to explain and defend or "prove" the predication. If the core sentence is to be expanded only into a paragraph, the writer will limit explanation and defense accordingly. If it is to be expanded into an essay, he will plan to take one paragraph or several for each of his obligations. If it is into several paragraphs that the expansion is to fall, each of those paragraphs, too, will have its core sentence, and each core sentence will likewise be divisible into subject and predicate, laying upon the writer obligations like those already illustrated.

As long as he fulfills his obligations, the writer is free to devise whatever strategy he thinks most likely to suit his matter, his purpose, and his reader. For that reason, what is conventionally called the "topic sentence" may be broken into parts or, if kept intact, may be placed at one of several places in the paragraph, or be so transformed by rhetoric that its presence comes more through the "sense" of the paragraph than through any explicit statement. A paragraph picked almost at random from the writing of an English essayist and novelist will illustrate the point:

> No, I distrust Great Men. They produce a desert of uniformity around them and often a pool of blood too, and I always feel a little man's pleasure when they come a cropper. Every now and then one reads in the newspapers some such statement as: "The *coup d'état* appears to have failed, and Admiral Toma's whereabouts is at present unknown." Admiral Toma had probably every qualification for being a Great Man —an iron will, personal magnetism, dash, flair, sexlessness—but fate was against him, so he retires to unknown whereabouts instead of parading history with his peers. He fails with a completeness which no artist and no lover can experience, because with them the process of creation is itself an achievement, whereas with him the only possible achievement is success.
>
> E. M. FORSTER, *Two Cheers for Democracy*

The paragraph is not so much an expansion of any stated proposition as the progress through several propositions which, taken together, culminate in a core of meaning, a something which we might say the paragraph is "about":

> Those men who are conventionally called "great," unlike those who act out of love or out of the desire to create, leave nothing behind them if they fail.

The author's assertion of distrust, his many ironic turns of phrase, his fictitious Admiral Toma are all stratagems, and it is to them that the richness of the paragraph is almost entirely indebted.

The sentence which comes closest to being a "topic sentence" in the paragraph just quoted is the last one. In another paragraph, it might be the second or a middle sentence. The location of the topic sentence, then, if indeed it is ever stated in so many words, will vary. The paragraph may move from or toward it, or it may rise to it and fall away from it like a wave sweeping the shore.

2/ Devices of Expansion

Whatever the location of the core sentence, its work is carried on by the other sentences of the paragraph. The division of that work—explanation of subject, explanation and defense of predication—has already been presented. Now it is important to examine the means by which writers do the explaining and the defending. The warning that appears again and again in this book deserves repetition at this point: to describe the devices of expansion is not to suggest that writers think of them as devices or that they consciously "fill out" each statement as though they were stuffing a pillowcase with feathers. To repeat, the expansion is (a) a necessary explanation of the core substance and (b) a part of the strategy by which the author contrives to render his full meaning. It is not separate from the core of the paragraph but is actually the medium through which the core of meaning is transmitted. Treating each device in isolation falsifies the actual situation somewhat, but it is the most convenient and useful procedure and is therefore the one chosen.

The writer's most common device for development is *restatement*. Despite the dangers of repetition, the simple fact is that a certain amount of repetition is necessary in the use of language, not only for emphasis, but quite as much for full expression of whatever is to be said. Restatement is not a completely literal repetition, of course, and that is why it succeeds. It is a second or a third attempt to weave a design from the strands of thought; if the first does not succeed, one of the later ones may, or all of them together will give a fuller reproduction than any one. Note how restatement works in this paragraph:

> Each generation takes a special pleasure in removing the household gods of its parents from their pedestals and consigning them to the cupboard. The prophet or pioneer, after being at first declared to be

unintelligible or absurd, has a brief spell of popularity, after which he is said to be conventional, and then antiquated. We may find more than one reason for this. A movement has more to fear from its disciples than from its critics. The great man is linked to his age by his weakest side; and his epigoni, who are not great men, caricature his message and make it ridiculous. Besides, every movement is a reaction, and generates counter-reactions. The pendulum swings backwards and forwards. Every institution not only carries within it the seeds of its own dissolution, but prepares the way for its most hated rival.

W. R. INGE, *Outspoken Essays*

No one would characterize this paragraph as repetitive; yet it is full of restatement. The second sentence is the first sentence looked at in different perspective; the "pendulum" sentence uses a metaphor to restate the on .hat precedes it; and the final sentence, which is as close to being tl topic sentence of the paragraph as any, is an accumulation and repetitic of parts of the first, the fourth, and the fifth sentences. Good restatement enriches and colors explanation and is therefore invaluable as a means of conveying the complexity of thought.

Example provides the most obvious means of expansion, and just because it is obvious it is uniquely suited to the job of clarifying the obscure and of making the general specific and the abstract concrete. Although they do not constitute formal proof—one swallow does not make a summer, as the saying goes—examples are really attempts at proof because they display the phenomenal evidence which is the ground for general statements. For that reason, they must be treated with respect; a faulty example is bad not simply because it is in itself inappropriate but because its failure detracts from the authority of the generalization it is supposed to support.

Whether or not an example needs to have attention called to its character as example depends on its context and its length. An example which is only a phrase or single sentence will generally not need any indicator of its presence:

The most enlightened members of the state—*the scribes, the councilors, and the wise men of the inner temple*—have for a long time predicted this event.

Men of lofty vision and deep conviction are often regarded with suspicion by their fellow men. *Socrates was condemned to die for corrupting the youth of Athens; Jesus was crucified for blasphemy.* Yet vision and conviction, being themselves incorruptible, have their way in the world.

Examples of greater length are sometimes treated more formally. Either they are set off from the main body of the text, as the examples above are set off, or they are preceded by a signal of some sort:

> The life of a President is so exacting that it must be relieved by regular periods of physical exertion. Every President within recent memory has found need for the stimulation of muscle tone and the relaxation of nervous tension which come from a vigorous hour or so of brisk activity. Mr. Eisenhower, *for example,* played golf several days a week; Mr. Truman used to take a fast morning walk; Roosevelt and Kennedy swam daily in the White House pool, and Hoover was an ardent fisherman.

> The fable has a double tradition in Western literature. From Æsop it inherits a certain moral solemnity; from La Fontaine, the habit of ironical reflection on the disparity between appearance and reality and between precept and practice in human affairs. Although the fable is no longer so popular as it once was, its modern practitioners have found it a useful instrument for satire of man and morality alike. *The two modern fabulists who come most quickly to mind*—Edward Lear and James Thurber—are both swift to detect the ludicrous in action and precept, but neither is so blunt as La Fontaine in exposing it.

The use of *supporting data* for statements, like that of examples, is a convenient and obvious means of clarifying and documenting whatever is predicated. The kind of data will be determined, of course, by the nature of the statement, and no illustrations are necessary here: statistics, tables, graphs, enumerations, diagrams, and citations of text, for instance, are all relevant. The means of handling such material within an essay are as varied as the nature of the material, and generalization about procedures is therefore difficult. The practice of relegating extensive documentation to footnotes or appendixes is, in the main, a wise one, particularly if the exposition in the text itself does not depend on such documentation for its clarity. Where clarity is at stake, the supporting data should remain in the text and there be exposed as economically and attached as organically as possible.

Both example and supporting data are largely substantive, though they have strategic value, too. Some other devices of expansion have less to do with support, or proof, of assertions than with their illumination. Among them, *anecdote* is one of the most valuable. Now it is clear that an anecdote is, in one sense, also an attempt to insist on the soundness of a statement by showing its representation in experience. But the sense of the particular and informal which is part of an anecdote detracts from its value as documentation at the same time as it adds to its value as illustration. Whether the anecdote is historical or contemporary, about the actions of someone well known or about the writer's personal experience, it adds the power that storytelling has for all readers. Abstractions, after all, are the dried leaves of event; to use anecdote as an expansion of a general statement is therefore to do no more than bring it back to life.

Like anecdote, *quotation* and *allusion* are more dramatic than substantive in character. They are different from anecdote, however, in being oblique aids to clarity and completeness. They suggest the rightness or the meaningfulness of preceding statements by proposing corollaries in the experience of writer and reader, corollaries which are called to mind by a familiar phrase or by mention of some figure or event which has taken on a particular character in the public consciousness. To describe Woodrow Wilson as "America's Robespierre" is to clarify and, at the same time, to add information so extensive that it would take pages of exposition to equal it. The problem which rises from the use of allusion is readily apparent from the example: if the allusion is within the reader's range of experience, it may be wonderfully effective; if it is outside that range, it may be annoying and will certainly do little to clarify. To some extent, the same thing may be said of the use of quotations, especially when they are presented elliptically:

> The medieval warning, *De gustibus* . . . , is more pertinent to fashions in clothing than to styles in art.

Many quotations, however, are so much a part of the public treasury that a writer may be almost sure of his reader's familiarity with them. The problem with them is that their very familiarity may annoy. A writer must simply steer his way carefully between obscurity and triteness if he chooses to amplify meaning by the use of allusion and quotation. Moreover, if he is wise, he will be sparing of both, for a text which relies on these two devices very heavily is likely to look like a connoisseur's display of dainties rather than a firm and rich elucidation of thought.

3/ Order

The classical structure of the oration was for a long time the model for ordering expository prose. Its three main divisions provide a scheme which is at once handsome and comprehensive: introduction (*exordio*), body (*praecognitio, partitio, explicatio, amplificatio, applicatio*), and conclusion (*peroratio*). There is a brief rhetorical opening; then a careful statement and dissection of the thesis, followed by an analysis of each part, an elaboration and a direct application to the life of the listener; finally, a summation designed to bring the weight of the thesis to bear on the listeners' feeling and on their desire for action. Implicit in the scheme is a recognition that reason is paramount but that it must be linked with feeling before it will produce action. And implicit also is the condition of argument—an assertion whose truth it is the purpose of the exposition to prove beyond question. Everything is taken care of in the most orderly fashion: terms are defined, possible ambiguities eliminated, implications and assumptions explained, proofs adduced, and examples provided. Beneath the formal structure an almost infinite variety is possible in the organization or order of matters in each part. One section may proceed by classification, another by contrasts, a third by chronology, and so on. Yet, whatever the internal variety, the enclosing structure remains firm and almost relentless.

The formal pattern of the classical oration is no longer in fashion, not even in sermons, which for a long time continued to exploit it after it had largely disappeared from general use. In its place—partly, no doubt, from analogy with discoveries in the natural sciences—there has grown a tendency to make even expository writing "express" in its form the nature of its substance. It is not easy to say how form and substance can be made one, and it may be exaggeration to speak of equivalence where only appropriateness is possible. Yet, whatever the formula, it is certainly true that some material, used for a particular purpose, is better dealt with in one form than in another. A particular argument, for instance, may achieve its greatest clarity and power in the form of a dialogue; one sort of proof may be most appropriately presented by the orderly tracing of cause and effect, another by the uninterrupted accumulation of supporting data; classification may best suit analysis; or chronology, narration. No general rule is possible, of course, for writers' intentions vary so widely that only ingenious combinations of form are sufficient to satisfy them. It is possible, however, to describe several kinds of organization and to point out uses and abuses of each.

Order by *classification* is the most obvious means of organization for expository prose, and it comes closest to the oratorical pattern mentioned above. The proposition which is the core of the essay (e.g., "Washington's policy of avoiding 'foreign entanglements' is no longer possible for any civilized country") is first divided, as suggested above, into "subject" and "predicate." The subject ("Washington's policy of avoiding 'foreign entanglements' ") is explained by reference to his Farewell Address and, in order that the policy may be accurately represented, by some account of the events during his tenure of office. Then the predicate ("is no longer possible for any civilized country") is developed—in this case, "proved"—by a presentation of arguments classified, let us say, as "economic," "political," and "moral." The classification itself arises from an initial listing of arguments and from the observation of similarities among those arguments. A decision about which of the three classes to present first depends in part on the strength of the evidence for each and in part on the particular emphasis a writer wishes to provide. A contributor to the *Christian Century,* for instance, might discuss all three classes but elaborate only "moral" intensively, placing it third in the series so that it might come as a climax to the whole line of argument. A political analyst in *The New York Times* might subordinate "moral" and "economic"; an editorialist for *New Masses* would undoubtedly make "economic" the climatic classification. Classification always depends in part on the observer's way of looking at a matter, so it is not surprising at all that various writers will classify and develop the same matter differently. Nor is it undesirable that they do so. The important thing is that the classifications, whatever they are, be borne out by the material and that they be sufficient to encompass it.

It is clear that order by classification requires that the subject matter be such as to lend itself to categories, to more or less watertight compartments. Classification is the handmaiden of analysis when analysis is concerned with what is static. To use it as the order for explaining a process is therefore inadvisable, for it reduces emphasis on action, which is the heart of process.

A second, and also common, order is that of *cause and effect.* Where classification throws emphasis on substance, cause and effect throws it on the active relationship between substances, on the alteration which results from their coming into contact with each other. Obviously, then, it is particularly useful for the explanation of process. At its simplest, this kind of order may seem to present no problems: cause precedes effect in fact and should therefore precede it in report on fact. Yet even to explain the chain of events which turns water into ice requires attention to more than one cause—to pressure as well as to temperature. Perhaps it is the term itself that misleads one into thinking of cause and effect as simple; "causes and effects" would be far more accurate, for few things happen in this world as the result of a single cause and few causes have only a single effect. This multiplicity and variety require that the writer select among causes and effects those relevant to his purposes (all are relevant to the action itself), and it is in the act of selection that trouble is likely to occur.

The writer who uses cause and effect as a principle of order must be alert to causes and effects which do not at once meet the eye. He must be ready to explore for more of both and should perhaps begin from the assumption that apparent causes and effects may or may not be the most important or even the real ones. Once he has made his selection, he can proceed from one to the other in either direction, making the choice of direction depend on whether he wants emphasis to fall on causes or effects. If he finds, and decides to deal with, a plurality of causes and effects, he will also find the order of cause and effect insufficient and will almost certainly have to call on another principle of order to act in subordinate capacity. Think, for example, of the problem of explaining the causes of so simple an event as a summer shower. Do we begin with today's wind and heat or with the warm front which began to develop last week in Texas and the breakup of an ice pack in Greenland? For practical purposes the writer must restrict the causes and effects he considers according to their proximity to the event and according to their necessity; those that are distant and, though relevant, either not absolutely necessary to the effect or not of major importance, he must perforce ignore or skim over lightly. Those that are immediate and essential he retains or brings to the fore, marshaling them in such fashion as to make their relationships apparent. The dominant connection which he must exploit in this procedure is a hybrid, a cross between "therefore" and "thereafter" which unites time and cause. Where relationships are purely associative, of course, that order is manifestly improper; but even where they are derivative, it may be misleading. Unless the lines of causation and response can be clearly sorted and exposed, it may be better to limit oneself to simple succession, carefully avoiding any indication of another relationship. The cumulative effect will be much the same, and the particular links of the chain will not then be subject to criticism.

In human experience, events seem to be inevitably related in time, whatever their other relationships may be. It is natural, therefore, that *chronology* should be an important principle of organization, even in nonnarrative prose. Its importance is enhanced, however, by the fact that all writing and speaking are also involved in duration so that even in pure description of a static object chronology is implicated: "What shall I describe *first?*" the novice asks. There would seem, then, to be two kinds of chronological order: that which records the actual progression of events (real chronology), and that which represents the experience of the observer (subjective chronology).

Real chronology may be manipulated for effect, the writer beginning, as Horace advised poets to do, in the middle of things, or at the beginning, or at the end. Subjective, or psychological, chronology is already a manipulation of the fact, generally a manipulation for the sake of emphasis: the writer begins by describing the nose because it is the nose to which he wishes to give prominence, or he holds back from describing the nose until the end of his account for the very same reason. Most expository prose stays within the sphere of real chronology, but the informal essay and, in recent years, even the speculative essay have shown a disposition to take liberties with it, to fuse the time of conscious, rational experience with the time of memory and feeling in which conventional order is inverted, distorted, or reduced to simultaneity. The effects achieved by such freedom are its best defense; like syncopation in music, they are achievable only when a strong sense of real chronology lies behind them. The amateur writer does well, then, to make sure that he can manipulate the patterns of ordinary chronology before he attempts to represent the extraordinary chronologies of subjective experience.

Aristotle noted that the ability to detect likeness is one of the sure signs of intelligence, and it is on this ability (which, of course, implies the ability to detect differences) that he based his system of classification and his theory of definition. The habit of creating order by *comparison* and by *contrast* seems, as a matter of fact, to be almost as natural to man as thought itself. Metaphor lies at the root of language and is fundamentally comparative in nature, exposing a linkage which is not patent but which is nonetheless real. To some degree all comparisons are useful in the same way—they call attention to characteristics which might otherwise escape the eye. An exposition of the concept of piety in The Book of Job may be greatly enriched by a comparative exposition of the same concept in Aeschylus' *Prometheus Bound,* the details of one revealing the absence or transformation of those details in the other. A discussion of a republican government's right of eminent domain profits from comparison of that right with a king's prerogative of entry and use for defense of the realm, the extent and power of the former becoming apparent only when the much more limited royal authority is described. Besides calling attention to detail, comparisons are particularly useful when the purpose of an exposition is to aggrandize or to demean; setting two objects or events against each other makes one into a touchstone or foil, a standard by which the other can be measured.

Managing a comparison is not easy, whether its purpose is simply to describe likenesses and differences or to solicit approval of one matter at the expense of another. If the explanation of each is developed separately, the force of comparison is diminished; if the objects or events are developed concurrently, each characteristic being balanced immediately against its foil or counterpart, the comparison becomes an annoying see-saw. Somehow the sense of integrity and the force of relationship must both be retained, a feat best accomplished by a judicious use of both procedures, coupled with another ordering device, perhaps that of classification. To return to the "piety" example mentioned above: the comparison might begin with a brief account of the cultural context of each of the works, using their approximate dates of composition as the initial links between them, then touching on the differences in the cultural context, and finally drawing the two together again on the subject matter of the essay—the embodiment in each of a concept of piety. At this point there comes an opportunity for further unifying by definition and by classification: determining the meaning of "piety" for this essay and stating the considerations relevant to exploration of the concept in these two works. The "body" of the essay may well continue the alteration between union and division: for each of the considerations to be developed, a sentence or more to point out the relevance of that consideration to both the Greek and the Hebrew work, then a point-by-point comparison of passages which illustrate the similarity or difference. And so on until the entire ground is covered.

Most comparisons, of course, are a compound of likenesses and differences, and the order of presentation is affected by the general rule of emphasis: the subordinate precedes the principal. This is true of a whole essay as well as of paragraphs or sections within it. By the same token, the place for concession or qualification is early rather than late. In the example given, if the differences between the two concepts of piety outweigh the likenesses, it is with the likenesses that the essay should begin. The essay thus falls "naturally" into two major divisions. Within each, subdivisions will more or less imitate the arrangement of the larger unit to which they belong.

Because comparison implies a balancing, this kind of order provides opportunities for rhetorical parallels of all kinds, an opportunity not really satisfied by bare connectives like "on the other hand" and "in contrast."

> The uppermost idea with Hellenism is to see things as they really are; the uppermost idea with Hebraism is conduct and obedience. Nothing can do away with this ineffaceable difference. The Greek quarrel with the body and its desires is that they hinder right thinking; the Hebrew quarrel with them is that they hinder right acting. "He that keepeth the law, happy is he"; "Blessed is the man that feareth the Eternal, that delighteth greatly in His commandments";—that is the Hebrew notion of felicity; and, pursued with passion and tenacity, this notion would not let the Hebrew rest till, as is well known, he had at last got out of the law a network of prescriptions to enwrap his whole life, to govern every moment of it, every impulse, every action. The Greek notion of felicity, on the other hand, is perfectly conveyed in these words of a

great French moralist: *"C'est le bonheur des hommes"*—when? when they abhor that which is evil? no;—when they exercise themselves in the law of the Lord day and night? no;—when they die daily? no;— when they walk about the New Jerusalem with palms in their hands? no;—but when they think aright, when their thought hits: *"quand ils pensent juste."* . . . The governing ideas of Hellenism is *spontaneity of consciousness;* that of Hebraism, *strictness of conscience.*

MATTHEW ARNOLD, "Hebraism and Hellenism"

Because comparison emphasizes extremes of likeness and of difference, its strategies are useless when emphasis on *degree* is what the writer wants to achieve. Pairing the abstract and concrete, for example, calls for the procedures of comparison. Pairing the general and particular calls for something quite different. Abstractness is a matter not of degree but of kind: a word is either abstract or concrete. But a word may be more or less general, more or less particular. For this condition of more-or-less, a rhetoric of gradualism is necessary. The scale from particular to general may begin or stop wherever the writer finds his purpose best served. A girl in Thornton Wilder's *Our Town* awes her friends by displaying a letter addressed to: "Jane Crofut; The Crofut Farm; Grover's Corners; Sutton County; New Hampshire; United States of America; Continent of North America; Western Hemisphere; the Earth; the Solar System; the Universe; the Mind of God." The pattern in this instance is that of completeness. Whether complete or partial, the only cautions necessary are against confusing the distance between leaps and against leaping in both directions at once or successively in opposite directions.

The five principles of organization discussed so far rely more or less heavily on a sixth, that of *climax,* or order of importance. It is no secret that emphasis, in a sentence as in a paragraph or an essay, is stronger at the beginning and at or near the end than in the middle. The order of the English sentence is partly responsible for that fact, no doubt, but more responsible is the human habit of expectation. Impressive climaxes and satisfying resolutions depend on the preparation that precedes them, and for that reason the usual order of matter is from the less to the more important. Now, as in chronological order, a writer may achieve special effect by doing the unexpected, by using an anticlimactic order. In general, however, that practice is useful only for surprise or for brief and violent emphasis, and it imposes upon its user the problem of retaining the reader's attention and of developing a stable perspective on the subject matter once the opening cannon has been fired.

Few essays of any length depend on a single organizing strategy for the good reason that readers expect a measure of variety in prose just as they expect a measure of uniformity in verse. Moreover, a single principle of order is seldom sufficient to provide for the complexity of the matter it is intended to control. A flexible strategy, on the other hand, makes it possible for a writer to exploit the full resources of whatever material he has at hand. The professional writer is able to shift from one kind of order to another without taking thought. The tyro may have to lay out his strategy well in advance and follow its successive maneuvers scrupulously to avoid a rout. For him an *outline* is important and often essential.

4/ The Outline

As the underlying metaphor implies, an outline describes the circumference of an essay and of each of its various parts. If, then, the earlier contention about topic sentences is sound, an outline is the orderly presentation of main assertions, those which are to be expanded by various devices. To make it any less than that is to respect form and to ignore substance. An outline for the projected essay on piety, for example, is little short of useless in this state:

    I. Introduction
   II. Body
        A. Similarities
            1. Idea of God
            2. Idea of man
            3. Idea of punishment
        B. Differences
            1. Idea of God
            2. Idea of man
            3. Idea of relationship
            4. Idea of afterlife
                . . .
                . . .
  III. Conclusion

Yet that is what "outline" means to many who have been taught to look upon it as a kind of ritual preliminary to writing. A good outline is not a ritual; it springs from thought and should capitalize on its origin. In its early state it may be no more than a series of assertions, set down (elliptically, perhaps) just as they occur to the writer:

1. Job and Prometheus know their inferiority in power
2. Job habitually dutiful, Pr. habitually resentful
3. Greeks thought of afterlife as a dark continuation of existence, not punishment or reward
4. Job patient under affliction, rationalizing at first
5. Both fall from high to low estate: Pr. for deliberate acts of rebellion, Job not
6. Hebrew idea of Sheol (afterlife) as a comfortable extension of life after death
7. Both pieces probably written in 5th century B.C.
8. Hebrew and Gr. culture separate but both Asian
9. Hebrew culture more isolated than Greek
10. *PB* a religious drama; Job half drama, half poem?
11. *PB* not a speculation but a demonstration of agreed-upon concepts

One assertion suggests another and the accumulation soon suggests the possible combinations and the appropriate means of organization. From the list an outline grows which not only guides the writing of the essay but stimulates it and provides a clearly focused test for its achievement. Any outline developed from such a series of assertions is immediately useful to the writer. With the outline before him, he can work swiftly and efficiently, explaining and expanding each assertion, "filling in" the outline with the corroborative and illustrative data he has accumulated by research and reflection.

THESIS: The treatments of piety and impiety in *Job* and *Prometheus Bound* reflect the most important differences between traditional Hebraic and early Greek religious belief.

1. Although Hebraic culture is more isolated than Greek, both are Asian.
2. Fatalism, strong sense of human inferiority, common to both; so also a vigorous tradition of the hero and saviour of a group or people.
3. Hebraic view of afterlife (Sheol), like Greek Hades, reflects uncertainty about judgment hereafter for acts committed here. Importance of justice vs. rule of inscrutable God.
4. Main difference between concept of single God and of a pantheon; distance between Job and God greater than that between Prometheus and Zeus.
5. Difference reflected in the two works.
   a. Job habitually dutiful; Prometheus independent.
   b. Job patient under affliction; Pr. resentful.
   c. Job finally distrustful of reasoning; Pr. full of reasoning on his own account.

6. Idea of a "testing" of Job consistent with relationship (See 4); Prometheus' ordeal not a test but a punishment.
7. Forms of the two works also reflect difference.
   a. *Job* part drama, part poem of speculation; its drama full of suspense (wagers, tests, peril, victory, reward).
   b. *PB* a religious drama designed to illustrate orthodox concepts; drama ritualized, outcome foreknown.
8. Form and content together develop attitude toward piety in each work.
   a. *Job*—piety is waiting patiently to understand will of God.
   b. *PB*—(by negative illustration) piety is obedience.

There is another use of the outline which must not be overlooked. Besides serving as a guide to composition, it may be a tool for reorganizing what has already been composed. Some writers like to release the pressure of thought within them by writing it out without preliminary concern for neat and efficient order. When they have temporarily exhausted their resources, they turn a critical eye on what they have produced, summarizing it in outline form just as it occurs and then rearranging sections for clearer directions and sounder emphasis. The procedure is attractive insofar as it allows a writer to rely on the rush of thought as long as it lasts; it is perhaps less attractive in the later stage, when by rewriting and reorganizing he must make up for the inadequacies of what he has produced. An early outline will reduce the amount of reconstruction necessary when the first draft is completed, though it may not eliminate all reconstruction and certainly will not eliminate some amount of rewriting. Most people who have something to write use outlines both at the head and the tail of their work, even when they do not write them down. The form in which they cast the outline, if they do write it down, is of relatively small importance as long as the principal assertions are precisely stated and then arranged so that their relationships are made clear and so that the whole plan displays a steady forward movement.

5/ Coherence

The three traditional goddesses of rhetoric—unity, coherence, and emphasis—are, suitably, the deities which all of the matters discussed in this section are supposed to serve. Of the three, *coherence* calls for special attention. Although sheer bulk may impose emphasis and a rough unity on the matter of an exposition, it is no aid—and is often a detriment—to coherence. Now coherence can be best defined by reference to its etymology; literally, it means a "sticking together," and in rhetoric it is the term used to designate the connectedness between parts large and small. Although it is clear that coherence will be affected by the degree to which the materials of an essay are congruous (a discussion of three battles of the Civil War would achieve some coherence simply as a by-product of the unity of its subject matter), congruity is not alone sufficient.

The basic means of achieving coherence is by rational *arrangement* of material, a matter already adequately discussed. A second means is by the judicious use of *connectors,* a matter treated at the end of this chapter under the heading "transitions." Both means are largely structural, that is, concerned with the manipulation of blocks of expository matter. Within the blocks, of whatever size, and controlling their internal chemistry, several other means of achieving coherence may come into action. *Repetition,* for instance, whether of a key word or of the pattern of phrases, clauses, and sentences (parallel structure), calls attention to the relationship between parts and thus increases coherence. The use of a *key metaphor*, whose terms are introduced obliquely and unostentatiously over a long passage of prose, may draw the whole passage together most subtly. More effective and less "literary" than either repetition or the use of a key metaphor, however, is the development of coherence by control of *actor and action.*

A subject—personal or impersonal—performs an action which begins, proceeds to climax, and ends. The essay remains coherent as long as the actor and the action make their presence constantly felt; it becomes disconnected and diffuse when their presence is obscured. This theatrical metaphor shows its relevance most clearly, of course, when the subject is personal:

> With regard to this system, Ammianus has but two general comments to offer, and, of these, the first concerns the Roman aristocracy. In a number of striking passages, which have been used by Gibbon as the basis for a brilliant portrayal of contemporary imperial society, Ammianus lets himself go in a scathing indictment of this class. With Juvenalian scorn he stigmatizes the aimless frivolity of lives made possible only through swollen incomes derived from the exploitation of the provincials and consecrated to no purpose worthier than the ostentatious display of wealth and pride. He describes the incessant round of amusements, bathing, driving, hunting, yachting, and the exchange of hospitality, whereby the worthless aristocrats of his day sought to conceal the futility of their existence. He points with disgust to their moral and spiritual shortcomings, their cowardice and effeminacy, their avarice and wastefulness, their quickness to borrow, their slowness to repay;

above all to the childish superstition which prompts them to resort, on the slightest pretext, to diviners and soothsayers who prey upon their fears. This superstition he attributes to the lack of any serious principles of conduct, a defect for which they have themselves to blame, inasmuch as they have turned from the cultivation of the mind, rejecting the heritage of philosophy through which alone such principles may be attained, in order to immerse themselves in mere sensationalism. Accordingly, among their retainers, the crooner has replaced the philosopher, the teacher of histrionics that of oratory; they seal their libraries like tombs, but construct for themselves hydraulic organs.

CHARLES NORRIS COCHRANE, *Christianity and Classical Culture*

Any subject may be treated as though it were personal and thus become the dominant presence in its development. Obviously, a lavish sequence of "he did" or "it did" sentences will be as annoying as a series of abrupt movements on stage, and it is to avoid abruptness that Cochrane varies the structure and length of sentences so carefully in the excerpt just presented. But there is no need for a slavish sequence in the first place. The actor may be given many names, by use of synonym and paraphrase; a series of actions may be so attached that only one mention of the actor is necessary for all; artful manipulation of syntax can place the actor at other than initial positions in the sentence without altering his grammatical and logical authority. All that is necessary is that the central figure and the central action dominate.

Now there is no denying that this formula for coherence is oversimple. It is nonetheless a useful one, often useful for actual composition, nearly always useful for clearing up passages which have become muddled and directionless. Its weakness is that it operates from a fixed element, the actor, and this limits flexibility and movement. Some of that weakness is easily overcome by taking liberties with the "actor." For instance, in this opening paragraph from an essay about an English novelist, "novel" is the actor for the first two sentences and "novelist," for the ones that follow:

> The English novel has traditionally admitted of no exact definition, no generic purity. Written by all sorts and conditions of men, as was the poetic drama of the Elizabethans, it has been designed for as many kinds of readers. The responsibility of the nineteenth-century novelist was to offer his readers a "story"; apart from that, and within the bounds of Victorian taste, he might provide what *extras* he would—sociological, psychological, moral. Sweeping his puppets aside, he might preach the new ethics, expound the nature of things, prophesy the future actions of his characters or the future of human character;

returning again to his puppets, he was free to pass in and out of their minds, now seeing through this pair of subsidiary eyes, now through that, now exerting the omniscience of his own sight.

AUSTIN WARREN, *Rage for Order*

In the end, coherence is always a quality of thought rather than a manner of expression. The confused mind cannot produce coherent prose. On the other hand, the deliberate effort to make an obscure or muddled passage coherent by the use of rhetorical procedures often helps to reduce the mental confusion in which it originated.

6/ Introductions

The frustrating experience of trying to find "a way to begin" is common to amateur and professional writer alike. Basically, it is usually a compound of dread and perplexity: dread of the labor involved in translating thought into language, and perplexity about which spring to touch first in order to set the machinery of composition going. Most writers resign themselves to the fact that they will begin a half-dozen times, throwing away one effort after another, until something satisfies enough so that writing can continue. Not infrequently, the sentence or paragraph which succeeded will later be abandoned entirely or completely altered, but if it has served its purpose the loss is a gain of one kind.

Because most serious writing goes through several stages, what is said about composition may apply to one stage but not to all. That is particularly true of introductions. It is more important to a writer that he get started than that his introduction be, at the outset, all that he wants it to be. Later, when he is revising, he can afford the energy to "polish up the handle on the big front door" of his essay, and these remarks are therefore directed to that final stage of his work.

The cursory glance taken in an earlier chapter at the articles in a single issue of the New York *Times Magazine* disclosed several strategies for introducing the subject and for engaging the reader's attention. The more "popular" the magazine, the greater will be the effort to relate the text to the reader's casual experience and the less will be the effort to make him rise out of his casual concerns into the particular world of the article before him. Ordinarily, the superficiality and sensationalism of an introduction will be consistent with the quality and manner of the exposition which follows it. For the writer of serious expository prose, directed in the main at those who may be assumed to have an initial readiness to be informed, it is therefore not necessary to provide further discussion of the opening maneuvers of less sober writing.

The aim of the introductory sentence or paragraph of a critical essay should be to get things moving: to indicate the topic of discussion, to give information about the limitations to be placed on that topic, and to set, or at least hint at, the tone of what is to follow. All this should be done as compactly as possible. Purely mechanical interposition of the writer is the sure mark of the amateur. This does not necessarily mean that use of the first person is bad, although it is true that "I" is a difficult pronoun to manage in many ways. Consider this example:

> I firmly believe that the honor system should be substituted for the present proctored examination system. I shall attempt in the following paragraphs to convince the reader of this.

Now, the first "I" is without question justifiable because this is an expression of opinion, and the writer wants the reader to know that it is his own opinion he is expressing. He could have done so, of course, by writing, "An honor system should be substituted for the present proctored examination system," and before he is done, having hunted for phrases to keep the "I" going—"in my opinion," "it seems to me," "as I see it"—he may wish he had. But "I firmly believe" is not entirely bad and even has the advantage of directness and simplicity on its side.

The same cannot be said for the second sentence. Here the writer enters though his presence has no value. At the moment he should be getting on to defend his revolutionary proposal, he is holding up a placard which reads, "This way to the main works."

The series of introductory sentences below illustrates clearly the process of improvement in the making of introductions which a student might practice in his own writing.

1. In the following paragraphs I shall compare and contrast views on American society as they were expressed by two foreigners writing about one hundred and fifty years apart.
2. Although one hundred and fifty years separate their views on American Society, there are many similarities between the observations of Crèvecœur and Müller-Freienfels.
3. Although their observations are separated by one hundred and fifty years of extensive social change, both Crèvecœur and Müller-Freienfels see that the most distinguishing characteristic of American society is the leveling process.

7/ Conclusions

There are two common faults in the concluding sections of students' papers. One is the reintroduction of the mechanical "I."

> Thus I have shown how one can obtain a synthesis of Martius yellow in shorter time by a reduction of the number of steps in the initial process.

The other might be called the "pious hope." It usually appears in some such form as this:

> If more men today would capture the great vision of St. Augustine's *City of God,* there would perhaps be no need for a United Nations.

The faults point to their own correction. A conclusion should be no more general than the essay it concludes; its job is to restate, as adroitly as possible, the principal matter and the tone of the preceding text. Rewritten, the examples given above might read:

> This eliminates a third step in the initial process for synthesizing Martius yellow and reduces the time for the whole operation to two hours and thirty-five minutes.

> The *City of God* is all of these things—history and theology, philosophical speculation and textual criticism—but above all it is a vision of the world redeemed by a "new Adam," Jesus Christ.

8/ Transitional Words and Phrases

If there is one difficulty that harasses students more than any other, it is the linking together of sentences and paragraphs. In large part, good transitional structures are a corollary of good organization; the author who is completely in command of his work, who knows just where he is going as he writes, will have no trouble with transitions. But even for the professional writer, the occasions are few in which he knows exactly where his writing will lead him. For him, transitional words and phrases are a means of tacking down the gains he has made, the ground he has covered. For his reader, they become signals of considerable importance.

Literally, "transition" means "a crossing." In the practice of exposition, the transition acts as a bridge between sentences, between groups of sentences, between paragraphs and sections. Moreover, it is a bridge with a direction sign: it not only takes the reader across but it tells him where he is going and where he has been. Explicitly, *a transition reveals relationship*. The possible relationships are many: cause to effect, general to particular or particular to general, supplementation, restriction, concession, and so on. The writer can readily decide which relationship exists between units by asking such questions as these:

> What do I want to accomplish in the sentence I am about to write? Am I simply adding information to that already given? Am I presenting conflicting matter? Do I wish to make a concession? prove a point? present a reason for something's being so? show the next step in a process? Is this sentence to be illustrative only or will it further the discussion? Does it define? assert? support?

Once the relationship is known, a proper connective can be selected. To make that selection, one must know the precise effect of conjunctions and other transitional words and phrases. Even the most common ones regularly suffer misinterpretation and should, for that reason, be listed here.

and moreover furthermore	These expressions indicate that what follows is supplementary to what precedes. They should, therefore, link matters of like kind and grammatical form.
but however yet	These mark a change in direction or the introduction of material which conflicts with what has gone before. Since opposition is intended, they, too, should link matters of like kind and grammatical form.
still nevertheless notwithstanding	The sense of an opposing current is conveyed by these words, also, but they generally come after some sort of concession has been made.
although though while	These words are concessive. They always require a balancing principal statement.
for because	Both introduce the *reason for* another statement or condition.
then since as	As conjunctions, these three words may be used to show cause or they may simply indicate a relationship in time.

in order that ⎫
so that   ⎬ These show purpose.

provided that ⎫
in case that   ⎬ These restrict.

Complete command of these connectives is a requisite of good writing, but they will not alone give all that is needed for free and forward movement of discourse. In fact, overuse of them can easily become an impediment to the easy flow of good prose. A page spattered with *however's* and *for's* and *then's* is as unsightly as a garment held together with safety pins. The kind of transition that does best service is the unobtrusive one, the one that comes from making the language of the text provide its own connections, the transition known—for want of a less pretentious word—as the "organic transition." It is not nearly so mystical as it sounds, and a little practice will give any student confidence in its use.

To create an organic transition, a writer may think of it as looking in two directions at once: back to what has been said and forward to what is to be said. The trick—and it is a kind of trick—of delivering that sense of double awareness lies simply in picking up a word or a phrase or the main idea of the preceding passage and touching it lightly, with or without some change, in the connecting term. Examples will make that procedure clearer than will further explanation.

The student who wrote the following paragraph has used both formal and organic transitions within the paragraph.

> For several reasons the convention is sometimes considered better than the primary system. *In the first place,* it is obvious, from the small number of voters in primary elections, that the public generally cares little about them. *Moreover,* the convention system allows selection of candidates so that the ticket is balanced to give all groups representation. *This kind of selection* has the *additional* advantage of providing a guarantee against the nomination of "crackpot" candidates and of sharply curtailing campaign expenditures, itself an important matter if one realizes that, in politics, support is always accompanied by the expectation of favors and patronage. *All these* are valuable considerations. *Yet,* in the face of the one great objection to conventions—machine domination—they lose their importance.

This kind of selection uses a key word in the preceding sentence and leaves to *additional* the work of showing that this statement is supplementary to its predecessor. *All these* gathers the four arguments advanced in favor of party conventions, and the sentence it introduces reinforces the tone of approval.

The following selection is another example of a tightly knit paragraph:

> . . . and throughout the first chapter of *Walden* there is a note of impatience, sometimes an almost feverish desire to get the world to shake itself clear of clutter and complication, to give up the velvet cushion for a pumpkin, to stop the trains from running, the newspapers from pouring out their daily rush of words, the housewives from adding to the useless piles of stuff in the attic, and their farmer husbands from adding shed to outhouse and barn to shed and mortgage to all. The *impatience and the fever* well up in a great cry, "Simplify! Simplify! Simplify!"
>
> But simplification was the one thing the world had no intention even to consider. The steam engine had come, and soon there would be. . . .

In the foregoing passage, a good part of the unity of the paragraph is achieved by the series of parallel phrases. The repetition of "impatience" and "fever" adds to the unity by drawing the examples together in the generalization originally proposed; and the turning of "Simplify" into a noun gives the paragraph that follows an emphatic but unmechanical link with the paragraph just concluded.

The more skilled the writer, the more subtle and varied will be the devices he employs for binding sentences and paragraphs together. The relationships conveyed by those devices will nonetheless be the same as those mentioned earlier, and a student can for that reason properly begin with them and with the rudimentary transitions as a means of coming to realize which connections between statements are common. Once he has those connections firmly in mind, he can learn to handle the many devices for making a paragraph or an essay appear as inevitable in its progress as a river.

chapter eight

Glossary of Usage

It is not at all easy to make definitive statements about this or that matter of usage, for three reasons: (1) "proper" usage varies from place to place and group to group; (2) it changes from century to century, even from generation to generation; (3) it develops changes, especially in these days of wide and rapid communication, quite unsystematically. Yet it is also true that the basic sentence patterns and grammatical structures, those that govern nine-tenths or more of our speech and writing, are fairly stable from one part of the country to another, from social group to social group, and even from century to century. It is also true that writing is more stable, more "standard," than speech.

The distinctions and judgements recorded below deal only with the matters of usage, verbal and grammatical, that are sufficiently argued about to make their separate listing worth while. Now the fact that they *are* argued about means that people do not agree about them—or, at least, do not make the same choices when they speak and write them. Therefore, there would seem to be two obligations paramount for this kind of book. First, it should specify what its authors observe to be the usage of writers who, in other ways, display respect for language as a vehicle of accurate expression. Secondly, it should give some indication of allowable differences, defining "allowable" as "sanctioned by the fact that even among writers of excellent reputation usage varies." The analogous obligations for the student are these: to respect the language of those who use English most carefully; and to distinguish between allowable differences, as defined above, and those that have no sanction but general currency. In short, the purpose of this checklist is not to teach you to write like everyone else, but to keep you from doing so.

References in these listings to Fowler and others may lead you to acquire one of several useful handbooks of usage. Some good ones are: Fowler, *Modern English Usage;* Nicholson, *A Dictionary of American English Usage;* Partridge, *Usage and Abusage;* Hook, *Guide to Good*

Writing; Bryant, *Current American Usage.* Wherever in our discussion the epithets *overused, pretentious, hackneyed* and the like appear, we rely on such handbooks as well as on our own experience for the advice implied.

ability, capability, capacity.   *Ability* means *power to perform; capability* adds a sense of endowment: *capacity* means *power to receive* or *hold.* Idiomatic: ability to swim (*not* ability of swimming); capability for unremitting effort; capacity to absorb, or capacity for absorbing (*not* capacity of absorbing); able to, capable of.

age, aged (as adjective).   In modifying expressions: seven men, *aged* forty or over. . . . The jargon of advertisement (from classified advertisements to information-wanted posters in the post office) has led some to substitute *age* for *aged* in such expressions.

aggravate, irritate.   *Aggravate* means *increase; irritate* means *excite anger in, cause soreness:* He *irritates* me and then *aggravates* my anger by pretending not to notice that I am *irritated.* Obviously, a useful distinction but one often ignored in speech, where *aggravate* is a common synonym for *irritate.*

all ready, already.   *Already* is an adverb; *all ready,* a pronoun modified by an adjective: They are *all ready* to go; they are *already* there.

all right, alright.   Conservative editorial practice rejects the second form, which seems to have developed by analogy with *all ready, already,* though the ground for such analogy is not a semantic one.

all the time.   When the time is clearly defined by context (She sat there *all the time* he worked), the expression is unquestionably acceptable. When there is no such clear definition and the phrase means something like "constantly" (Actors act while they are on the stage, but he acts *all the time*), Fowler classifies it as slang. The distinction is so nice that few observe it, though placement of the undefined phrase does, in some instances, give it an unidiomatic ring (*All the time* he takes money from the till; he *all the time* looks at her). Place the phrase at the end of either sentence, and the expression becomes idiomatic, though still informal.

almost, most.   *Almost* means *nearly; most* means *preponderant part* or *to a high degree.* He was *most* eager to criticize what *almost* everyone else approved. *Most* of his remarks showed little more than irritation.

and/or. This shorthand expression, once the subject of legislation in Georgia (where *andor* was temporarily given legitimacy), has crept into general use probably from law and business. Its purpose is to indicate a double set of alternatives. "Eat this food with butter or with mustard or with butter and mustard" becomes "Eat this food with butter and/or mustard." We have seen very few instances of its use by literary men, but the expression occurs with increasing frequency in political and sociological writing, even in conservatively edited journals. It is called "unlovely," "un-English," and "ugly" by various arbiters, and that should be warning enough about the displeasure it provokes in many readers. "Eat this food with butter or mustard, or with both" solves the problem—but does not satisfy the argument, of course.

and etc. Redundant, since *etc.* is the abbreviation for *et cetera,* meaning "and others." (And, by the way, it should not be pronounced *ek-set-er-a.*)

and which. As a coordinating conjunction, *and* requires an element of the same kind on each side of it. The common error involving *and which* goes like this: They read all six of the books *and which* I didn't really expect them to do. Two corrections are possible: omission of "which" and "do"; omission of "and." This sentence, of course, is correct: The six books which he read, *and which* I expected him to read, cover the field satisfactorily.

anxious, eager. As for *aggravate, irritate* the distinction between these words, though little observed, is worth preserving since it gives a meaningful discrimination between states of mind. *Anxious* means *worried; eager* means *keenly desirous.* I am *anxious* about his health and *eager* to see him recover.

any (place, thing, one, body, where). *Any* combines with these words —though not regularly with *-place*—when there is no special stress (*Anything* you can do, I can do better). When emphasis is desired, the words separate (*Any one* of us would have done as well). Fastidious writers used to avoid *anybody,* preferring *anyone,* but few are so fastidious now. One use, with *more,* is colloquial but is occasionally found in respectable writing: He doesn't do it *any more.* What is true of *any* in such constructions is true of *some.*

apt, likely, liable. The distinctions here are less tenuous than that between *anyone* and *anybody* but not so clear-cut as that between *anxious* and *eager.* The expression *likely to* is reserved by many writers for matters of more or less agreeable or neutral outcome. He is *likely* to show up before noon. *Liable* to, by contrast, introduces unpleasant consequences. He is *liable* to be left behind. In careful usage, *apt* is an adjective meaning *quick to learn* (an apt pupil) or *appropriate* (an apt solution). Its use as a synonym for *liable* is colloquial (He is apt to come late).

area. The metaphorical use of *area,* like that of *field,* or *region,* is convenient but jargonic and sometimes pretentious. "In the *area* of concern for social welfare," will reduce to "Concern for social welfare" without loss.

as, like. Conjunctive use: *as* is so ubiquitous in its temporal sense that its conjunctive use in a causal sense often makes rereading a line necessary and should therefore be avoided (Compare: "The duchess swept into the room *as* he was leaving" with "The duchess swept into the room, *as* she intended to make a good impression at once"). In the comparative sense, it has long shared honors with "like," though writers who are punctilious about diction scorn "like" in any conjunctive situation (Compare: "They came home *as* they said they would" with the rejected "They came home *like* they said they would"). Anyone who cares can keep that distinction in mind. The difficulty comes when following pronouns are involved. "They know me *as* well *as* she" means something different from "They know me *as* well *as* her." In the following pair of sentences, however, meaning is the same: He is twice *as* heavy *as* I; He is twice *as* heavy *as* me. In "He is twice *as* heavy *as* me" the conjunctive rule (see *and which,* above) is ignored; the sentence is ungrammatical though well on its way to becoming idiomatic in speech. To avoid such an error, Nicholson faces the most strained construction without a tremor: You dressed up *as* she. Any American writer of English would try to avoid that strangeness. You dressed up to look *like* her.

being that, being as. In constructions like *"Being that* he has no more money," the phrase is apparently a vestige of some formal locution possibly derived from schoolboy translations of the Latin absolute construction. Use *because* in its place.

between, among. The simple distinction that requires *between* for two instances and *among* for more than two is not enough. *Among* emphasizes participation in a group: He is one *among* many. *Between* emphasizes particularization, distinction, difference, even opposition of members of a group: There is no way of discriminating fairly *between* the seven owners. It is true, however, that *among* is never used when fewer than three are in the group referred to.

beside, besides.   *Beside* is a preposition meaning *near by* and, therefore, from force of fact, *compared with:* sitting *beside* me; looks cheap *beside* this one. *Besides* is a preposition or adverb meaning *in addition to* or *other than: Besides* running the store, he acts as postmaster (prepositional); *Besides,* he is a boxer (adverbial).

bi-, semi-.   Though dictionaries disagree, soundest practice appears to sanction *bi-* as two and *semi-* as half. *Biennial* means *every two years; semiannual* means *every half-year.* However, *Webster's Collegiate* lists *biannual* as meaning the same as *semiannual.* Informed use equates *biweekly* with *fortnightly;* popular use is ambivalent. One way out is to avoid the Latin prefixes altogether: twice a week, every two weeks, yearly, every other year. If used, the prefixes are hyphenated only before proper names (semi-Socialist) and before the letter *i* (semi-incapacitated).

burst, bust.   *Bust* is a corrupt form for the past tense both of *burst* and of *break* (for which *busted* is an additional corrupt form). It has made its way into a good many rather slangy expressions and is unchallengeable within them; fit to *bust.* By some sort of alchemy, the corruption has also become a noun (The whole effort is a *bust*), but the use is slangy.

but that, but what.   The first is preferable to the second on sheer grammatical grounds, but both are widely used in good writing: I don't know *but that* you are right.

can, may.   The traditional distinction remains a useful one, though frequently ignored. *Can* deals with ability, power (*Can* he move his injured arm at all?); *may* deals with permission (*May* he attend, too?). In either of these examples, a substitution may be made, and that is exactly the point of distinction: a substitution can be meaningful if the distinction is preserved.

can but, cannot but, can't help but.   The first two locutions sound very formal to the American ear: He *can but* consent (can only consent); He *cannot but* consent (cannot do anything other than consent). The third is a loose construction substituted for a tighter one: He *cannot help* (*can't help*) *but* think; He *can't help* thinking.

case.   The word has uses but it is much overused and often conceals vagueness. Fowler and Quiller-Couch object to *in any case,* but on no very satisfactory grounds; it is clearly an idiom. *In the case of* is usually superfluous altogether (In the *case* of the third member of the group, we think . . . ; We think the third member of the group . . .). As a substitute for *often* or *usually,* such a phrase as *in many cases* is wordy; as a substitute for nouns of specific reference, *case* is lazy ("in such *cases*" for "in such situations, operations, places, examples, etc.").

certain.   Loosely and inelegantly used simply for emphasis: I have a *certain* distaste. Curiously enough, in this use, *certain* seems to indicate a considerable degree of uncertainty, indefinability. This use, like that of *definite* to mean *strong* (He has a *definite* tendency . . .) is rather faddish.

common, mutual.   *Common* means *shared* (our *common* heritage); *mutual* means *reciprocal* (their *mutual* hatred, that is, of each other). But *mutual* may also be used as a synonym for *common* (our *mutual* preference for quiet).

[comparatives].   Two faults are common: doubling of the comparative form (These are far *more richer* forms than those); omission of a needed element in the comparison (Capitalism is *more* successful in developing means of production). For the second example, the comparison may develop either the subject (. . . more successful *than* communism) or the predicate (. . . means of production *than* in controlling means of distribution"). It should not fail to do one or the other.

compose, comprise.   *Compose* means *make up; comprise* means *include.* Five members *compose* a basketball team; Great Britain *comprises* England, Wales and Scotland. The passive form of *comprise* (*is comprised*) usurps the meaning of *compose.*

contact.   The most careful writer undoubtedly limits *contact* to use as a noun. Therefore: "He made a contact with the enemy agent," and not "He contacted the enemy agent." But like *blame* and a hundred other nouns-made-from-verbs, this one is accepted in even the best company today.

consensus.   The meaning of the word makes a following *of* opinion unnecessary.

continual, continuous.   Another useful distinction, though much ignored. *Continual* means *occurring in steady but not unbroken succession;*

continuous means *without interruption:* a day of *continual* interruption, an hour of *continuous* quiet.

contrary. In an introductory or connective phrase, the idiomatic expression is *on the contrary*. In an adjectival phrase, the idiomatic expression is *to the contrary: On the contrary,* the simple truth is that . . . ; Whatever he says *to the contrary,* the simple truth is that. . . .

contrast, compare. *Contrast* emphasizes difference; *compare* emphasizes likeness. Idiomatic: *contrast with; compare to* or *compare with,* tenuously distinguished according to the breadth of the comparison (Shall I *compare* thee *to* a summer's day? If we try to *compare* practices of the reigning monarch *with* those of his predecessor. . . .).

couple together. Like *combine together* or *attach together,* redundant. When redundancy produces emphasis, it is excusable, though emphasis achieved by such means raises some question about the general economy of the prose in which it occurs.

criteria. Plural only. The singular is *criterion.*

data. Used for both singular and plural. This liberty with a grammatical form is the result of ignorant borrowing. *Datum* is singular in Latin; *data* is plural. Therefore, by derivation: this *datum* is, these *data* are. However, the distinction between these words is not strictly observed even in edited written prose.

decimate. Strictly, *reduce by one-tenth.* Loosely used to mean *destroy the greater part of.*

deprecate, depreciate. *Deprecate* means *disapprove; depreciate* means *make less, reduce in quantity, quality or stature:* His father *deprecated* his decision to study law. He *depreciates* every noble motive to the principle of self-interest.

desirous of. High-flown for want: He is *desirous of* obtaining some assistance; He *wants* some assistance.

discussant. A relatively new word, apparently built on analogy with *inform, informant* or *participate, participant.* Its sudden fashionableness has given offense, but the word is here to stay.

disinterested, uninterested. The distinction, abused by many, is a useful one. *Disinterested* means *impartial; uninterested* means *lacking* *interest:* The best judge is a *disinterested* one. The worst audience is an *uninterested* one.

dive, dived, dove.   In the United States, at least, this weak verb is becoming a strong one, hence *dove* is an acceptable though not required past-tense form. The past participle remains *dived:* He *dove* (*dived*) into the pool. He has *dived* ten times already.

different from, different than, different to.   The cultivated idiom in American English is *different from:* His theory is *different from* any other I have heard. *Different than* frequently introduces a clause, as an alternative to *different from what:* College life is *different than* (from what) I thought it would be. His way is *different from* mine. He does it *differently than* I do. Colloquially, *than* frequently replaces *from:* His theory is *different than mine. Different to* is strictly British idiom.

due to.   *Due* is an adjective. It therefore needs, and originally had, a noun which it modified: His illness is *due to* exposure. The idiomatic use of *due to* as alternative to *because of* (*Due to* unforeseen circumstances. . . .) is, however, so widespread that grammatical origin has been all but overwhelmed.

each, every.   Two errors are common: use of a plural verb with these singular pronouns (*Each* of them *have studied*), and use of a related plural pronoun or a pronoun of the second, rather than the third, person (*Each* of them will take *their* lessons alone. When *each* of you stood up, *you* volunteered). Despite slack colloquial usage, edited written prose holds firm for these correct forms: *Each* of them *has studied.* Each of them will take *his* lessons alone. When *each* of you stood up, *he* volunteered. Formal use requires a matching possessive adjective when *each* follows the verb (They have rendered *each his own* talent), but a more natural phrasing would be: *Each* has rendered *his own* talent.

end up.   In this expression *up* is an intensifier and otherwise meaningless. It is common in modern speech, frequent in written prose, but rare in the prose of literary writers.

enormity, enormousness.   Dictionaries allow the words as synonyms, but commonly *enormity* means *great badness* (the *enormity* of his crime) and *enormousness* means only *greatness in size* (the *enormousness* of the universe).

enthuse.   A verb developed from the noun and adjective but abhorrent to many. Still, it is common in speech, even in the speech of cultivated people, and it occasionally appears in prose of indisputable propriety.

equally as. The words overlap completely (He is *equally as* tall as I am). Corrected: He is *as* tall as I am. His height is *equal* to mine.

evaluate. A perfectly good word, meaning *judge* or *measure,* which has been so much abused, especially in the derived form *evaluation,* that sensitive writers often avoid it.

except. As a conjunction, the word is now unacceptable (He would go *except* she doesn't want him to) though it was once not only acceptable but elegant (*Except* ye become as little children, ye shall not enter . . .).

extra. This is a short form for *extraordinary,* therefore *something in addition to or beyond the normal.* It has long been used in combination with some adjectives (*extracurricular, extramural*) and has in recent years extended itself to other adjectives with somewhat altered meaning (*extra-special* means very special, *extra-heavy* means very heavy). In this adulterated sense, the word is gaining currency but is still rare in conservative prose.

fact. From f*actus,* past participle of *facio,* I make; *something made.* Facts are. Therefore, the expression *true fact* is a tautology. A factual statement (that is, one that purports to contain a fact or facts) may be true or false, but a fact simply is a fact.

farther, further. The traditional limitation of *farther* to physical distance lingers, but general practice in the best modern prose seems to make choice more by personal preference of the sound of one over the other than by any semantic distinction. The words have a different origin and once had distinguishably different meanings, but context appears to serve well enough to identify the specific meaning so that the two have blurred.

feature. As a verb in the passive (This is *featured* by), this word has come into colloquial currency through its jargonic employment in advertising. It doesn't mean anything very precisely, is already hackneyed, and therefore offends a discriminating reader on two scores. As a noun meaning *aspect* or *lineament,* it is, of course, standard: His *features* are sharp, almost ferret-like. As an adjective or noun-surrogate (the *feature* story, the page-ten *feature*), it is the jargon of journalism for *main* or *principal* or *special.*

firstly. Though *secondly, thirdly,* etc., have survived, *firstly* became obsolete in respectable prose decades ago. It is common now for the other ordinal forms to receive similar reduction; therefore: *First,* it should be noted that . . . ; *second,* it must be admitted. . . .

flammable, inflammable, nonflammable. The first two words are synonyms; the third is an antonym to the other two.

forward, forwards, toward, towards. Reputable practice is to use the form without *-s* for all purposes.

future prediction. A tautology, easily corrected by omitting *future.* There is a sense, it is true, in which this phrase is acceptable, meaning *a prediction yet to be made.*

graduate. For good usage as a verb meaning *leave after completing a course of study,* it requires the preposition *from:* He will *graduate from* high school, *not* He will graduate high school. Stricter use in such an expression requires the passive: He will *be graduated* from high school.

guess. Used to mean *estimate,* or *calculate,* the word is entirely acceptable in all contexts; used to mean *suppose* (I *guess* so), it is colloquial at present, but may not remain so (If he is, as I *guess,* a sympathizer, I want nothing more to do with him).

had better, had rather, had ought. *Had better* is used for command and warning. (He *had better* get ready); *had rather,* and its alternative form, *would rather,* for wish or preference (He *had rather* stay than go). *Had ought* is a solecism (He *had ought* to go), corrected by dropping either of the words, depending on the intent. He *had* to go. He *ought* to go.

hang, hanged, hung. The verb *to hang,* meaning *to suspend by the neck until dead,* is a weak verb. Therefore: they *hang* him, they *hanged* him, they have *hanged* him. The verb used with reference to inanimate objects is a strong one. Therefore: They *hang* it up, they *hung* it up, they have *hung* it up.

hardly, scarcely. Negative in force as adverbs, these words are therefore complete without *not, none, etc.* They have *hardly* begun. She had *scarcely* any money left when she came.

healthy, healthful. A distinction, seldom closely observed even by good writers, uses *healthy* to mean *having good health* and *healthful* to mean *health-giving.* A *healthy* mushroom might be anything but *healthful.*

human, humane.   The tendency to use *human* as a noun (These *humans* are . . .) as well as an adjective (These *human* beings are . . .) is increasing and will undoubtedly prevail. As adjective, *human* means *characteristic of man, humane* means *kindly, decent* (the *humane* thing to do).

hurt.   Only colloquially used as a noun, and then either entirely uncultivated or unbearably arch: Does it have a *hurt* in its paw?

identical same.   Tautological, colloquial, uncultivated.

imply, infer.   Implying is the action of the speaker or writer; inferring is the action of the listener or reader: Do you *imply* that he is a fool, or am I making a false *inference*?

individual.   Colloquially used as substitute for *person* (This *individual* thinks . . .). In such use the special referential aspect of the word —to distinguish one from many (An *individual* may achieve more than a group)—is lost.

in, into.   As prepositions, *in* is for position, *into* for direction of movement: He was *in* the dining-room and went directly *into* the kitchen. The use of *in* for both meanings is common in speech, rare in careful writing.

inside of.   So written, and not as a single word. But *on-to* has achieved union (He steps *onto* the terrace). A related expression is *in back of,* or *back of;* it, too, remains ununited. *Inside of, onto, back of,* and *in back of* are almost universal in speech and very common in writing, but some very good writers resent the prepositional doubling and either drop one preposition altogether (*inside* the room, *to* the terrace) or use another word (*behind* the barn). Though common in speech, *in under* is not yet used by any serious writers. Obviously, no rule will hold here. The matter is one of gradual shifts and developed tastes.

irregardless, disregardless.   Vulgarisms.

interpretative, interpretive.   Some arbiters admit only the second form, but both are widely used without difference in meaning.

kind, sort.   As nouns, singular and therefore to be used with singular adjectives and verbs: This kind is less expensive than that. *Kind of* and *sort of,* used to mean *somewhat* (He is *kind of* soft-hearted), are colloquial and uncultivated.

last, latest. A useful distinction assigns *last* to the terminal member of a group or series (the *last* game of the year) and *latest* to the most recent one (the *latest* effort to embarrass this country). *Last* is widely used, however, where the distinction would require *latest* (His *last* operation was unsuccessful, but his next . . .).

lay, laid, lie, lain. *Lay* (past form *laid*) takes an object: He *lays* the tie on the table; He *laid* it there; He *laid* his hand on the board. *Lie* (past forms *lay* and *lain*) is intransitive: He *lies* down; They *lay* without moving; We have *lain* asleep too long.

lend, loan. As verbs, interchangeable now, though once *lend* was reserved—by handbooks, at any rate—for the verb, *loan* for the noun (*Lend* me some money. Make me a *loan*). *Lend* shows no signs of becoming a noun (but see *hurt,* above).

less, fewer. Like *amount, number,* a pleasant distinction widely ignored. *Less* is used of amount (*less* money), *fewer* of number (*fewer* coins): If *fewer* members attend, we shall need *less* food.

may, might. *May* is used in the present-tense sequence, *might* in the past-tense sequence: If he *may* enter, she will want to; If he *might* enter, she would want to. *May of* and *might of* (He *may of* gone) are corruptions of *have* into *of.*

maximize. A relatively new word, developed by analogy with *minimize.* (See *discussant,* above).

moral, morale. The adjective *moral* means *right and proper.* The noun (with an -e added from the French form of the adjective and the accent shifted) means *spirit.*

neither, nor; either, or. One careless construction is common: failure to observe the coordinates (He is not *either* clever *nor* honest. Corrected: He is not *either* clever *or* honest. He is *neither* clever *nor* honest). One awkwardness is almost unavoidable: selection of verb form when the nouns coordinated are of different person or number (*Neither* he *nor* I is? am? *Neither* the Senator *nor* his constituents has? have?). The best solution, not entirely arbitrary since it exploits proximity, is to match the verb form to the nearer of the two nouns or pronouns: *Neither* he *nor* I am. *Neither* the Senator *nor* his constituents have. If *Neither he nor I am* sounds too precious to be borne, avoid the problem: *Neither of us is.* But if the significance of *neither* amounts to anything at all, not *Neither of us are.*

nice, nice and. An exhausted adjective at best (a *nice* day) and, at worst (*nice and* helpful), merely a colloquial intensive.

none. Since the word is a shortening of *no one,* the argument for its use with a singular form of verb is logical. But *none* is so widely used in plural references and with no intention to sort the group into single units that a plural verb is common, both in speech and in cultivated writing: *None* of them are more convinced now than they were before he spoke.

no one. So written.

noted, notorious. *Notorious* has a pejorative sense (a *notorious gambler*); *noted* and *famous* are roughly synonymous (a *noted* author, a *famous* person).

nowheres, noways, anywheres, anyways. In all four words the terminal *-s* is colloquial and uncultivated.

off of, off from. See *inside of,* above.

official, officious. Both adjectives obviously derive from *office.* The distinction between them is that between what genuinely belongs to an office (an *official* communication) and what merely assumes the airs of official authority, with or without warrant but always with imperiousness (an *officious* manager). We admire, or at least put up with, what is official; we resent what is officious.

old-fashioned. So written. *Not* old-fashion.

one of. A common mistake is this one: He is *one of those men who spends* more than he makes. The position of *one* coerces the verb-form even though the subject (*who*) of the verb clearly refers to the plural noun *people* and requires a plural form of the verb. Equally common is an error involving person: You are the person who are responsible. Corrected: He is *one of* those men who spend more than they make. You are the person who is responsible.

oneself. Preferred to *one's self* unless an attempt is being made to create a distinction (*one's self* and one's body, *one's self* and all the other selves in the world). Note the trouble this reflexive suffix makes in English. We say *myself* (*my,* possessive) but *himself* (*him,* objective). By analogy, then, *meself* (now obsolete) and *hisself, theirself* (uncultivated but far from obsolete). Since the reflexive is also intensive, you may hear and read *Between him and myself,* but fastidious writers retain parallel pronouns: *Between* *him and me.* The plural pronoun requires plural reflexive form: *ourselves, themselves,* not *ourself, themself.*

overall.   Imprecise and overused word meaning *general* (*overall* tendency) or *comprehensive* (*overall* view).

over with.   See *inside of,* above.

owing to.   A genteel, and grammatically questionable, substitute for *due to* (see above), apparently intended to regularize an idiom into decency. Two resolutions are possible. Instead of "Due to the heavy rain" or "Owing to the heavy rain," write "Because of the heavy rain"; or, better, make the construction unnecessary: "The heavy rain obliterated all tracks," rather than "Because of the heavy rain, all tracks were obliterated."

particular.   See *certain,* above.

party.   Legal jargon for *contracting person.* Colloquially, *any person* (A certain *party* is interested in knowing more about you). In this use, uncultivated.

percent, per cent., per cent.   Alternates, equally acceptable. All derive from *per centum,* L., meaning *by* (or *calculated in terms of*) *the hundred.*

personal.   Coupled with some nouns metaphorically used (personal equation, personal factor, personal coefficient), it is jargonic.

personal, personnel.   *Personal* is an adjective (*personal* affairs). *Personnel* is a noun meaning *employees* or *staff* (military *personnel*) and, by derivation, an adjective meaning *having to do with employees or staff* (*personnel* officer). A *personal adviser* and a *personnel* adviser may have very different relations with those whom they advise.

phenomena.   Colloquially used for both singular and plural, but in written edited prose plural only (These *phenomena* indicate that . . .). But for the future of this word, see *data,* above. *Phenomena* suffers from another misuse. It means *objects known through the senses* and is meant to distinguish those objects from *noumena, objects known through thought or intuition only.* To use *phenomena* as a synonym for *facts* or *events* is both inaccurate and pretentious.

plausible, feasible, conceivable.   *Plausible* means *believable; feasible* means *practicable; conceivable* means *within the range of rational understanding.*

plenty. Used colloquially to mean *for the most part;* resembles *maybe* in its growing acceptance in edited written prose (There is *plenty* of competition but *maybe* not enough to suit a real scrapper).

plan on. *Plan on doing* is primarily colloquial; *plan to do* is more common in good written prose.

potful. As for all such compounds (cupful, handful), the plural adds *-s* (potfuls) unless the intent is to indicate plurality of the noun itself, in which case the compound disappears (He has his *pots full* now; *But* He has two *potfuls* of dirt).

potential. As a noun (He has a great *potential*), perhaps jargonic, certainly pretentious. Better: He is a promising athlete, student, musician, etc.

premium. By etymology, *only.* Its use to mean *of high quality* (a *premium* food, a *premium* performance) is hackneyed in advertising, reviewing, and the like.

pretty, pretty much. American idiom for *rather,* more colloquial than not.

prone, supine. *Prone* means *lying face down; supine* means *lying on one's back.* Metaphorical: *prone* means *inclined* (He is *prone* to hesitate); *supine* means *passive* or *cowardly* (He takes her remarks *supinely*).

proof, evidence. *Proof* is evidence sufficient to establish a conclusion. *Evidence* is whatever is brought forward in the attempt to establish a conclusion.

provided (-ing) that, if. Either *providing that* or *provided that* is an acceptable form, when the form is desirable at all. In the main, its formality suggests something contractual rather than something causal, for which *if* is more appropriate: If the rain falls, we shall get wet. *Provided* that you supply the funds, we agree to let you use our name as sponsors.

queer. As a verb (Their conduct *queered* the deal), both slangy and colloquial.

quote. A verb of unimpeachable reputation, but as a noun a colloquial shortening of *quotation* (This *quote* is taken from . . .). Also, shortening for *quotation marks* (Put it in *quotes*).

raise, rise. As verbs, these words distinguish actions in the same way as *lay, lie* and *set, sit.* As nouns, they are more interesting. They

seem to be synonymous, but they are not in all instances interchangeable. We say *a raise in pay* but *a rise in the cost of living.*

reason is because, reason why.   *The reason is because* is obviously redundant, but that does not keep it out of general colloquial use.
It is seldom found in edited written prose. *Reason why,* on the
other hand, though almost as obviously redundant, is common in
both cultivated speech and cultivated writing. For the tender of
ear, *reason is that* and *reason that* sound better.

refer back.   So obviously redundant as to be admissible only for emphasis.

regarding, as regards, in regard to.   Overused as synonym for *about.*

respective, respectively.   Words meant to clarify relationship (Henry
and John presented their gifts, a tin of ham and a pound of coffee
respectively, and then left). The most common abuse reflects mis-
placed preciseness (They put their *respective* coats on the rack).
Not to be confused with *respectfully.*

right off.   Colloquial only, as are *right away, right now, right then.*
Right soon, right pretty, right new, and the like are colloquial and
regional.

round.   Or *around.* Needs no preceding apostrophe since *round* is the
older form.

same.   With or without a preceding *the,* this word is jargonic if it is
used as a substitute for *it* (Having gathered this matter, we shall
now assess *same* in the light of . . .). As elliptic for *the same thing*
(The *same* may be said of . . .), it is common in good speech, perhaps a little less common in good writing, where the noun is more
likely to be supplied (the *same* remark, the *same* intention).

said.   Used as an adjective meaning *previously mentioned* (*said* document), the word is legal jargon. See *party,* above.

sensual, sensuous.   Though efforts have been made to link *sensual* with
the psychology and *sensuous* with the physiology of sense impres-
sions, actual distinction now seems to be one of value. *Sensual* is at
least mildly pejorative; *sensuous* is neutral or approbatory.

shall, will.   Though a moderately useful distinction is commonly
taught (*shall* for first person, *will* for second and third, except
when determination or promise is involved), it is little observed
and has no strong historical sanction. *Will* has largely supplanted

shall, and the distinction between simple future and indication of promise or determination is left to context.

size, sized.   As hyphenated to make an adjective, the proper form is *-sized* (pint-*sized*). See *age,* above.

slow, slowly.   *Slow* is both adverb and adjective; *slowly* is an adverb. As adverbs, the two may or may not have exactly the same sense (same: drive *slow,* drive *slowly;* not the same: *slow*-moving car, *slowly* moving car).

soluble, solvable.   Some writers use *solvable* only in referring to problems, *soluble* only in referring to physical elements. Negatives are *insoluble, unsolvable.* The noun *solution* serves both.

[split infinitive].   For strong emphasis, an adverb may sometimes split the *to* and verb of an infinitive (If you want *to* really *destroy* the program . . .). Generally the infinitive is best left intact (He decided *to read* through the last chapter hastily, *not* He decided *to* hastily *read* . . .). Except for eccentric stylistic effects it is almost never separated by more than a word (They hope *to,* in a manner of speaking, *"subsidize"* the enemy).

status.   Has two common uses, the first one derived from the Latin original, *status quo* (His *status* at the time of the incident was entirely regular). The second use is apparently an extension of the first (They are trying to get *status* by moving to a suburb).

superior.   Followed by *to,* not by *than.*

suspicion.   Colloquially, both verb and noun; but in edited written prose, usually a noun only (He suspected me of perjury, *not* He *suspicioned* that I had perjured myself).

that, which.   This distinction is sometimes made: *that* for restrictive clauses (The box *that* you want is there); *which* for nonrestrictive clauses (The box, *which* you need not take unless you want to, has no cover). The demonstrative adjective should not be used to modify a word also modified by a restrictive clause (The box *that* you want, *not That* box *that* you want). It is only fair to admit that these usages are not always observed even by impeccable stylists, partly because the discriminations are not essential and partly because euphony sometimes overrules.

till, until.   Equally acceptable in speech or writing, but *until* is more common in writing.

too, very. *Too* is superlative; *very* is intensive. Colloquially, *too* is common as a substitute for *very,* though it obviously begs the question (He isn't feeling *too* well). When *very* is used with a passive participle, conservative usage requires an intervening *much* (very much improved), though some unsupplemented uses of *very* are now idiomatic (*very* interested, *very* tired). A rather recent substitute for both *very* and *too* is *that* (He isn't *that* serious about it), but it remains colloquial.

try and, try to. *Try to read* makes better sense for what is meant than *try and read,* but colloquially *try and* is used frequently.

type. As an adjunct word, it is jargonic (Hollywood-*type* setting, roller-*type* bed); it is hackneyed as a noun meaning no more than *kind* (that *type* of person).

unpractical. Or *impractical.*

upon, on. See *in, into.* Much depends on sound and something on idiom (*Upon* my word! *on* the house).

utilize. Means *use,* but some appear to find it more indicative of calculated action. Often merely pretentious.

used to. So written except in the negative (didn't *use* to) when customary past action is meant. In passive constructions of the verb *to use* (It is used for painting; it was used for painting), the negative form does not change (it is not *used* for painting).

various, different. A useful, but not essential distinction, assigns *various* to general distributive meaning (various members agree) and *different* to discrimination (He gave it to different members each time), but cultivated colloquial practice uses the words interchangeably.

who, whom. Traditionally, *who* is used as subject of verb, *whom* as object of verb and preposition. Colloquially, *who* is superseding *whom* especially in questions (Who are you speaking to? Who did you give it to?), but edited written prose does not admit the locution intentionally. One sign of the confusion these pronouns produce appears in the substitution of *whom* for *who* in interrupted relative structures (This is the man whom I think would be most likely to help you). In such a sentence the strength of *I think* seems to attract the object-form even though the subject-form is needed to govern the verb *would be.* Like *Between him and I,* this mistake generally comes from a self-conscious effort to be correct, coupled with ignorance of grammatical form.

-wise, -ways. In many words, interchangeable (*endways, endwise*); in a few, only *-wise* occurs (*clockwise, likewise, otherwise*). Recently, the fashion has grown for attaching *-wise* to every noun in sight (policy-*wise,* money-*wise,* statistics-*wise*).

without. A preposition, not a conjunction, in cultivated usage: He goes *without* me. "He won't do it *without* I come" should be corrected to "He won't do it unless I come" or "He won't do it without my coming." *Without hardly* is a kind of double negative and should be corrected to *with hardly* or *almost without.*

yet. When *yet* is used adverbially, it takes the perfect tense forms (He has not done it yet, *not* He didn't do it yet).

chapter nine / *Mechanics*

This brief chapter on mechanics is intended to be simply a convenient source of information about the technical matters most frequently troublesome to college students.

1/ Capitalization

1. *Names.* Capitalize proper nouns and the adjectives derived from them. Darwin, Darwinian theory; France, French policy; Republican party; Roman Catholic Church. When such adjectives come to be part of the name of an object in common use, capitalization generally disappears; china cups, india rubber, italic type, french fries, bermuda shorts, graham cracker.

2. *Honorifics.* Capitalize titles of honor which are followed by a proper noun: Rabbi Wise, President Hayes, Professor Wilson, Mr. Eliot. Capitalize titles of honor when they refer to a specific person: the President of the Board of Overseers, the Mayor of Cleveland. *But:* A corporation consists of a president, secretary, treasurer, board of directors. . . .

3. *Titles.* Capitalize the first word, the last word, and all other words except articles, one-syllable prepositions, and conjunctions in the titles of books, stories, poems, plays, essays, lectures, paintings, sculptures, motion pictures, and songs: *Twenty Thousand Leagues Under the Sea, Ode on a Grecian Urn, The Adoration of the Magi, Moonlight and Roses.* Within a sentence do not capitalize "the" if it is the first word in the title of a newspaper or magazine: the *London Times,* the *American Scholar.*

4. *Courses of Study.* Capitalize as for (3) if the course of study has a formal title: Economic Theory, Drama since Ibsen. Do not capitalize such terms otherwise: Capitalism represents a change in economic

theory from . . . . ; the development of the drama since Ibsen shows the influence . . . .

5. *Geographic Areas.* Capitalize words referring to geographic areas: the Far West, the Near East, the Old South. When the reference is adjectival, the word is sometimes capitalized and sometimes not, depending on the tastes of the writer or the practice of a publisher: a Western sandwich, a western sandwich; but if the reference is to an area of land or water whose boundaries are clearly fixed, capitalization will occur: the Atlantic coast. Words indicating direction only are not capitalized: They will go west this summer. (*But:* They will visit the West this summer.)

6. *The Deity.* Capitalize nouns and pronouns referring to a deity: Our God Who made heaven and earth sets His laws in the hearts of men; Jehovah; Lord; Saviour; Allah; Zeus.

7. *Historical Matters.* Capitalize the names of historical events, personages, places, institutions, artifacts, memorials, and documents: the French Revolution, General Taylor, Faneuil Hall, the Shenandoah Valley, the Washington Monument, the Bill of Rights.

8. *Family Relationships.* Capitalize words indicating family relationship when they are used in conjunction with proper names and when they are used as a substitute for proper names: Uncle Tom; my surprise at seeing Grandfather alone. Do not capitalize such words when they are used generically or when they are modified by possessives: the three sisters; my father, Mary's uncle (*But:* my Grandfather Perkins, Mary's Uncle John).

9. *Quotations.* Capitalize the first word of a quotation, if the quotation is itself a complete sentence, not if it is only part of a sentence: They answered together, "We have done nothing wrong." (*But:* They swore that they had done "nothing wrong.") If the quotation is interrupted, capitalize wherever a new sentence begins: "They have done it again," he observed, "and they deserve to win." "Don't put it there," he warned. "The water may damage it."

Do not capitalize

10. *Seasons.* fall, winter, spring, summer, autumn, springtime.

11. *Phrases or sentences following a colon.* The long months had restored his health: he was almost a new man. However, capitalization may occur if the colon is followed by a rule, a proverb, a sentence cited from a familiar text, an example, or the like.

12. *Parentheses within sentences, even if they are complete sentences.* He stepped further into the room (it was a library, he noted)

and cleared his throat noisily in hope of attracting attention. Again, capitalization may occur if the parenthetical interruption is used for providing examples which are complete sentences.

2/ Spelling

Spelling is a matter of convention based on linguistic development. Without the convention, communication would be much more difficult than it is. For that reason the convention deserves respect. Although it is true that some people have what appears to be a genuine inability to spell even simple words correctly, the condition is so rare that no college student can use it as an excuse; if he has reason to think his disability is physical or psychological, he has an obligation to seek help from an oculist or a counselor.

The only "cure" for most bad spellers is the replacing of bad habits by good ones: each must discipline himself in proportion to his need. These procedures will help:

1.   Always keep a dictionary within reach as you write; consult it, during revision of your text, whenever you are in doubt about the correct spelling of a word.

2.   Check the spelling of words you seldom use.

3.   If you habitually misspell some words, make a list of them and keep it where you can consult it readily.

4.   Learn by heart the distinction between such similar-sounding words or frequently confused words as these:

accept, except	costume, custom
affect, effect	coarse, course
all ready, already	council, counsel, consul
altar, alter	deceased, diseased
assent, ascent	decent, descent, dissent
breath, breathe	desert, dessert
capital, capitol	device, devise
censure, censor	diary, dairy
choose, chose	dual, duel
climactic, climatic	eminent, imminent
coma, comma	euphemism, euphuism
compliment, complement	foreword, forward
conscience, conscious	formally, formerly
corps, corpse	genteel, gentle, gentile

genus, genius
hear, here
hoard, horde
idle, idol
illicit, elicit
illusion, allusion
immanent, imminent
ingenious, ingenuous
irrelevant [irrevelant]
its, it's
knew, new
know, no
later, latter
loose, lose
moral, morale
of, off
past, passed
peace, piece
psychological, physiological
plain, plane
pore, poor, pour
precede, proceed
precedents, precedence
presence, presents
principal, principle
prophecy, prophesy
quiet, quite
raise, raze

receipt, recipe
recent, resent
respectively, respectfully
rite, right
route, root, rout
sense, since
sight, site, cite
sleight, slight
stationary, stationery
statue, statute, stature
straight, strait
suit, suite
their, there, they're
then, than
threw, through
to, too, two
vain, vein, vane
venal, venial
vice, vise
weak, week
weather, whether, wether, whither
which, witch
whose, who's
wrack, rack
wrapped, rapt
wry, rye
your, you're

5. If you are not certain about the spelling of words containing one of the following combinations, *always check by dictionary*. There are "rules" for each combination, but if you have not learned them by now, the likelihood is that you will master the combinations only by forcing yourself to check until they stick permanently in your mind.

    a. *ie* and *ei* (*believe, receive, weigh*)
    b. final consonants before suffix (*refér, referring; trável, traveling*)
    c. final vowels before a suffix (*arrange, arrangement; desire, desirable; change, changeable*)
    d. final *y* in plurals and verb forms (*lady, ladies; alley, alleys; stay, stayed; pay, paid*)
    e. final *o* in plurals (*radio, radios; potato, potatoes*)

f. final *fe* in plurals (*wife, wives*); final *ff* in plurals (*sheriff, sheriffs*); but final *f* in plurals is variable (*shelf, shelves; chief, chiefs*)

g. plurals of compounds (*courts-martial, handfuls, menservants*)

6. Compound adjectives are hyphenated when they precede the noun unless the first part of the compound ends in *-ly* (*second-class citizen; poorly paid worker*).

7. Words at line end divide by syllable only (*pay-ing, be-gin-ning, un-pre-ten-tious, knowl-edge*).

8. Possession is indicated for personal nouns (not for personal *pronouns*) by an apostrophe with or without an inflectional *s*.

a. Singular nouns not ending in *s* take *'s*.

Gibbon's *Decline and Fall*

b. One-syllable singular nouns ending in *s* take *'s*.

James's pragmatic philosophy

c. Multisyllable nouns ending in *s* take only an apostrophe.

Collins' *Ode to Evening*

d. Plural nouns ending in *s* take only an apostrophe.

the Goncourts' journals

e. Plural nouns not ending in *s* take *'s*.

Gentlemen's Magazine

Possession may also be indicated by prepositional phrases (the pragmatic philosophy of William James) and is preferably so indicated when the relationship is not so much one of possession in the sense of owning as that of whole-to-part (the streets of Paris, the paintings of the Romantic Movement, the speeches in the Senate).

3/ Punctuation

Unlike spelling, punctuation is less a matter of convention than of common sense. Properly used, it indicates relationships within sentences and between sentences so that the reader may proceed without uncertainty. Improperly used, it misleads the reader.

1/ THE PERIOD
a. Declarative and imperative sentences end with a period.

b. Abbreviations require a period.

2/ THE COMMA

Nine tenths of the errors in punctuation on students' papers are due to misuse of the comma. These are the principal situations in which errors occur.

a. The use or omission of commas to set off appositive words and phrases depends on the relationship intended. If the appositive is an adjunct (Charles the Bald, Peter the Hermit), commas are omitted. If the appositive limits or restricts the word to which it stands in apposition, commas are likewise omitted:

> Europeans acclaimed the novelist James Fenimore Cooper as they had once acclaimed Scott.

If the appositive is simply supplementary—if it adds information but does not limit or restrict—commas separate it from the word it supplements:

> The author of *Pathfinder,* James Fenimore Cooper, was a native of New York State.

Note that, if the appositive expression is to be set off by commas, it must be *completely set off:*

> The last part of *Dead Souls,* Gogol's greatest work, appears to be irrevocably lost. NOT: The last part of *Dead Souls,* Gogol's greatest work appears to be irrevocably lost.

b. Restrictive clauses (those that materially qualify the referent) are *not* set off by commas:

> The chapters that remain show the powerful genius of that great novelist. (Restrictive)

> The remaining chapters, which have been translated into a dozen languages, show the powerful genius of that great novelist. (Nonrestrictive)

In the first example the phrase "that remain" limits the word "chapters." The subject of "show" is not merely "chapters" but "chapters that remain." In the second example the "which" clause adds information but does not limit "chapter" and does not govern "show." (See Glossary on *that, which.*)

c. Clauses joined by the conjunctions *and, but, or* ordinarily take a comma before the conjunction, unless both clauses are short.

> He wrote the essay, and I read it as soon as he brought it to me.

A comma is always helpful when *for* is used as a conjunction:

> I read it at once, for the publisher was calling for copy.

d. Commas separate items in series; their use before "and" in such a series is optional.

> The titles of books, stories, plays, and moving-pictures should be underlined in manuscript.
>
> A wordy, abtruse, pretentious statement is seldom clear. *But:* A wordy, abstruse, pretentious introductory sentence may easily discourage a reader.
>
> (In this example the adjective "introductory" has a different relationship to "sentence" from that of the other adjectives; "introductory sentence" is a unit of the same kind of "moving-pictures," but does not have enough use to gain the hyphen of "moving-pictures.")

e. Participial phrases are *completely* set off by commas—

> Reading the report again, he discovered the important detail he had missed.
>
> He discovered, by reading the report again, that he had missed several important details.
>
> He spent the remainder of the day at home, reading the report once again.

—unless they follow the main clause and are very short:

> He came home singing lustily.

f. Dependent clauses that explain or give a reason for the main clause are sometimes set off by commas:

> Ortega rejects this definition, for he believes "mass" is not a matter of number but of mental habit.

BUT: He use the term "mass-mind" whenever he refers to the mental habit of rejecting the unique or the original.

When dependent clauses *precede* the main statement, they are always set off by commas unless they are very short (note the punctuation of this rule):

Whenever Ortega refers to the mental habit of rejecting the unique or the original, he uses the term "mass mind."

g.   Commas set off parenthetical expressions of various kinds:

Albert Einstein, the distinguished mathematician and physicist, was also an amateur musician. (appositive)

He said that, like other scientists, he found mathematics and music a congenial combination. (additive)

He insisted, moreover, that the two have fundamental similarities. (connective)

Both are, in their purest form, entirely abstract; both use an entirely symbolic, that is, nonrepresentational, idiom. (qualifying; explanatory)

h.   Occasionally, commas are needed where syntax does not require them simply to prevent misreading or to indicate a pause essential for correct reading:

In the open air drama takes on the dignity of its surroundings.

CORRECTED: In the open air, drama takes on the dignity of its surroundings.

What must be must be.

CORRECTED: What must be, must be.

i.   Commas are used to separate numbers, dates, and addresses:

There were 19,170 more votes cast this year than last.

He was born February 22, 1936, in Washington, D.C.

We are moving from Middletown, Connecticut, to Middletown, New York; our address will be 29 Park Street, Middletown 14, New York.

j.   Degrees and titles are separated from the names of their bearers by commas:

> This report is the work of Samuel E. Jones, M.D., a friend of the late Consul General, M. Georges Faivre.

k.   All forms of direct address are set off from the text proper:

> And these, my friends, are answers to your questions.

> If you want to come along, John, you are welcome to do so.

l.   Commas set quoted words off from other parts of sentences that contain them, unless the quoted words are interrogative or exclamatory:

> "Virtue," she said, "is not the prerogative of bachelors."

> "Isn't it?" he asked ironically.

> "No, it isn't!" she retorted with vehemence. "You men are all alike," she went on. "You think you own the universe."

3/ THE SEMICOLON

The semicolon is a connection between independent clauses not joined by a conjunction:

> History makes men wise; poetry makes them witty.

In such use, it suggests closer relationship and a more studied balance between units than is indicated by separate sentences. It may also separate a series of long, dependent clauses:

> When a man has read deeply in history; when he has come to appreciate the subtle illumination of poetry; when he has mastered the knowledge of nature, animate and inanimate; when he has examined the moral and religious thought of all time: then, and only then, can it be said of him that he has a liberal education.

There is often confusion about the use of the semicolon with such conjunctive words as "however," "therefore," "nonetheless," "consequently." If such words introduce a clause, a semicolon precedes them; if they interrupt a clause, they are set off by commas:

> He made up his mind without any investigation at all; therefore, his discovery of the truth taught him the folly of hasty judgment.

If he had investigated the matter, he would not have said what he did say. He blurted out his opinion, however, without making any inquiry at all.

4/ THE COLON

The colon is often confused with the semicolon. It has so definite a function in writing that every student should learn its particular uses and practice them frequently.

  a.   The colon may introduce an enumeration:

> Although he is known primarily as the author of the novel *Moby-Dick,* Melville wrote sixteen books in all, demonstrating his skill in four different literary forms: the novel, the short story, the account of travel, and poetry.

  b.   The more important structural use of the colon is in expanding, explaining, or illustrating what precedes it:

> *War and Peace* is the giant of Russian fiction: by sheer comprehensiveness it overshadows all other novels in the language. (explaining)

> Like a giant, it gazes down on the panorama of Russian life: the debt-ridden extravagance of urban aristocrats, the poverty and obduracy of the peasants, the disorderly yet impassioned life of the military, the cynicism and anguish of the spiritually uprooted. (expanding)

> And its gaze is not only wide but penetrating: it reveals the quiet nobility of Andrei as superbly as it displays the tumult and confusion of the battle of Novgorod. (illustrating)

  c.   If the enumeration or expansion or illustration is the grammatical object of a preposition or the grammatical object or complement of a verb, the colon does not occur:

> The nations attending the conference are England, Denmark, France, West Germany and the Netherlands.

> The cake is made of a rich batter filled with candied cherries, ginger, citron, and nuts.

5/ THE DASH; PARENTHESES

These two marks of punctuation are most frequently used to set off matter not grammatically related to its context. Of the two, the dash is the less formal.

> Both men contributed—Beethoven the more powerfully of the two—
> to the enlargement of musical form.

> Beethoven's third symphony (the *Eroica*) provoked a storm of protest.

The dash is also used—and too often so used—to produce emphasis:

> To Beethoven, protest meant nothing, favor meant nothing; his life
> was focused entirely on one passion—music.

6/ QUOTATION MARKS

Although the liberality with which quotation marks are used varies
from writer to writer, general publishing practice has more or less
established the conventions listed below.

> a.   Quotation marks are necessary for setting off phrases or pas-
> sages not one's own (see the section entitled "Plagiarism"). They
> enclose *only* the quoted words:

> > Plutarch tells us that, although the Athenians continued to observe
> > Solon's laws, they nonetheless "expected some changes and were de-
> > sirous of another government."

> > "Hence it was," Plutarch goes on, "that through the city. . . ."

Note that the commas fall *before* the quotation mark. That is true
also of periods, even if a single quoted word occurs at the end of
the sentence:

> Plutarch is not specific about what the Athenians expected; he limits
> himself to the general word "change."

The placement of other marks of punctuation in relation to quotation marks will depend on the sense of the passage:

> How does Plutarch know that "all expected some change"?

When a quoted passage continues for more than one paragraph,
quotation marks are set at the beginning of *each* paragraph but at
the end of the *last* paragraph only. If the citation is longer than
seven or eight lines, a more common practice is to indent the
quoted passage, *omitting quotation marks entirely.*

> b.   The terms of a formal definition and any other use of a word
> as though it were an object require quotation marks or italics:

In the title *Brave New World,* the word "brave" means something like "good" or "noble."

His "Yessir" was immediate but a shade contemptuous.

c.   Quotation marks may also indicate that a word is being used in a special sense, usually one which the author has established beforehand or feels will be readily understood by his reader:

He is genuinely an "amateur" tennis player, who plays for love of the game, not for money.

d.   Colloquial words and slang expressions, if used in a context that does not readily accommodate them, are often set off by quotation marks. The purpose of the usage seems to be largely protective, the author making sure by this means that the reader knows his choice of language to have been deliberate.

Apparently teen-agers no longer "dig" that crooner as they once did.

In our part of the country such "toney" people seldom have much to do with the hill dweller.

e.   The use of quotation marks to set off passages of dialogue from description and explanation has a long tradition in English. The convention is simple enough to illustrate, but it is no longer so invariably observed, even in novels, as it once was:

"You can do it, I think," he said, "but you will have to do it alone."

BUT: He said that you could do it but that you would have to do it alone.

A few contemporary writers omit the quotation marks, substituting a dash before the beginning of a speech or using no mark of punctuation at all:

—You can do it, I think. But you will have to do it alone, he added.

Or: He looked at her steadily. You can do it, he said, but you will have to do it alone.

Both of the foregoing examples get around the difficulty posed by the running together of "I think" and "he said" which is so neatly taken care of by quotation marks, but the fact that a difficulty arises may illustrate a sound reason for retaining the convention.

7/ BRACKETS

Brackets are commonly used as a means of indicating additions to a cited text which have been supplied by the citer of the text.

> The third of Haney's letters on the subject was more specific. It included full information about the location of the mine and an account of the operations so far completed. Then, in a sudden burst of candor, it concluded:
>
>> It is now only May [the letter is dated May 16] and already I have taken enough silver out of this hole to make me comfitable [*sic*] for the rest of my life.

(The bracketed *"sic"* is a device for indicating to the reader that the misspelling of "comfortable" occurred in the original text and is not a proofreader's or author's oversight.)

If a parenthetical expression occurs within another parenthetical expression, the internal one is set off by brackets.

8/ SUSPENSION POINTS

In citing a text, a writer may wish to omit parts that are irrelevant to the purpose for which it is being cited. An omission is indicated by the simple device of inserting suspension points, or ellipses, at the proper place in the text:

> The fourth and final letter has undertones of tragedy, but it begins with characteristic cheerfulness:
>
>> Today I am going back to see Melia [Haney's only living sister] and I plan to take what I have got saved back with me. There is enough . . . for both of us, and some to spare . . . . It is a long trek, and I don't like to go it alone, but I must. Anyone who can stick it out here for ten months sure don't need to worry much about lasting through a little ten-day ride on horseback.

The first appearance of suspension points in the passage above uses only three since the omission occurs within a sentence. The second appearance uses a fourth to indicate the period at the end of the sentence from which the last part has been omitted.

In order to accommodate the text he cites to the sentence introducing it, a writer may break into the middle of a sentence or paragraph, or he may break off before the end. To indicate such interruptions he uses suspension points.

In all the writing of these hardy adventurers there is something melancholy, a feeling—as one of them put it—of ". . . a hollowness inside that ore won't fill, a hole bigger'n a mine shaft and twicet as dark."

If a writer quotes a passage long enough to indent but still less (either at beginning or end) than the complete paragraph in the original, he indicates the omission of sentences in the same way that he indicates the omission of words from a sentence: by three suspension points before the quotation or four points after it.

chapter ten / *The Use of Sources*

1/ Definition of Plagiarism

The academic counterpart of the bank embezzler and of the manufacturer who mislabels his products is the plagiarist, the student or
scholar who leads his reader to believe that what he is reading is the
original work of the writer when it is not. If it could be assumed that the
distinction between plagiarism and honest use of sources is perfectly
clear in everyone's mind, there would be no need for the explanation
that follows; merely the warning with which this definition concludes
would be enough. But it is apparent that sometimes men of good will
draw the suspicion of guilt upon themselves (and, indeed, are guilty)
simply because they are not aware of the illegitimacy of certain kinds
of "borrowing" and of the procedures for correct identification of
materials other than those gained through independent research and
reflection.

The spectrum is a wide one. At one end there is a word-for-word
copying of another's writing without enclosing the copied passage in
quotation marks and identifying it in a footnote, *both* of which are
necessary. (This includes, of course, the copying of all or any part of
another student's paper.) It hardly seems possible that anyone of college
age or more could do that without clear intent to deceive. At the other
end there is the almost casual slipping in of a particularly apt term which
one has come across in reading and which so admirably expresses one's
opinion that one is tempted to make it personal property. Between these
poles there are degrees and degrees, but they may be roughly placed in
two groups. Close to outright and blatant deceit—but more the result,
perhaps, of laziness than of bad intent—is the patching together of random jottings made in the course of reading, generally without careful
identification of their source, and then woven into the text, so that the
result is a mosaic of other people's ideas and words, the writer's sole
contribution being the cement to hold the pieces together. Indicative of
more effort and, for that reason, somewhat closer to honesty, though still

dishonest, is the paraphrase, an abbreviated (and often skillfully pre-pared) restatement of someone's else's analysis or conclusion, without acknowledgement that another person's text has been the basis for the recapitulation.

The examples given below should make clear the dishonest and the proper use of source material. If instances occur which these examples do not seem to cover, conscience will in all likelihood be prepared to supply advice.

THE SOURCE

> The importance of the *Second Treatise of Government* printed in this volume is such that without it we should miss some of the familiar features of our own government. It is safe to assert that the much criticized branch known as the Supreme Court obtained its being as a result of Locke's insistence upon the separation of powers; and that the combination of many powers in the hands of the executive under the New Deal has still to encounter opposition because it is contrary to the principles enunciated therein, the effect of which is not spent, though the relationship may not be consciously traced. Again we see the crystallizing force of Locke's writing. It renders explicit and adapts to the British politics of his day the trend and aim of writers from Languet and Bodin through Hooker and Grotius, to say nothing of the distant ancients, Aristotle and the Stoic school of natural law. It sums up magistrally the arguments used through the ages to attack author-ity vested in a single individual, but it does so from the particular point of view engendered by the Revolution of 1688 and is in harmony with the British scene and mental climate of the growing bourgeoisie of that age. Montesquieu and Rousseau, the framers of our own Declara-tion of Independence, and the statesmen (or should we say merchants and spectators?) who drew up the Constitution have re-echoed its claims for human liberty, for the separation of powers, for the sanctity of private property. In the hands of these it has been the quarry of liberal doctrines; and that it has served the Socialist theory of property based on labor is final proof of its breadth of view.
>
> CHARLES L. SHERMAN, "Introduction" to John Locke, *Treatise of Civil Government* and *A Letter Concern-ing Toleration.*

1/ WORD-FOR-WORD PLAGIARIZING

It is not hard to see the importance of the *Second Treatise of Govern-ment* to our own democracy. Without it we should miss some of the most familiar features of our own government. It is safe to assert that the much criticized branch known as the Supreme Court obtained its being as a result of Locke's insistence upon the separation of powers; and that the combination of many powers in the hands of the executive under the New Deal has still to encounter opposition because it is contrary to the principles enunciated therein, the effect of which is not spent, though the relationship may not be consciously traced. The framers of our own Declaration of Independence and the statesmen who drew up the Constitution have re-echoed its claims for human liberty, for the separation of powers, for the sanctity of private property. All these are marks of the influence of Locke's *Second Treatise* on our own way of life.

In this example, after composing half of a first sentence, the writer copies exactly what is in the original text, leaving out the center section of the paragraph and omitting the names of Montesquieu and Rousseau where he takes up the text again. The last sentence is also the writer's own.

If the writer had enclosed all the copied text in quotation marks and had identified the source in a footnote, he would not have been liable to the charge of plagiarism; a reader might justifiably have felt, however, that the writer's personal contribution to the discussion was not very significant.

2/ THE MOSAIC

The crystallizing force of Locke's writing may be seen in the effect his *Second Treatise of Government* had in shaping some of the familiar features of our own government. That much criticized branch known as the Supreme Court and the combination of many powers in the hands of the executive under the New Deal are modern examples. But even the foundations of our state—the Declaration of Independence and the Constitution—have re-echoed its claims for human liberty, for the separation of powers, for the sanctity of private property. True, the influence of others is also marked in our Constitution—from the trend and aim of writers like Languet and Bodin, Hooker and Grotius, to say nothing of Aristotle and the Stoic school of natural law; but the fundamental influence is Locke's *Treatise,* the very quarry of liberal doctrines.

Note how the following phrases have been lifted out of the original text and moved into new patterns:

crystallizing force of Locke's writing
some of the familiar features of our own government

much criticized branch known as the Supreme Court
combination of many powers in the hands of the executive under the
New Deal
have re-echoed its claims for human liberty . . . property
from the trend and aim . . .. Grotius
to say nothing of Aristotle and . . . natural law
quarry of liberal doctrines

As in the first example, there is really no way of legitimizing such a procedure. To put every stolen phrase within quotation marks would produce an almost unreadable, and quite worthless, text.

3/ THE PARAPHRASE

PARAPHRASE: Many fundamental aspects of our own government are
ORIGINAL: Many familiar features of our own government are

apparent in the *Second Treatise of Government*. One can safely
apparent in the *Second Treatise of Government*. It is safe to

say that the oft-censured Supreme Court really owes its exist-
assert that the much criticized . . . Court obtained its being as

ence to the Lockeian demand that powers in government be kept
a result of Locke's insistence upon the separation of powers;

separate; equally one can say that the allocation of varied
and that the combination of many powers

and widespread authority to the President during the era of
in the hands of the executive under the

the New Deal has still to encounter opposition because it is
New Deal has still to encounter opposition because it is

contrary to the principles enunciated therein . . . . Once more it
contrary to the principles enunciated therein . . . . Again we see

is possible to note the way in which Locke's writing clarified
the crystallizing force of Locke's writing.

existing opinion.

The foregoing interlinear presentation shows clearly how the writer has simply traveled along with the original text, substituting approximately equivalent terms except where his understanding fails him, as it does with "crystallizing," or where the ambiguity of the original is too great a tax on his ingenuity for him to proceed, as it is with "to encounter opposition . . . consciously traced" in the original.

Such a procedure as the one shown in this example has its uses; for one thing, it is valuable for the student's own understanding of the passage; and it may be valuable for the reader as well. How, then, may it be properly used? The procedure is simple. The writer might begin the second sentence with: "As Sherman notes in the introduction to his edition of the *Treatise,* one can safely say . . ." and conclude the paraphrased passage with a footnote giving the additional identification necessary. Or he might indicate directly the exact nature of what he is doing, in this fashion: "To paraphrase Sherman's comment . . ." and conclude that also with a footnote indicator.

In point of fact, this source does not particularly lend itself to honest paraphrase, with the exception of that one sentence which the paraphraser above copied without change except for abridgement. The purpose of paraphrase should be to simplify or to throw a new and significant light on a text; it requires much skill if it is to be honestly used and should rarely be resorted to by the student except for the purpose, as was suggested above, of his personal enlightenment.

4/ THE "APT" TERM

> The *Second Treatise of Government* is a veritable quarry of liberal doctrines. In it the crystallizing force of Locke's writing is markedly apparent. The cause of human liberty, the principle of separation of powers, and the inviolability of private property—all three, major dogmas of American constitutionalism—owe their presence in our Constitution in large part to the remarkable *Treatise* which first appeared around 1685 and was destined to spark, within three years, a revolution in the land of its author's birth and, ninety years later, another revolution against that land.

Here the writer has not been able to resist the appropriation of two striking terms—"quarry of liberal doctrines" and "crystallizing force"; a perfectly proper use of the terms would have required only the addition of a phrase: *The Second Treatise of Government* is, to use Sherman's suggestive expression, a "quarry of liberal doctrines." In it the "crystallizing force"—the term again is Sherman's—of Locke's writing is markedly apparent. . . .

Other phrases in the text above—"the cause of human liberty," "the principle of the separation of powers," "the inviolability of private property"—are clearly drawn directly from the original source but are so much matters in the public domain, so to speak, that no one could reasonably object to their re-use in this fashion.

Since one of the principal aims of a college education is the development of intellectual honesty, it is obvious that plagiarism is a particularly serious offense, and the punishment for it is commensurately severe. What a penalized student suffers can never really be known by anyone but himself; what the student who plagiarizes and "gets away with it" suffers is less public and probably less acute, but the corruptness of his act, the disloyalty and baseness it entails, must inevitably leave a mark on him as well as on the institution of which he is a member.

2/ Making a Bibliography; Using Footnotes

Essays written for college courses generally require the use of "sources": books, periodicals, and newspapers containing information relevant to the topic of the essay to be written. The citation of such sources occurs in one or both of two places: in footnotes; in a bibliography appended to the essay.

Very simply, a bibliography lists the books, periodicals and newspapers, and other documents actually used in the preparation of the essay; a footnote indicates very precisely the source of a quotation or specific statement occurring in the text of the essay. For both, a more or less standardized system has been developed so that readers anywhere can turn quickly from the footnote or the bibliographical listing to the proper source and be sure that they have at hand the correct volume of the correct edition of the cited work. This section provides, in a form as abbreviated as clarity permits, the fundamental information you will need about these two tools of scholarly work.

BIBLIOGRAPHY

A bibliography lists the books, periodicals, and newspapers, and other documents actually used in the preparation of an essay. (There are bibliographies, to be sure, which do more than that, but for present purposes the definition given above is accurate.) It is, therefore, a record for the reader of the kind and amount of research done in preparing the essay and, as such, it enables him not only to verify the documentation but also to make at a glance an estimate of the probable value of the paper. It is this latter function which occasionally leads the writer to make one of two errors in the compilation of a bibliography: (1) the listing of everything read during the period of research, whether or not it has any revelance to or value for the essay, a completeness that is both pretentious and wasteful of the reader's time and energy; (2) the listing of important or important-sounding volumes which have not been read at all or have only been "looked into," clearly a dishonest procedure.

The following examples illustrate the common kinds of bibliographical entry.

    1. Lunt, W. E. *History of England.* New York, 1947.

The author's name is given as it appears on the title page of the book itself, but with surname first so that alphabetization of entries will be obvious.

The title is italicized. (This is the equivalent of underlining in typescript and manuscript.)

The place of publication and date of publication are listed in that order.

    2. Crosby, John. "Speechlessness at Great Length," New York *Herald Tribune,* CXI (July 23, 1951), p. 13.

The title here is set in quotation marks because it is only an article, a part of a larger work. Italicizing is reserved for the larger work (New York *Herald Tribune*). The simple rule for capitalization of titles explains usage here and elsewhere: *capitalize all words in a title except articles and one-syllable prepositions and conjunctions, and always capitalize the first and the last word.*

The volume number is given in Roman numerals to distinguish it from the numbers that follow. It is necessary for periodicals and newspapers because back numbers are bound by volumes for library storage.

The date of the issue and the page on which the article can be found provide all the additional information that is needed for quick access to the source. Commas separate each piece of information from the next.

    3. "Haiti." *Encyclopædia Britannica,* 14th ed. (1936), XI, 81–83.

As is common in encyclopedias, the author of this article is not indicated. The entry therefore begins with the title of the article.

It is important that the edition be noted because the content of the article might be different in another edition and the location of it within the set would almost certainly be different.

    4. Turgot, Anne Robert Jacques. *Œuvres de Turgot,* ed. Eugène Daire. 2 vols. Paris, 1844.

The title appears exactly as on the title page (is not translated). In this case the author's name is implicit in the title, but is listed nonetheless so that the entry may be alphabetically placed. The man who prepared the *Œuvres* (*Works*) for publication is listed after the abbreviation "ed." ("edited by").

Note that the number of volumes has been stated. This is customary procedure if the work has more than one volume. Some bibliographers give the number of pages in one-volume works, but that is not necessary. Page numbers *are* given, however, in the second and third examples above because the source cited forms only part of a larger work whose other parts are not necessarily germane to the topic.

A final note: the items in a bibliography should be arranged alphabetically, the first word in an item determining its alphabetical placement, unless the first word is an article (the, a, an); in that case, the following word is the basis for alphabetization.

FOOTNOTES

A footnote indicates very precisely the source of a quotation or specific statement occurring in the text of the essay. (It may also give incidental or supplementary information, of course.) There is some variation in the form of footnotes from one publishing house to another and even from one scholarly society to another. The instructions that follow, however, have the authority of most of the university presses in the United States and conform, as do those on bibliography, to the style sheet of the Modern Language Association. Only the most commonly used terms are presented for study. These few simple generalizations deserve prior attention and observance:

1. Number the footnotes consecutively throughout an essay.

2. Place the footnotes for each page at the bottom of that page; or, if you want to save yourself a great deal of space calculating, assemble them all on a separate sheet at the end of the essay.

3. Make sure, in the final draft, that the numbers in the text correspond to the numbers attached to relevant footnotes.

4. Indicate the presence of a footnote by an Arabic numeral in the text. Ordinarily, this numeral should come at the end of a sentence. It should always be raised above the line of text:

Jones vehemently denied the report.[6] When the . . .

When footnotes are infrequent, an asterisk or other symbol may be used in place of numbers.

5. Use footnotes sparingly. Their purpose is to inform the reader, not to impress him.

The following series of footnotes satisfies the most common situations. A full explanation follows the series.

[1] Theodor Wilhelm and Gerhard Graefe, *German Education Today* (Berlin: Terramare, 1936), pp. 3–5.

[2] James Bryant Conant, "The Advancement of Learning in the United States in the Post-War World," *Science* XCIX (February 4, 1944), 91.

[3] Ibid., p. 92.

[4] *Jahrbuch des Reichsarbeitsdienstes,* 1937–38 (Berlin, 1937), S. 34.

[5] Conant, p. 94.

Explanation. The first footnote is a reference to three pages in a book published by Terramare in Berlin and written by two men. Their names appear in the order in which they are found on the title page. Note that they are not reversed so that the surname comes first as in bibliographical entries; this is simply because there is no purpose in making the adjustment necessary for alphabetization when arrangement is by order of occurrence in the text.

The second note refers to one page in an article that appeared in volume ninety-nine of *Science* magazine. In such an instance it is not necessary to name the publisher or place of publication if the magazine is at all well known, but it is advisable to give the date of issue as well as the volume number. Note that the page reference for a publication does not use the abbreviation "p." (for "page") or "pp." (for "pages") if the volume number is given. In the first example (where there is no volume number indicated because the work is published in a single volume) the abbreviation *is* used.

The third note is a reference to a different page of the same work as that referred to in (2). "Ibid." is an abbreviation for the Latin word *ibidem* meaning "in the same place" and always points back to the immediately preceding work.

The fourth note refers to a yearbook, a compilation of statistics (in this case, concerning state work projects). Such a volume is the work of a host of men, and there is no point in indicating either editor or author for any particular section. The abbreviation "S." stands for "page" in German.

The fifth note is also a reference to the article by Mr. Conant. This time, however, "Ibid." could not be used since another reference intervenes. Therefore, the author's name and the page number alone are given.

These additional footnote abbreviations occur frequently in scholarly texts:

cf.	*compare*	loc. cit.	*in the place cited;* (different from op. cit. because it refers to the same *passage,* not simply to the same work, as previously cited)
ch.	*chapter*		
et al.	*and others*		
ff.	*following*		
l.	*line*		
ll.	*lines*	passim	*throughout the work, here and there*
v.	*see*		
viz.	*namely*		

Just as honesty requires quotation marks around any statement copied directly from a written source, it requires a footnote to indicate the place from which information has been gathered or from which paraphrased reconstructions are woven into the text.

A fine bibliography and careful footnoting, no matter how ably prepared, will not make up for deficiency in reasoning, style, and substance of the essay proper, but they do enhance the value of good scholarly writing because they act as auxiliary agents in the process of communication.

Index